INFERNAL
GEOMETRY
AND THE
LEFT-HAND PATH

"Toby Chappell has revealed a pragmatic, powerful, and magical secret of the Western Left-Hand Path, according to a strict and hidden calendar. Great forces are made available for the talented and daring magician who uses this book. Greater forces still are unleashed upon the sleeping world with its publication. At times the face of the serpent is seen among men. This is such a time. This erudite and practical book is such a veil render. This is literally a moment when Western magic will be changed forever."

DON WEBB, AUTHOR OF *OVERTHROWING THE OLD GODS: ALEISTER CROWLEY AND THE BOOK OF THE LAW* AND COAUTHOR OF *SET: THE OUTSIDER*

"Our existence is built out of 11 dimensions, as Benoît B. Mandelbrot (1924–2010) has shown, but humankind is only aware of 4—space (3D) and time (4D). The research of Mandelbrot was paradigm-shifting and gave birth to chaos mathematics and the fractal theories. To most people interested in these fields, it stays as a theory, but for the true magician it is a call that there are 7 dimensions unexplored. These unexplored dimensions are dealt with in H. P. Lovecraft's horror fiction, which echoes a genuine description of the worlds beyond the Newtonian laws of physics—dark unknown worlds that Toby Chappell, the author of *Infernal Geometry and the Left-Hand Path,* gives us access to through a system developed by the Church of Satan and the Temple of Set but that has a history that goes back in time to the mystery cults of ancient days."

THOMAS KARLSSON, PH.D., AUTHOR OF *NIGHTSIDE OF THE RUNES: UTHARK, ADULRUNA, AND THE GOTHIC CABBALA*

INFERNAL GEOMETRY

GEOMETRY

AND THE

LEFT-HAND PATH

The Magical System of
the Nine Angles

TOBY CHAPPELL

Inner Traditions
Rochester, Vermont

Inner Traditions
One Park Street
Rochester, Vermont 05767
www.InnerTraditions.com

Text stock is SFI certified

Cataloging-in-Publication Data for this title is available from the Library of Congress

ISBN 978-1-62055-816-4 (print)
ISBN 978-162055-817-1 (ebook)

Printed and bound in the United States by Lake Book Manufacturing, Inc.
The text stock is SFI certified. The Sustainable Forestry Initiative® program
promotes sustainable forest management.

10 9 8 7 6 5 4 3 2

Text design and layout by Debbie Glogover
This book was typeset in Garamond Premier Pro with Botany, Tide Sans, and Gill
Sans MT Pro used as display fonts

Excerpt from pp. 181–193 [1580 words] from THE SATANIC RITUALS by
ANTON LAVEY. Copyright © 1972 by Anton LaVey. Reprinted by permission of
HarperCollins Publishers.

To send correspondence to the author of this book, mail a first-class letter to the
author c/o Inner Traditions • Bear & Company, One Park Street, Rochester, VT
05767, and we will forward the communication, or contact the author directly at
geometer@fastmail.com or visit his blog at **stonyrubbish.tumblr.com** or his
twitter **@motiondemon**.

Without the pioneering work of Anton Szandor LaVey, Michael A. Aquino, Ph.D., and Stephen E. Flowers, Ph.D., this book would not exist. I have been deeply inspired by all three and am grateful for having had the opportunity to know and work with Aquino and Flowers (as well as Don Webb, himself a formidable practitioner and Teacher of the subject matter of this book). May this humble text bring honor to your teachings and spread your renown.

For their valuable contributions, encouragement, and/or feedback on the subject of the book and the writing process itself, I thank the following: Patty Hardy, Tim McGranahan, James Fitzsimmons, Ingvild Clark, André Harke, Mark Luskin, and Chris Merwin. Thanks also to James S. and Jarl T. for my original introduction to the Nine Angles; what seemed just a fascinating curiosity at the time has grown into a life-changing area of study, of which this book is but one manifestation.

I would also like to thank Jon Graham and all at Inner Traditions for their enthusiasm toward this project and hard work to help it become a reality.

CONTENTS

The Appendices

"FOREWEIRD"

BY MICHAEL A. AQUINO, PH.D.

In trying to make sense of the natural environment in which they found themselves, the ancient Egyptians discerned regularities in phenomena, from the courses of the stars to the annual cycles of the Nile. As these phenomena recurred with inevitable regularity and predictability, the Egyptians further recognized determining and enforcing agencies behind them, each of which they identified as a *neter* (from which we retain the modern word & concept "nature").

All but one of the *neteru*—whom later, duller cultures would call "gods"—created and ordered the physical environment; collectively, they would later comprise "Natural Law" (or, mythologically, various "gods" or a combined "God").

So sensible humans learned about the *neteru* that impacted them and harmonized their lifestyles with them as much as possible, both to benefit and to avoid harm. Priesthoods and later scientists were/are entrusted with the task of understanding the *neteru* and devising optimal human cooperation with them.

To their marvel and delight, humans also discovered that the mechanisms and regularity of the *neteru* have æsthetic aspects. They are harmonious, beautiful to the sight, pretty to the ear. Applying musical scales makes possible complex symphonies; using *pi* and *phi* in art and architecture ensures both strength and attractiveness.

If this were all there is to nature and human interaction with it, there would be no reason or need for this book. If in Tolkien's Middle-earth there had been only the 3 Rings of the Elves, the 7 of the Dwarves, and the 9 of Men, the Ages of Arda (Earth) would have glided along placidly and unremarkably.

But there was another Ring there, and there is one here too: that "other *neter*," which positions individual human consciousness independent of, hence external to the natural universe and its laws. The Egyptians knew this "*neter* not of the *neteru*" as Set; later cultures would echo him as "Satan" and similar deities of separateness.

It is this conscious separateness that enables humans to identify Natural Law and intentionally use it harmoniously. Yet intriguingly, it also enables them to use those laws in all sorts of ways they would not "naturally" manifest on their own. By itself, nature produces elements and substances such as iron, electricity, rubber, and combustible chemicals. But it takes human ingenuity and creativity to first imagine and then actualize combining these into a Ferrari.

The natural *neteru* don't go out of their way to make Ferraris. Set does.

But that's still not the whole story. This book tells the rest of it.

What happens when Set, or Set-inspired humans, start tinkering with Natural Law? You get mathematics wherein 2 + 2 no longer equals 4, art and architecture that seem impossible, music that your ears can't believe they heard.

Some of this stuff is amusing and entertaining: listening to a Charles Ives symphony or viewing M. C. Escher's drawings. NonNatural æsthetes have even built themselves "Klein-bottle" homes with "no inside/outside," as the curious may easily discover with an internet Google search.

But where it gets really weird is in the effects of such NonNaturalism on consciousness itself. One's mind and brain are accustomed to function amid rigid, reassuring regularity. Knock this skeleton away and the result is absolutely independent, unconstrained creative power, which the pedantic might mistake for "insanity."

The first artists to realize and explore this realm were the

Expressionists of the early twentieth century, most famously in Weimar, Germany. Hence the stunning and shocking impact of films such as *The Cabinet of Dr. Caligari, The Golem,* and *Metropolis.* The first performance of Stravinsky's *Rite of Spring* in Paris resulted in an audience riot and the orchestra's percussionist famously breaking his drumsticks over his knees because of the blasphemy they had helped to create. It was scarcely surprising that a few years later Expressionism would be suppressed in a near-hysterical reactive rush to neorealism. Horror writers such as H. P. Lovecraft and Clark Ashton Smith were prescient to see in NonNaturalism a panoply of terror far greater than the old imagery of vampires and werewolves. Along with their tales came a bibliography of forbidden books, telling the courageous (and usually fatally foolish) reader how he "may gett beyonde Time & ye Spheres."

Most of those tomes, such as Lovecraft's *Necronomicon,* are fictional.

There are a few that aren't, like this one. If you don't want to be discovered tomorrow morning crouched in a corner and shrieking incantations to Yog-Sothoth, you had better throw it into the fireplace and dash for the door.

MICHAEL A. AQUINO, PH.D., is a Lt. Colonel, Psychological Operations, U.S. Army (Ret.). He earned a B.A., M.A., and Ph.D. in Political Science from the University of California, Santa Barbara. Since 1975 he has been a Priest of the ancient Egyptian god Set and served as High Priest of the international Temple of Set until 1996. He is the author or editor of numerous books on political, military, and initiatory subjects, including *The Church of Satan, The Temple of Set, MindWar, MindStar,* and *Extreme Prejudice: The Presidio Satanic Abuse Scam.* He, his wife, Lilith, and inevitable, innumerable, and immortal cats live in San Francisco, California.

1 & 2 · *See Appendix A — pp. 265-267*

WEIRD TALES, SEMIOTICS, GEOMETRY, AND THE LEFT-HAND PATH

In 1972, Anton Szandor LaVey's follow-up to his 1969 book *The Satanic Bible* was published. In this companion volume, entitled *The Satanic Rituals,* LaVey revealed public versions of many of the internal rites of the Church of Satan.

Most of the contents of the book focus on "traditional" black-magic topics, such as the Black Mass, but there are three rituals and a concluding essay that stand out as something very different in their conception and purpose.

The first of these rituals, *Die Elektrischen Vorspiele,* is a combination of text and ideas from Frank Belknap Long's Cthulhu-mythos story "The Hounds of Tindalos" and occultist Maurice Doreal's supposedly ancient text *The Emerald Tablet of Thoth,* rendered through the visual aesthetic of German Expressionist film.

The other two rituals (*The Ceremony of the Nine Angles* and *The Call to Cthulhu*) are directly influenced by the writings of H. P. Lovecraft, and both make use of an elaborate magical language inspired by the scant phrases of the "language of the Great Old Ones" (dubbed Yuggothic) in Lovecraft's works. These rituals were not, in fact, written by LaVey, but were contributions from Michael Aquino (who was LaVey's "left-hand man" in the Church of Satan at that time).

The concluding essay, "The Unknown Known," gives LaVey's theory that nine is the most magical of all numbers and that humans and their institutions adhere to cyclical behavior patterns based on periods of nine years. LaVey's musings on cycles were heavily inspired by German engineer Hanns Hörbiger's pseudo-scientific *Welteislehre* (or "World Ice Doctrine," discussed in more detail in chapter 3).

The three rituals all include references to magically potent **angles**, and build on their significance as alluded to in LaVey's version of the Enochian Keys, which concludes *The Satanic Bible*.

The Nine Angles referred to in their eponymous Ceremony are visualized as an inverse pentagram superimposed on a trapezoid, the nethermost point of the pentagram extending beyond the lower horizontal of the trapezoid, with the upper points of both figures coinciding. Since a regular pentagram embodies the Golden Ratio, and the connected trapezoid is drawn in proportions derived from the distance between the two upright points of the pentagram, the combined figure is predominantly composed of line segments divided into the Golden Ratio. As such, the Angles function as a type of sacred (or perhaps more accurately, **infernal**) geometry that provides a symbolic and practical model of transforming the Self through carefully measured introspection and action.

The Nine Angles describe a model for self-knowledge and self-transformation because at their core they are a cosmology—that is, a conception of the objective universe (the physical universe of matter and energy, and the laws that govern its existence) and its relationship to

The Nine Angles

the subjective universe (the individual knowledge, experience, and self-awareness of each sentient being within the objective universe). To begin understanding how the Angles can be used in magical practice, it may be useful to approach them as a map of how ideas, actions, and other products of the mind come into being, thus providing a way to quantify the different stages of this process and to aid in refining its results.

Each Angle has one or more *keywords* associated with it, which attempt to capture some aspect of the essence of that angle in the context of all nine. The keywords provide a semiotic map of how the Angles interact with each other as representations of different stages of the creative and transformative process, and they also serve as a common language for discussing the Angles. The magician may have both an understanding of the commonly accepted keywords, as well as their own personal keyword, all of which facilitate the practical use of the Angles.

THE NINE ANGLES AND THE LEFT-HAND PATH

Magic as used in this book refers to the **process by which perceptual changes are created and made permanent within the inner world, and which may, when needed, create phenomenal change in the outer world.**

The use of a keyword associated with each of the Angles is an application of the semiotic theory of magic, which posits that results depend on finding the proper symbols and mode of address/communication, combined with ascriptive thinking (assignment of meaning) regarding the otherwise hidden aspects of reality and their influence on the desired results. The semiotic theory of magic is a postmodern replacement for the previously in vogue sympathetic theory of magic (popularized by James George Frazer and others), which was predicated on the assumption that magic was flawed thinking [or ignorance of science] and thus ineffective. The semiotic theory proceeds from the assumption that magic **does** work, and attempts to quantify the means by which it is effective (particularly as an outgrowth of effective symbolic communication between the practitioner and that which is to be affected). This crucial aspect of the theoretical background behind angular magic is discussed in detail in chapter 5.

The Nine Angles as put forth in this text are a purely **Left-Hand Path** (LHP) system, neither derived from, nor predicated on any traditional system. The concept of the Left-Hand Path as used in this book is **the unending pursuit of enhancing and perpetuating the magician's self-aware, psyche-centric existence** (i.e., the subjective universe, as defined above). In doing so, the individual becomes a more potent actor within the objective universe and seeks to know his or her own positive transformations as reflected by their effects on the outer world. The term Left-Hand Path implies no moral judgment (that is, choosing a side in simplistic notions of good and evil); it is merely a particular approach that emphasizes enhancing the sense of Self and Being, with its own techniques and aesthetics, and which is imperative to pursue responsibly and ethically.

The system of the Nine Angles shows the influence of such diverse sources as Platonic number theory, Germanic cosmology, the works of H. P. Lovecraft (and other authors exploring similar themes), and the mathematical perspectives of the visual arts. At their core, however, the Angles are a relatively new development that transcends and unifies all of these into a coherent yet continually evolving system of magic.

This book is about the Nine Angles—and the theory and practice of angular magic—as developed within and practiced by the Temple of Set and its internal body the Order of the Trapezoid; however, it is not a doctrinal statement about either organization. Many timeless ideas and influences from the Western esoteric traditions in general, and the Germanic esoteric traditions in particular, converge in the Nine Angles. As a primordial expression of the human psyche, their use is not exclusive to any one organization—just as work with the runes is not limited to the Rune-Gild, or Thelema to the Ordo Templi Orientis (O.T.O.). Nonetheless, the Temple of Set and the Order of the Trapezoid remain the most authentic—and advanced—schools for developing understanding and mastery of the Angles. This book represents a distillation of two decades of reflection and practice based on the Nine Angles, which have been an integral part in my becoming both a Master of the Temple of Set and the current Grand Master of the Order of the Trapezoid. The synthesis I share here honors and expands on the work begun by Michael Aquino, Ph.D., and Stephen Flowers, Ph.D., which has been pursued and enhanced by many other talented magicians of the Temple and the Order over the decades.

CHAPTER PREVIEW

Chapter 1 is an overview of the Nine Angles as a magical system, including further background about its conception in *The Ceremony of the Nine Angles.*

Chapters 2 and 3 explore the historical antecedents of the Nine Angles and the development of the system within the Church of Satan and Temple of Set.

Chapter 4 covers various geometric concepts that are the basis for understanding the symbolism of the Nine Angles.

Chapter 5 discusses the semiotic theory of magic, placing it in the context of historical theories of magic as well as delving into the "Command to Look" of photographer William Mortensen, which was a primary influence on Anton LaVey's Law of the Trapezoid.

Chapter 6 draws on the historical, geometrical, and theoretical material presented in the previous chapters to analyze in detail *Die Elektrischen Vorspiele, The Ceremony of the Nine Angles,* and *The Call to Cthulhu.* These three rituals are the foundational works of angular magic, and are critical to understand and study for their inspiration in crafting your **own** rituals.

Chapter 7 establishes the foundations for magical work with the Nine Angles. This groundwork includes suggestions for preparing and dedicating a chamber to the practice of angular magic, as well as the basis for daily practices that will awaken the reader to the possibilities within this system.

Chapter 8 presents a variety of examples of illustrative and operative uses of the Angles. The illustrative operations—that is, the introspective and reflective applications of the Angles—explore such topics as a uniquely Left-Hand Path form of divination, sigils and symbols, and developing mindfulness. The operative applications focus on the use of the Angles to facilitate discernible change within the Self or in the objective universe. The chapter also includes suggestions for developing your **own** practices, which are a necessity for truly under-standing the Left-Hand Path underpinnings of the Angles.

W   The book concludes with the appendices that provide deeper historical context about angular magic through some of the rituals and essays that have been profound influences on its develop-ment within the Order of the Trapezoid.

My desire is to empower and inform those who may resonate with this system—one which until now has only been hinted at in materials available to the public—through my two decades of work with it. Above all, the Nine Angles must be **worked with** and **experienced** in order to gain the most from their study. True transformation cannot come from reflection alone, and a system such as the Angles, which is dynamic and ever-evolving, must be approached with an equally dynamic, flexible, and experimental mind-set.

Let us now begin with a more thorough look at what the Angles are and how you might begin to use them in your own practices.

Author's Note: The use of gender-specific pronouns in the various rituals is intended in a purely literary sense; all of the rituals may be performed by magicians of any gender identification.

The Ceremony of the Nine Angles

By Michael A. Aquino, Ph.D.

[This ceremony is to be performed in a closed chamber containing no curved surfaces whatsoever. No open flames are to be present in the chamber, except a single brazier or flame-pot to be used where indicated. General illumination is provided either through controlled starlight or moonlight, or via concealed ultraviolet devices. Above and behind the altar platform should appear the outline of a regular trapezoid. The celebrant and participants all wear masks or headpieces to blur or distort the true facial features.

All participants assemble in a half-hexagonal formation facing the large trapezoid emblem. The celebrant stands before the altar, facing the participants. He raises his left hand in the Sign of the Horns:]

CELEBRANT:

N'kgnath ki'q Az-Athoth r'jyarh wh'fagh zhasa phr-tga nyena phragn'glu.

Let us do honor to Azathoth, without whose laughter this world should not be.

[Participants answer the gesture.]

PARTICIPANTS:

Ki'q Az-Athoth r'jyarh wh'fagh zhasa phr-tga nyena phragn'glu.

Honor to Azathoth, without whose laughter this world should not be.

CELEBRANT:

Kzs'nath r'n Az-Athoth bril'nwe sza'g elu'khnar rquorkwe w'ragu mfancgh' tiim'br vua. Jsnuf a wrugh kod'rf kpra kybni sprn'aka ty'knu El-aka gryenn'h krans hu-ehn.

Azathoth, great center of the cosmos, let thy flutes sing unto us, lulling us against the terrors of thy domain. Thy merriment sustains our fears, and we rejoice in the World of Horrors in thy name.

PARTICIPANTS:

Ki'q Az-Athoth r'jyarh wh'fagh zhasa phr-tga nyena phragn'glu.

Honor to Azathoth, without whose laughter this world should not be.

[Celebrant lowers hand, then renders the Sign of the Horns with his right hand. All participants echo the gesture.]

CELEBRANT:

N'kgnath ki'q Y'gs-Othoth r'jyarh fer-gryp'h-nza ke'ru phragn'glu.

Let us do honor to Yog-Sothoth, without whose sign we ourselves should not be.

PARTICIPANTS:

Ki'q Y'gs-Othoth r'jyarh fer-gryp'h-nza ke'ru phragn'glu.

Honor to Yog-Sothoth, without whose sign we ourselves should not be.

CELEBRANT:

Kh'run-mnu kai Y'gs-Othoth hrn-nji qua-resvn xha drug'bis pw-nga s'jens ni'ka quraas-ti kno'g nwreh sho-j rgy-namanth El-aka gryenn'h. Ky'rh-han'treh zmah-gron'tk'renb phron-yeh fha'gni y'g zyb'nos vuy-kin'eh kson wr'g kyno.

Yog-Sothoth, master of dimensions, through thy will are we set upon the World of Horrors. Faceless one, guide us through the flight of thy creation, that we may behold the Bond of the Angles and the promise of thy will.

PARTICIPANTS:
Ki'q Y'gs-Othoth r'jyarh fer-gryp'h-nza ke'ru phragn'glu.

Honor to Yog-Sothoth, without whose sign we ourselves should not be.

> [Celebrant raises both arms away from him at a sharp angle. Participants do likewise.]

CELEBRANT:
Z'j-m'h kh'rn Z'j-m'h kh'r Z'j-m'h kh'rmnu. Kh'rn w'nh nyg hsyh fha'gnu er'ngidrg-nza knu ky cry-str'h n'knu. Ou-o nje'y fha'gnu qurs-ti ngai-kang whro-kng'hrgh-i szhno zyu-dhron'k po'j nu Cth'n. I'a ry'gzenghro.

The Daemons are, the Daemons were, and the Daemons shall be again. They came, and we are here; they sleep, and we watch for them. They shall sleep, and we shall die, but we shall return through them. We are their dreams, and they shall awaken. Hail to the ancient dreams.

PARTICIPANTS:
I'a ry'gzenghro.

Hail to the ancient dreams.

> [The celebrant now turns to face the altar.]

CELEBRANT:
Kh'rensh n'fha'n-gnh khren-kan'g N'yra-l'yht-Otp hry'n chu-si whr'g zyb'nos thu'nbyjne'w nhi quz-a.

I call now to the unsleeping one, the black herald, Nyarlathotep, who assureth the Bond between the living and the dead.

PARTICIPANTS:
I'a N'yra-l'yht-Otp.

Hail, Nyarlathotep.

CELEBRANT:

Kh'rengyu az'pyzh rz'e hy'knos zhri ty'h nzal's za naagha hu'h-nby jne'w nhi quz-al hjru-crusk'e dzund dkni-nyeh ryr'ngkain-i khring's naaghs pyz'rn ry'gzyn rgy-namanth El-aka gryenn'h tko f'unga l'zen-zu dsi-r p'ngath fha'gnu nig-quz'a I'a N'yra-l'yht-Otp.

O dark one, who rideth the winds of the Abyss and cryeth the night gaunts between the living and the dead, send to us the Old One of the World of Horrors, whose word we honor unto the end of the deathless sleep. Hail, Nyarlathotep.

PARTICIPANTS:

I'a N'yra-l'yht-Otp.

Hail, Nyarlathotep.

CELEBRANT:

I'as urenz-khrgn naaghs z'h hlye fer-zn cyn. I'as aem'nh ci-cyzb vyni-weth w'ragn jnusf whrengo jnusf'wi klo zyah zsybh kyn-tal-o huz-u kyno.

Hail to thee, black prince from the Barrier whose charge we bear. Hail to thee and to thy fathers, within whose cycle thou laugh and scream in terror and in merriment, in fear and in ecstasy, in loneliness and in anger, upon the whim of thy will.

PARTICIPANTS:

I'a N'yra-l'yht-Otp urz'n naagha.

Hail, Nyarlathotep, prince of the Abyss.

CELEBRANT:

V'hu-ehn n'kgnath fha'gnu n'aem'nh. Kzren ry'gzyn cyzb-namanth El-aka gryenn'h kh'renshz k'rahz'nhu zyb'nos y'goth-e vuy-kin'eh nals zyh.

In thy name let us behold the father. Let the Old One who reigneth upon the World of Horrors come and speak with us, for we would again strengthen the Bond that liveth within the angles of the Path of the Left.

[The celebrant stands directly before the altar, clenching both fists and crossing the left hand over the right against his chest.]

CELEBRANT:
I'a Sh'b-N'ygr'th aem'nh El-aka gryenn'h. I'a aem'nh kyl-d zhem'n. I'a
zhem'nfnin'quz n'fha'n-gn ki-qua hu-ehn zyb'nos.

Hail, Shub-Niggurath, father of the World of Horrors. Hail, father of
the hornless ones. Hail, ram of the Sun and deathless one, who sleepest
not while we honor thy name and thy bond.

PARTICIPANTS:
I'a Sh'b-N'ygr'th.

Hail, Shub-Niggurath.

> [The Goat of a Thousand Young appears. All participants clench
> their fists after the fashion of the celebrant.]

CELEBRANT:
I'a aem'nh.

Hail, father.

PARTICIPANTS:
I'a aem'nh.

Hail, father.

SHUB-NIGGURATH:
Phragn'ka phragn. V'vuy-kin'e f'ungn kyl-d zhem'n k'fungn zyb'nos
Z'j-m'h kyns el-kran'u, Fungnu'h zyb-kai zyb'nos rohz vuy-kh'yn.

I am that I am. Through the angles I speak with the hornless ones, and
I pledge anew the Bond of the Daemons, through whose will this world
is come to be. Let us speak the Bond of the Nine Angles.

CELEBRANT AND PARTICIPANTS:
I'a aemn'h urz'vuy-kin w'hren'j El-aka gryenn'h. Fung'hn-kai zyb'nos
rohz vuy-kh'yn n'kye w'ragh zh'sza hrn-nji qua-resvn k'ng naagha zhem
v'mhneg-alz.

Hail, father and lord of the angles, master of the World of Horrors. We speak the Bond of the Nine Angles to the honor of the flutes of the laughing one, the master of dimensions, the herald of the barrier, and the Goat of a Thousand Young.

ALL:
V'ty'h vuy-kn el-ukh'nar ci-wragh zh'sza w'ragnh ks'zy d'syn.

From the First Angle is the infinite, wherein the laughing one doth cry and the flutes wail unto the ending of time.

V'quy'h vuy-kn hrn-nji hyl zaan-i vyk d'phron'h El-aka gryenn'h v'jnus-fyh whreng'n.

From the Second Angle is the master who doth order the planes and the angles, and who hath conceived the World of Horrors in its terror and glory.

V'kresn vuy-kn k'nga d'phron'g kr-a El-aka gryenn'h p'nseb quer-hga phragn uk-khron ty'h-qu'kre vuy-kin'e rohz.

From the Third Angle is the messenger, who hath created the power to behold the master of the World of Horrors, who giveth to thee substance of being and the knowledge of the Nine Angles.

V'huy vuy-kn zhem'nfi d'psy'h dy-tr'gyu El-aka gryenn'h f'ungn-ei si'n si-r'a s'alk d'hu'h-uye rohz.

From the Fourth Angle is the ram of the Sun, who brought thy selves to be, who endureth upon the World of Horrors and proclaimeth the time that was, the time that is, and the time that shall be; and whose name is the brilliance of the Nine Angles.

V'cvye vuy-kn kh'ren-i kyl-d zhem'n lyz-naa mnaa r'cvyev'y-kre Z'j-m'h gryn-h'y d'yn'khe cyvaalic h'y-cvy-rohz.

From the Fifth Angle are the hornless ones, who raise the temple of the five trihedrons unto the Daemons of creation, whose seal is at once four and five and nine.

V'quar'n vuy-kn fha'gn Z'j-m'h ki-dyus dyn-jn'ash cvy-knu ukr'n hy-rohz.

From the Sixth Angle is the sleep of the Daemons in symmetry, which doth vanquish the five but shall not prevail against the four and the nine.

V'try'v vuy-kn djn'sh dys-u n'fha'g-nir Z'j-m'h r'n hy-kre'snvy'k kr'n-quar.

From the Seventh Angle is the ruin of symmetry and the awakening of the Daemons, for the four and the nine shall prevail against the six.

V'nyr vuy-kn hrn-njir vu'a lyz-naa mnaa r'nyrv'y Z'j-m'h gry-h'y d'yn-khe cyvaal'k hy-cvy-rohz.

From the Eighth Angle are the Masters of the Realm, who raise the temple of the eight trihedrons unto the Daemons of creation, whose seal is at once four and five and nine.

V'rohz vuy-kn i'inkh-v zy-d'syn ur'bre-el hy'j whreng'n nakhreng'h yh'whreng'n kyenn'h.

From the Ninth Angle is the flame of the beginning and ending of dimensions, which blazeth in brilliance and darkness unto the glory of desire.

Shub-Niggurath:
K'fung'n zyb'nos Z'j-m'h kyns el-gryn'hy.

I pledge the Bond of the Daemons, through whose will this world hath come to be.

Celebrant and participants:
Ki'q zyb'nos k'El-aka gryenn'h.

We honor the bond upon the World of Horrors.

Shub-Niggurath:
Ki-iq kyl-d zhem'n.

Hail to the hornless ones.

CELEBRANT AND PARTICIPANTS:
Ki-iq Sh'b-N'ygr'th aem'nh El-aka gryenn'h.

Hail to Shub-Niggurath, father of the World of Horrors.

SHUB-NIGGURATH:
Zhar-v zy-d'syn.

Unto the beginning and the ending of dimensions.

CELEBRANT:
Zhar-v zy-d'syn.

Unto the beginning and the ending of dimensions.

> [The Goat of a Thousand Young no longer appears. The celebrant faces the participants.]

CELEBRANT:
Ty'h nzal's kra naaghs n'ghlasj zsyn'e ty'h nzal's za'je oth'e kyl-d zhem'n fungh'n.Nal Y'gs-Othoth krell N'yra-l'yht-Otp. I'a Y'gs-Othoth. I'a N'yra-l'yht-Otp.

The gaunts are loose upon the wold, and we shall not pass; but the time shall come when the gaunts will bow before us, and man shall speak with the tongues of the hornless ones. The way is Yog-Sothoth, and the key is Nyarlathotep. Hail, Yog-Sothoth. Hail, Nyarlathotep.

PARTICIPANTS:
I'a Y'gs-Othoth. I'a N'yra-l'yht-Otp.
I'a S'ha-t'n.

Hail, Yog-Sothoth. Hail, Nyarlathotep. Hail, Satan.

1

OVERVIEW OF
THE NINE ANGLES

As the prelude recounts, the first fully formed expression of the concept of the Nine Angles (in its visual representation as the trapezoid-plus-pentagram) emerged in *The Ceremony of the Nine Angles*. The *Ceremony* was written by Michael Aquino, and published in Anton Szandor LaVey's *The Satanic Rituals* (Avon, 1972).

Multiple threads of esoteric thought came together in the *Ceremony*. The number mysticism of Pythagoras plays an important role, as do Anton LaVey's ideas on the metaphysical significance of oblique (non-right) angles in architecture and art. The mathematical properties of the number nine (and the mystical significance of this in LaVey's thought) find a practical application, and Aquino's interest in the intellectual and magical implications of artificial language construction also figure prominently. All of this is presented through the aesthetics of the writing of Howard Phillips Lovecraft.

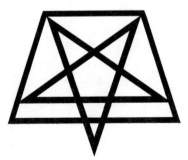

The geometric mystery that represents the Nine Angles

Chapters 2 and 3 explore in detail all the components of this amalgam of ideas and their historical antecedents.

In this chapter, we'll take a closer look at the Law of the Trapezoid, and its role in the development of the Nine Angles as a magical system. We'll also introduce two of the key aspects of their operative use: the Bond of the Nine Angles and a new perspective on the perception and manipulation of time. The chapter concludes with a pair of detailed examples of how the Angles progress, from two different vantage points of time.

THE ORDER OF THE TRAPEZOID

The Ceremony of the Nine Angles and its companion rite, *The Call to Cthulhu*, are both closely connected to the mysterious group called the Order of the Trapezoid. The Order first emerged from the shadows in an announcement by Anton LaVey in the December 1970 issue of the Church of Satan's newsletter, *The Cloven Hoof,* where he described it as the Board of Directors, security staff, and advisors of the Church of Satan.* Through various iterations of what exactly it signified within the Church, the emphasis always remained on the Order as the behind-the-scenes caretaker of those ideas and practices of which the Church was the public, active face. The Order of the Trapezoid finally took a definite form through the work of Michael Aquino in October 1982, and became one of the now oldest active Orders (or areas of specialization, under the leadership and teaching of a Grandmaster) within the Temple of Set.†

---

*John M. Kincaid, "An Explanation of the Role of the Council of the Trapezoid," *The Cloven Hoof* 5, no. 12 (December 1970). The name John M. Kincaid, although originally that of an actual member of the Church of Satan, later remained as a pseudonym used in administrative Church correspondence by Anton LaVey (and others). This both preserved the mystique of receiving rare actual correspondence signed by LaVey, as well as added to the appearance of a full staff of administrative workers at the Church headquarters at 6114 California Street in San Francisco.

†For a more complete account of the history of the Order of the Trapezoid, and its wide-ranging interests including angular magic, see chapter 3. The Order also maintains a public presence through its website.

The name of the Order of the Trapezoid refers to LaVey's **Law of the Trapezoid**, summarized by Aquino as:

> All obtuse angles are magically harmful to those unaware of this property. The same angles are beneficial, stimulating, and energizing to those who are magically sensitive to them.[1]

It is clear from LaVey's writings on the Law—covered thoroughly in chapters 3 and 6—that it refers to acute angles as well. It is thus curious to note that the trapezoid is the only convex polygon, in its standard forms, that contains both types of oblique angles (i.e., acute and obtuse), rendering the trapezoid as the figure that most fully encapsulates in symbolic form the hidden meaning of the Law that bears its name.

DEVELOPING THE SYSTEM

Though *The Ceremony of the Nine Angles* was published in 1972, it was not until March 1988 that a fuller exposition of the magical implications of the Nine Angles first surfaced in print.* The renowned runologist Stephen Edred Flowers, Ph.D., as a part of an exploration of the roots of the Order of the Trapezoid in the Church of Satan, wrote an article called "The Nine Angles of the Seal" for *Runes* (the private journal of the Order). This article put forth the first conception of the Angles beyond their roots in Pythagorean number mysticism and introduced the idea of the Nine Angles as a self-contained introspective and operative magical system.

The Ceremony of the Nine Angles will be analyzed in more detail in chapter 3 (focusing on its conceptual background) and chapter 6

---

*An article by Michael Aquino about the two Lovecraftian rites in *The Satanic Rituals* was published in 1978 in *Nyctalops* magazine; however this article was written for non-magicians and focused more on the construction of the rites (including explanations of some of the roots behind Aquino's creation of the "Yuggothic" language that have not been written about elsewhere). This article is reprinted as appendix A in the present volume.

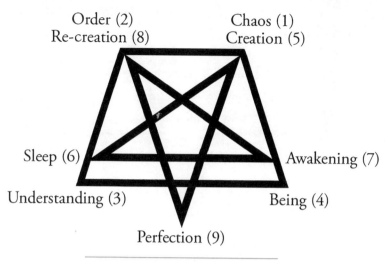

Order (2)   Chaos (1)
Re-creation (8)   Creation (5)

Sleep (6)   Awakening (7)

Understanding (3)   Being (4)

Perfection (9)

The keywords for the Angles;
1–4 corresponding to the trapezoid, 5–9 to the pentagram

(a magical analysis). However, in order to introduce the keywords associated with the various Angles by Stephen Flowers, we must first discuss briefly the section of the *Ceremony* known as the "Bond of the Nine Angles." The Bond speaks of each Angle, hinting at its meaning and significance in a manner similar to that of the rune poems in Germanic lore,* and the keywords themselves are part of a semiotic map of the Angles that point toward their essence. As the Nine Angles represent a dynamic, evolving magical system, the keywords associated with the Angles must themselves be refined along with further understanding; in later chapters, other possible keywords will be suggested, and the reader is encouraged to use those as guides to discover the most personally evocative set for him- or herself.

Tracing from the upper right corner of the trapezoid, the first

---

*The rune poems are a collection of poetic stanzas that reveal some of the meaning and significance of individual runes at various stages of their history. The three major rune poems are the Old English Rune Poem (eighth or ninth century), and the Old Norwegian Rune Rhyme (twelfth or thirteenth century), and the Old Icelandic Rune Poem (fifteenth century, but preserving lore from much earlier). For more information, see Edred Thorsson's *Runelore* (Red Wheel/Weiser, 2012), 93–112.

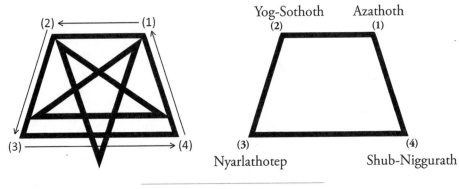

Tracing the first four Angles

four angles are associated with the Lovecraftian entities Azathoth, Yog-Sothoth, Nyarlathotep, and Shub-Niggurath. The overall purpose of the psychodramatic rite, which is written as a call and response between the participants and the chief celebrant, is to experience the shift in perspective and understanding that comes from working with strange angles. This theme is explored explicitly in Lovecraft's stories "The Haunter of the Dark" and "The Dreams in the Witch-House," and implicitly in many other places in his writings.

The fragments of the speech of the Great Old Ones, found in *The Case of Charles Dexter Ward* and "The Call of Cthulhu," were expanded by Aquino into a magical language somewhat reminiscent of Enochian. The entire ritual is written in this language, which Aquino dubbed Yuggothic, and also given in English translation. The intent is that the participants familiarize themselves with the English translation beforehand, while performing the rite itself exclusively in Yuggothic. For now, I'll limit the analysis to the English version, but will cover some of the more interesting aspects of the Yuggothic rendition in a later chapter.

INTRODUCING THE
BOND OF THE NINE ANGLES

From the First Angle is the infinite, wherein the laughing one doth cry and the flutes wail unto the ending of time.[2]

The keyword—or unifying concept—for the First Angle is **Chaos**. This is a state of unity, but which holds all possibilities (and polarities). The association of Chaos with the First Angle might suggest randomness or destructiveness, though it was originally intended to refer to the emergent properties of complex, dynamic systems that are highly sensitive to their initial conditions (such as those studied in the discipline of chaos mathematics). The implications of the First Angle emerge throughout the rest of the unfolding of the Angles. Geometrically, this is a single point, without dimension. In terms of Lovecraft's pantheon, the First Angle corresponds to Azathoth.

> From the Second Angle is the master who doth order the planes and the angles, and who hath conceived the World of Horrors in its terror and glory.[3]

The Second Angle refers to **Order**. Here the possibilities implicit within the Chaos of the First Angle begin to be glimpsed. The association of Order with the Second is not suggesting that it is the opposite of the Chaos of First, nor is it an attempt to obliterate the First Angle in lieu of the Second. Nothing could be further from the truth; if the First Angle implies unity, the Second implies a duality that allows the possibilities contained within that unity to begin to unfold. In terms of geometry, this is the extension of a point into a line, which only goes in a single direction even though it extends infinitely. The Lovecraftian deity implied by the Second Angle is Yog-Sothoth.

> From the Third Angle is the messenger, who hath created the power to behold the master of the World of Horrors, who giveth to thee substance of being and the knowledge of the Nine Angles.[4]

Understanding is the keyword of the Third Angle. Here, perspective is possible; a vantage point outside the simple binary dualism of the first two Angles allows for intentional differentiation between the two. Geometrically, the line becomes the triangle. As the bridge between worlds, the messenger of the Outer Gods, and the one who brings Understanding, Nyarlathotep is the essence of the Third Angle.

> From the Fourth Angle is the ram of the Sun, who brought thy selves to be, who endureth upon the World of Horrors and proclaimeth the time that was, the time that is, and the time that shall be; and whose name is the brilliance of the Nine Angles.[5]

The Fourth Angle has **Being** as its keyword. The perception possible through the Understanding of the Third Angle expands to include temporal awareness. Adding the perspective of time provides distinctly new possibilities for movement and the ability to observe the previous states of creation. The Lovecraftian Outer God associated with the Fourth Angle is Shub-Niggurath.

The Fifth Angle shares its vertex with that of the First, and the remaining five Angles are traced continuing in a counterclockwise direction.

> From the Fifth Angle are the hornless ones, who raise the temple of the five trihedrons unto the Daemons of creation, whose seal is at once four and five and nine.[6]

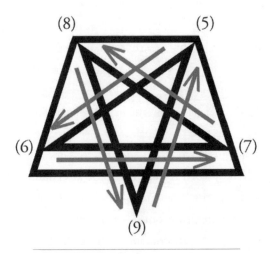

Tracing the remaining five angles

With the Fifth Angle, the vertices are now within the pentagram. The keyword for this Angle is **Creation**. The "hornless ones" referred to here are humanity, who can become an active, creative force in the world of matter and the senses. In his "Charter of the Order of the Trapezoid," Aquino writes, "It was the approach of the Church of Satan, and later of the Temple of Set, to single out self-consciousness as the characteristic feature of That which stood in contrast to the harmony of the natural cosmos."[7] There is no Lovecraftian entity associated with the Fifth through Ninth Angles, for reasons that will emerge in Chapter 3.

Also note that the point (vertex) at the tip of the Fifth Angle is the same as that of the First. There is a definite conceptual relationship between those two Angles; these resonances are one of the keys to working with the Nine Angles as a magical system.

From the Sixth Angle is the sleep of the Daemons in symmetry, which doth vanquish the five but shall not prevail against the four and the nine.[8]

The keyword for the Sixth Angle is **Sleep** (or alternately, **Death**). This refers to an incubation period where conscious thought and action regarding what is being brought into being are set aside for a while. By directing the active mind elsewhere, insights may now arise from the work and effort that have been internalized; this will necessarily be a reflection of the work that has been done through the previous Angles.

From the Seventh Angle is the ruin of symmetry and the awakening of the Daemons, for the four and the nine shall prevail against the six.[9]

Closely related to the Sixth Angle in concept, the Seventh Angle works through the keyword **Awakening** (or alternately, **Birth**). At this part of the cycle, that which has been incubating is brought forth again into conscious awareness and deliberate intention. This is the moment when the unbidden and unexpected "Aha!" moment arises, and previous mysteries or uncertainties suddenly begin to become clear.

From the Eighth Angle are the Masters of the Realm, who raise the
temple of the eight trihedrons unto the Daemons of creation, whose
seal is at once four and five and nine.[10]

The sequence from Sixth to Seventh to Eighth Angle is one of
the most important in the series. The renewal of purpose, intent, and
understanding gained from the transition of the Sixth to the Seventh
must now be used to bring forth the true form of that being created
through understanding and application of the Angles. All of the tools
needed for this creation are available, and the personal transformation
undergone thus far in the cycle can now be applied to the creation itself.
At this point in the process, creation folds back in on itself; thus, the
Eighth Angle is known by the keyword **Re-creation**.

Also note that the point at the vertex of the Eighth Angle is the
same as that of the Second. Just as with the First/Fifth, there is a vital
connection between those two Angles that provides a great key to working with this system.

From the Ninth Angle is the flame of the beginning and ending of
dimensions, which blazeth in brilliance and darkness unto the glory
of desire.[11]

The Ninth Angle is both the culmination of one cycle of the
Angles, and the beginning of a new one. It is referred to by the keyword
Perfection because it is complete in and of itself and also functions as
the ideal from which further creation can be sprung. Geometrically, it
is the Ninth Angle that functions as the point of dynamic balance for
the entire structure; it is dynamic because without constant effort and
motion to maintain that balance it will falter.

DIFFERENT VIEWS OF TIME

To approach the Nine Angles as a magical system, it is necessary to
introduce the notions of **curved time** and **angular time**.

In the cosmology of Plato, best exemplified in his dialogue *Timaeus,* the shape of the cosmos itself manifests as a sphere. The components of the cosmos form from the unmanifest void in the proportions of a Pythagorean musical scale, further tying this cosmology to notions of the Music (or Harmony) of the Spheres. The perfection of the sphere arises from all points on its surface being the same distance from its center, and it averages the shape of the other Platonic solids (themselves being composed of angles).

This geometrical/musical approach to cosmology was so influential that it has been implicit in much of Western esoteric thought for the past 2,500 years.

In 1929, *Weird Tales* magazine published a story by Frank Belknap Long (a member of Lovecraft's circle of admirers and correspondents) called "The Hounds of Tindalos." The titular hounds were able to move in and out of our world of three dimensions and linear time via gateways created by acute angles in the surrounding environment (e.g., a door frame or wall that is not quite square). Woe unto any whom the Hounds encountered, for they would surely meet their doom whether their transgression was intentional or not.

In terms of Plato, **curved time** is the time we experience as physical inhabitants of the orderly cosmos. These conceptions of curved time can be **linear** (time as a one-way arrow, limited and shaped by the curves of the "spherical" cosmos), or **cyclical** (like the progression of the seasons, or the connection to the sacred via the "eternal return" of Mircea Eliade's interpretation of mythology and religion as models of social structure).

Long's conception of **angular time**, however, was more closely tied to the subjective experience of time by the non-natural psyche. In angular time, much like the human thought process, ideas and awareness unfold in ways that are out of sync with the predictable processes of nature. A flash of insight may circumvent a much longer process of logical analysis; a moment of inspiration may create an entirely new worldview, or a previously undreamt-of work of art. The Hounds are the guardians against access to this non-natural aspect of the subjective universe, ready to strike against those who would dare transgress the orderly world of nature, convention, and conformity.

THE ANGLES AS SEEN
THROUGH CIRCULAR TIME

Let's look at circular time and angular time in terms of the Nine Angles, using the keywords given above as a shorthand for the significance of each Angle in the cycle as a whole. First, I'll trace the coming into being of a piece of music in circular time, starting from the bottommost Angle (which represents both source and destination for those processes that can be understood via the Nine Angles). The Nine Angles plus the circle, representing the objective universe (the entirety of what exists in time and space, whether known or unknown), form what Stephen Flowers calls the "Seal of Rûna." *Rûna* is an ancient Germanic word for "mystery" or "secret," and refers to the allure that the pursuit of the hidden and the mysterious holds. *Rûna* reminds us that there are always things that are outside of our knowledge and experience, and that the most essential quest for both scholars and magicians is to dig more deeply into the roots of things to uncover the mysteries that always lie behind them.

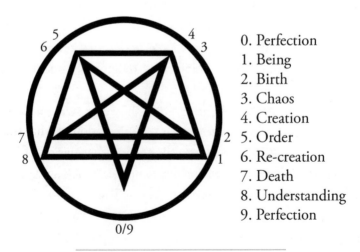

0. Perfection
1. Being
2. Birth
3. Chaos
4. Creation
5. Order
6. Re-creation
7. Death
8. Understanding
9. Perfection

The Angles through circular time

Impulse

0. **Perfection**: All possible combinations of notes and sounds reside in this state; some may be accessible by standard musical instruments, and some must be made real by electronic processes or the application of boundless imagination.

1. **Being**: The inspiration has struck; the idea has arisen. The desire to create has taken hold, and while the results are still unknown, *Impulse* the potential for a new musical creation has been established and recognized.

2. **Birth**: The framework for the composition is now in place. It will likely change and evolve, but the shaping process has now come alive.

3. **Chaos**: All of the potential directions the music can take swirl around it; some with form and pattern, others seemingly random. Out of this web of connections, the parts that seem to "fit" will begin to coalesce, hinting at a coherence that has not yet been fully realized.

4. **Creation**: What this particular inspiration might become has begun to take on a definite state. This is the point where—if you're in a band, for example, or have others whose musical opinion you value—you might share some of what is now taking shape.

5. **Order**: The piece of music is progressively refined, having been formed to the point that the vision of its eventual completion now draws forth its creation. It now exists in and of itself, and later changes will likely affect it only in subtle—yet important—ways.

6. **Re-creation**: In the wake of the form emerging from Order, the creator is now modified by her creation. This Re-creation is not the result of purely intellectual effort, but is a holistic transformation—it results from the integration of what the music reveals about its creator into the creator's new vision of herself.

7. **Death**: Active work on the music may cease for a while, but it is still in the "back of your mind." You'll find yourself humming it, or have it arise in your mind's ear spontaneously in moments of calm or quiet. It is no longer at the center of your conscious effort—but is always at the edge of conscious awareness, waiting

for the final details to be put in place in a moment of inspiration.

8. **Understanding**: What you've learned and created so far in this process can now be used in ways that were not available to you before. For example, you discovered a new way to use an old and familiar scale (or finally realized a way to incorporate a new one); these are all borne of the newfound understanding of your craft, as you have begun to reflect the transformations expressed through the music. Music can function as a magical diary through its connections to new Understanding of how to express your inner desires and feelings in the world outside your Self.

9. **Rebirth, or Perfection encountered anew**: The piece of music may be complete at this stage (although the creator knows that there is always more music to bring forth from the unmanifest), or it may serve as the beginning of a new cycle of creation. In either case, the creator has brought something new into the world, and the creator has transformed herself by the act of creating. The Nine Angles illustrates the idea that the ending of one cycle often merely reveals the pathway to the beginning of a new one, the difference being that the transformation gained by the enacting of one cycle opens possibilities that were previously out of reach or beyond imagination.

Note the various references to "inspiration" in the preceding description. This is a hint of two important ideas: (1) the general applicability of Nine Angles to the creative process (regardless of the medium that process works in); and (2) the influence of the Germanic cosmology centered on the emergence of Óðinn—the roots of whose name mean "master of inspiration"—which is important in the further development of the Angles by Stephen Flowers.

UNFOLDING THROUGH ANGULAR TIME

The way an idea or creation unfolds in angular time is more direct, but also more mysterious because it does not follow an expected linear timeline. Viewing the Angles in this way provides clues for magical timing (by being able to see events and ideas from a point of view that reveals different opportunities than those apparent from the perspective of linear time). Even with this knowledge of the Angles, it still holds true that the closer an event is to the present in *linear* time, the easier it will be to affect its unfolding in *angular* time.

To illustrate this angular perspective on the realization of an idea (and its effect on the one bringing it into being), let's trace the meaning and significance of the stages arising from this ordering. These can be interpreted in both a macrocosmic sense (pertaining to the phenomenon of consciousness itself) and a microcosmic sense (the particular experiences of a self-aware individual).

0. **Perfection**: Out of this idealized but fleeting state comes the desire for the magician to become more than she has been. (Contrast this with the religions and practices of the Right-Hand Path, where this perfected state is the final goal, instead of the Left-Hand Path ideal of a progressively refined jumping-off point for further realization of what the self might become.)

1. **Chaos** is the feeling that existence and self-awareness are beginning to unfold into something new, but it is not clear yet what that might be, or even ultimately which direction it needs to

0. Perfection
1. Chaos
2. Order
3. Understanding
4. Being
5. Creation
6. Sleep/Death
7. Awakening/Birth
8. Re-creation
9. Perfection

The Angles through angular time

take. The desire to seek out inspiration has been sensed, however, and can't be ignored. If we answer the call of the Hidden instead of retreating into the innumerable ways the world provides for shunning growth through action, we may arrive at

2. **Order.** This is the point at which we're faced with a crucial choice: whether to embrace the responsibility for being the active force in our lives, or to retreat into servitude masquerading as comfort. When we realize that, within the subjective universe, meaning exists only insofar as we are able to create and assign it, we come to

3. **Understanding.** The source of self-consciousness itself can be apprehended, and significant change can be brought about through knowledge of where to apply the pressure. Even though great transformation is possible here, without the wisdom that comes from experience, this is a dangerous state despite the apparent power it brings; by using this state to bring clarity, we can gain access to more

4. **Being.** By drawing forth an aspect of the objective universe that is recast according to our newly evolved Understanding, our transformations now begin to affect others in ways we could have scarcely imagined. We have become more aware and potent in the process, but while this leads to greater control, the uncertain destiny of these actions must then lead to true

5. **Creation.** Once the creator unleashes her creation on the world, it no longer belongs solely to her. An idea or thing, cast loose from its creator, thrives or perishes depending on how well it allows *others* to create meaning. The creator, having sent forth a creation communicating some part of their own essence which takes hold within the subjective universes of others, may then progress into a state that appears as

6. **Sleep.** Paradoxically, this newly enhanced power to create must be kept in check so that it doesn't dissipate too quickly. Rather than unleash what we are now capable of creating all at once, we must preserve this creative ability so that it arises only in

response to true need. To do otherwise would be to lose what has come before in gaining sovereignty, as the creative act is at its most individualistic when its possessor alone controls its manifestation. Now when the creator does choose to bring forth this capacity, she has chosen the moment for

7. **Awakening.** Emerging from self-imposed rest when the time and need are there allows the magician to be an active force within the universe in a completely new way. Those ideas and innovations already brought into being can be rebuilt according to the new vision of their creator, which opens the possibilities of

8. **Re-creation.** This occupies the same point in the Angles as **Order**, and what once seemed a profound and difficult choice was anything but that. Only the choice of ownership was possible, if the desire were there to continue unfolding oneself via the Angles. Neither the beginning nor the destination of the quest are where they were once thought to be, but both spring from

9. **Perfection.** The principle of Becoming **itself** is the driving force that must be connected with, dynamic yet kept in balance through motion. The creator and her creation have become unified, although for the quester along the Left-Hand Path, this glimpse of perfection (completion and self-coherence) then leads to awareness of the pull of *Rûna*, and the cycle of the Angles remains in motion.

2

HISTORICAL ANTECEDENTS

Ideas are like hardy spores, and sometimes the presumed origin of a concept may be only the reappearance of a much more ancient idea that had lain dormant.[1]

CARL BOYER, *A HISTORY OF MATHEMATICS*

Before we can talk about the Nine Angles, we must explore the mysteries of the numbers **three** and **nine**. Three—and its product when multiplied by itself, nine—figure prominently in the lore of Indo-European language and mythology. This significance carries through to much of the numerical symbolism Anton LaVey employed in his theories of cycles of human behavior; in the essay "The Unknown Known" in *The Satanic Rituals,* he sums this up as "Nine is the number of the Ego, for it always returns to itself."[2]

In this chapter, we'll look at the fascinating history of the numbers *three* and *nine* in folklore and mythology. Then, the arithmology—or number mysticism—of the Pythagoreans reveals some crucial keys to understanding the Nine Angles, followed by an unexpected reappearance of Pythagoreanism in a Germanic context. We'll also discuss the history and significance of other nine-angled figures, such as the so-called *Valknútr* and the *Enneagram.* The chapter concludes with an examination of the essential influence of John Dee and Howard Phillips Lovecraft on angular magic.

Trifunctional Hyp.: Georges Dumezil (1898-1986)
Sovereignty, Martial, Generative

* INDIA CASTE *
SYSTEM

CULTURAL AND MYTHOLOGICAL
OCCURRENCES OF THREE

The significance of the numbers three and nine is well-attested in ancient Indo-European mythologies and cultures, and especially in northern Germanic lore. What follows are some of the more prominent occurrences.

A fundamental pattern of a threefold division of social class in Indo-European societies—known as the tri-functional hypothesis—was identified and thoroughly documented by the French philologist Georges Dumézil (1898–1986). These divisions were:

- **Sovereignty**—the ruling class of leaders and priests.
- **Martial**—segments of society engaged in military action (in dealing with those outside the tribe or societal unit) or enforcement of the laws (within the tribe or societal unit).
- **Generative**—the groups responsible for crafting, farming, and productivity in the society.

In keeping with the idea that mythology often functions as the basis for the ideal arrangement of society, Indo-European peoples tended to have gods or goddesses exemplifying each of these important divisions. For example, in Norse mythology these functions were represented by Óðinn (sovereignty), Tyr (law and justice), and the Vanir (various fertility deities). Further examples of this tripartite division include the caste system in India (Brahmans, Kshatriya, and Vaishya fulfilling the respective roles).

Also in northern Germanic lore, the triple god Óðinn (whose name derives from a Proto-Germanic root meaning "inspiration") and his "brothers" Vili (cognition) and Vé (sacred power) represent another significant occurrence of this important number. Additionally, there are the three Norns—rulers of human destiny—named *Urðr* (whose name means "what has turned or become"), *Verðandi* ("what is turning or becoming"), and *Skuld* ("what should be").[3] Yggdrasill—the tree that connects the nine worlds—is supported by three great roots.

As an important example of the occurrence of three outside of

Mulas, Egyptian; Xeper; Runes

the northern European realm, the Mediterranean figure of Hermes Trismegistus—"thrice-greatest Hermes"—is well known as the mythical author of the *Corpus Hermeticum*. Hermes Trismegistus was said to know the three parts of the wisdom of the entirety of existence: alchemy, astrology, and theurgy.

The Number Three in Magical Formulas

The number three also appears as a structural element in magical formulas, both within and beyond the Indo-European cultural sphere. The transcultural appearance of such tripartite formulas implies that this numerical significance may precede the prehistoric splitting-off of various different cultures from their common ancestors.

A significant non-Indo-European example is from the Egyptian text of *The Book of Knowing the Spiral Force of Re and the Felling of Apep*. Reflecting its self-referential nature, the formula of the "spiral force" was inscribed around a column as part of a monument created by Ramses II ("the Great"). In Egyptian, it can be expressed as **Xepera Xeper Xeperu**, or in Don Webb's rendering:

> I have come into being, and by the process of my coming into being the process of coming into being is established.[4]

In a more modern example, yet still rooted in archaic cosmology and folklore, the early twentieth-century Austrian occultist Guido von List* saw the runes as part of a threefold formula:

> *Entstehen, Sein, Vergehen zum neuen Entstehen* ("Arising, being, passing away to a new arising")[5]

---

*List (1848–1919), an Austrian occultist, journalist, and writer, was a key figure in the Germanic pagan revivalism of the early twentieth century. While temporarily blinded (due to a cataract operation) for about eleven months in 1902, List synthesized his understanding of the runes and later taught a system he called the Armanen runes. His most well-known book, *Das Geheimnis der Runen,* has been translated into English (along with commentary and biographical information) as *The Secret of the Runes* by Stephen E. Flowers (Destiny, 1988).

List's formula emphasizes the ideal of eternal, cyclical evolution as applied in both an organic sense (life/death/rebirth) and a cosmological sense that can be reflected in an individual's own development.

All of these formulas reflect the use of the number three in cycles that are self-perpetuating; that is, the formulas describe the subject (the doer) of an act being transformed by it and then becoming the object (or recipient) of the same act. We will discuss this connection between "magical" numbers and self-evolving patterns in more detail, and specifically in the context of the Nine Angles, in chapter 5.

CULTURAL AND MYTHOLOGICAL OCCURRENCES OF NINE

Nine—three amplified through multiplication with itself—is also widely attested as a significant number in Indo-European mythologies and cultures. Again, the mythological importance of the number is especially pronounced in the lore of the northern Germanic cultures.

Two of the most well-known instances of the number nine as a central measure in Norse cosmology are the Nine Worlds, and the nine nights when Óðinn sacrificed himself to himself following which he won knowledge of the runes. Both of these are centered around the World Tree, Yggdrasill, the holy ash tree that connects earth and the heavens. Yggdrasill—whose roots extend to unknown depths—acts as the axis around which the cosmos revolves, and provides the connections between the ninefold division of reality represented by the various worlds (or realms).* During the Ordeal of Yggdrasill, Óðinn hung from the tree for nine nights with no sustenance, wounded by his own spear,

---

*The names of the nine realms are not preserved in existing lore; however, the general consensus assigns them as: **Muspellsheimr** (realm of fire), **Niflheimr** (realm of mist), **Vanaheimr** (home of the Vanir, the fertility and nature gods/goddesses), **Jötunheimr** (home of the giants), **Ljóssálfheimr** ("light-elf" realm), **Svartálfheimr** ("dark-elf" [i.e., dwarf] realm), **Hel** (home of the souls of the dead that are not able to renew themselves), **Ásgarðr** (fortress of the Aesir, the gods of consciousness), and **Midgarðr** (home of humans, able to become fully conscious through work with and emulation of the Aesir). See appendix E for more on the magical applications of this arrangement of the cosmos.

and at his moment of deepest despair was suddenly infused with knowledge of the fundamental mysteries of the cosmos (the runes themselves).

Also in northern Germanic lore, the symbol of the so-called *Valknútr* embodies both three and nine, being composed of three interlocking triangles. This is one of the antecedents of the nine-angled magical figure, and will be discussed more fully in that context in chapter 5. The symbol is a common one carved onto various objects as early as the seventh century of the Common Era in Sweden. The word *Valknútr* (Old Norse for "knot of the slain/fallen") is a modern name created for the symbol; its true name is unknown. On historical artifacts the symbol almost exclusively appears as part of other imagery of Óðinn; given the other significance attached to the number nine, it is likely connected in its meaning with the Nine Worlds, and the nine nights during which Óðinn overcame death itself in order to win knowledge of the runes.

Some other notable instances of the number nine in Indo-European culture and myth are:

- The Old English *Nine Herbs Charm* (tenth century), full of mentions of three and nine, provides a recipe for a salve to treat poisoning and infection. The poem contains one of the two major mentions of Woden (the Old English cognate of Óðinn) in Anglo-Saxon texts, thus providing another reference for the important connections between Óðinn and the number nine.

The *Valknútr*

- In Greek Mythology, the Muses were nine goddesses (or, rarely, three in some accounts) providing the source of inspiration in the arts and sciences. Their various realms of influence provided a means of categorizing knowledge and art forms.
- In the *Inferno* section the fourteenth-century epic poem *The Divine Comedy*, Dante Alighieri famously divided Hell into nine concentric circles. The journey through these circles is illustrative of the path of the individual in overcoming and rejecting sin; to begin the journey, the narrator must first confront and overcome three beasts that are also symbolic of the three groupings of the circles.
- The 1923 Talbot Mundy novel, *The Nine Unknown*, tells a story about the legendary Nine Unknown Men; this group is a secret society claimed to have existed since 270 BCE and founded by the emperor Ashoka to safeguard knowledge that would be dangerous for the rest of humanity to possess. In the 1960 book *Le Matin des Magiciens* (*The Morning of the Magicians*), the authors Pauwels and Bergier recounted the legend without regard to its fictional origins—thus contributing it to various other suppositions about the history of secret societies. The Nine Unknown also appear in the dedication section of the early editions of Anton LaVey's *The Satanic Bible;* we will discuss the influence of *The Morning of the Magicians* on LaVey in more detail in chapter 3.
- The Austrian mystic Karl Maria Wiligut—later occult advisor to *Reichsführer*-SS Heinrich Himmler under the pseudonym "Weisthor"—included among his writings on ancient Germanic religion a set of precepts called **The Nine Commandments of Gôt**. This credo is most readily understood as a Germanic recasting of Pythagorean number symbolism of the numbers one through nine (along the same line as Michael Aquino's adapting Pythagorean numerology into his conception of the Nine Angles). Later in this chapter, in the section on Pythagoras, we will cover these nine laws in their full context.
- The diagram in the Shri Vidya school of Hinduism called the **Sri Yantra** includes four upward pointing triangles (representing

the masculine) combined with five downward pointing triangles (the feminine). The union of these two principles, in the proper ritual contexts, is a method for knowing Tripurāsundarī (beautiful goddess of the three cities). Thus, the symbol utilizes both three- and nine-based imagery. Certain rites of union in the Western ceremonial magic tradition such as Aleister Crowley's *Star Sapphire* reflect similar symbolism. Peter Levenda, drawing on the works of Kenneth Grant, connects Tripurāsundarī (sometimes referred to as the "Red Goddess") with the Scarlet Woman archetype,[6] with all its associations between Indian Tantra and Western sex magic and continuations of older, forgotten traditions from the dim past. This connection is thus deeply enmeshed in Grant's synthesis of the primal archetypes gaining expression through the fiction of H. P. Lovecraft, Tantra, and Crowley's Thelema.

Origins of the Name for the Number Nine

The name of the number nine in English and many other Indo-European languages has roots in a Proto-Indo-European word that has been reconstructed as $h_1néwn$. Curiously, the word *new* in many Indo-European languages can be traced to the very similar reconstructed term *néwos*. This similarity is readily seen in languages such as German (*neu*, "new"; *neun*, "nine") and Latin (*novus*, "new"; *novem*, "nine"). While it is considered somewhat controversial, and far from proven, historians of mathematics as well as some linguists have proposed that this similarity is not a coincidence. Rather, it is conjectured to be evidence of count-

The Triangles of the Sri Yantra

ing and number systems based on four and/or eight, where nine would represent the beginning of a new cycle.

This supposition cannot be proven with currently available historical evidence, but its symbolic implications do however fit very neatly with our uses of nine in a magical sense. Since we are concerned with symbolic behavior, and our ability to use it to modify the content and significance of our own unique experiences as conscious and self-aware beings, the actual truth of this linguistic assertion is not nearly as important as what we are able to do with it. In other words, it is the significance and degree of truth we ascribe to it that matters; we need merely distinguish it as symbolically true in order not to confuse it with the linguistic truth, which it may or may not possess.

PYTHAGORAS AND NUMBER

The philosophy of Pythagoras of Samos (ca. 570–495 BCE) has been profoundly influential on Western Philosophy of the past 2,500 years. This philosophy—based primarily on the symbolism behind numbers as a means of comprehending the universe and the magician's place within it—provides a significant basis for the original conception of *The Ceremony of the Nine Angles*. The idea of the fundamentally mathematical nature of the cosmos is further developed by the most important figure in the development of Western Philosophy, Plato (428–348 BCE).

The meaning of numbers in the teachings of the Pythagoreans is to be interpreted arithmologically (i.e., by the concepts of "oneness," "twoness," etc.) and not strictly arithmetically (the numbers as a sequence used in counting or other mathematical operations). The arithmological symbolism and meaning the Pythagoreans associated with the first ten numbers (the **decad**) can be summarized as follows:

1. The **monad**: the singular, self-contained aspect of existence; the primordial **one**; associated with chaos (in the sense of the unformed matrix from which greater order is formed). Geometrically, it is a single point in no dimensions.

2. The **dyad** (or **duad**): the monad divided into two polar opposites, undifferentiated and with no means of choosing or comparing between them—leading to ignorance—since each has no meaning or significance without the other. The Pythagoreans regarded the **dyad** as the "mother" of ignorance, which provides the background against which true wisdom is developed and attained. In terms of geometry, it is a line (extending infinitely in one direction and in one dimension).

3. The **triad**: a third element provides for perspective on the **dyad**, ultimately leading to wisdom. With three (the **monad** combined with the **dyad**), the perceiver can now conceptualize past, present, and future. The Pythagoreans associated the **triad** with the disciplines of geometry, astronomy, and music; in terms of the faculties of Man, it is spirit, mind, and soul. With two dimensions, the line extends into a plane.

4. The **tetrad**: considered to be the most perfect number, as it is the final component needed to create the **decad** ($1 + 2 + 3 + 4 = 10$). The **tetrahedron**—a four-sided pyramid—is the simplest geometrical solid. It is also the number of the elements of the physical world: earth, air, fire, and water.

5. The **pentad**: to the Pythagoreans, the five-pointed pentagram was a sacred symbol of life and vitality, and a gateway to otherwise inaccessible realms of awareness beyond the normal senses. Indeed, the pentagram was the secret sign of their Brotherhood. The pentagram, both in its symbolism and its encoding of the Golden Ratio, forms an integral part of the information in chapter 4.

6. The **hexad**: the hexagram (composed of two triangles implying the union of **triads**) represented harmony and union—opposites or other disparate elements are neutralized by canceling each other out. The **hexad** is a place of rest and symmetry.

7. The **heptad**: associated with life, birth, and spiritual law. The union of three (the spirit, mind, and soul of Man) and four (the world—the elements of earth, air, fire, and water).

8. The **ogdoad**: significant as the cube, which has eight corners; the perfect number four added to itself; divides into two 4s, which each divide into two 2s, which each divide into two 1s, thus reestablishing the monad.

9. The **ennead**: the number of man (perhaps because of the nine months of gestation); the **triad** multiplied by itself; associated with things then considered boundless, such as the ocean and the horizon (nine is limitless because there is nothing beyond it but the idealized perfection of the **decad**).

10. The **decad**: the greatest of all numbers; the gateway of return to the **monad** in ever greater cycles of regeneration; symbolic of the stages of creation (represented in a four-row pyramid of dots stacked on each other: 4, then 3, then 2, then 1).

The Pyramidal Dots

THE NINE COMMANDMENTS OF GÔT

The Austrian mystic Karl Maria Wiligut* (1866–1946) took inspiration from other leaders of *völkisch* pagan revivalism in late nineteenth- and early twentieth-century German-speaking lands. From the teachings of

---

*The definitive biography of Wiligut is Rudolf J. Mund's *Der Rasputin Himmlers: Die Wiligut-Saga* (Volkstum, 1982), which includes much information directly from surviving associates and students of Wiligut, combined with rare writings by Wiligut himself. While that book has never been fully translated into English, it was a primary source for Stephen E. Flowers and Michael Moynihan's *The Secret King: The Myth and Reality of Nazi Occultism* (2nd ed., Dominion/Feral House, 2007).

Guido von List and Jörg Lanz von Liebenfels,* combined with a personal interpretation of the runes and claims of an ancient family tradition passed from father to eldest son, Wiligut synthesized and taught his own unique version of the "original" Germanic religion.

A decorated army officer in World War I, Wiligut was later to become a high-ranking advisor responsible directly to Heinrich Himmler in the SS. Many of the writings containing Wiligut's teachings in his own words only survive as memos to Himmler.

Both indirectly through Guido von List, and perhaps directly although he never explicitly acknowledges this as a source, some of Wiligut's writings show the influence of the works of Madame Blavatsky.† There are references to and speculation on the so-called root races of humanity, as well as bits and pieces of philosophy and number mysticism from Pythagoras interpreted through a decidedly Theosophical lens.

It is in the context of the Pythagorean influence that we now examine **The Nine Commandments of Gôt**. Allegedly first written down in 1908, the only known surviving manuscript of the Commandments is a typewritten memo to Himmler in 1935, with the handwritten note "For the authenticity of the tradition."[7] Annotated in a complex

---

*Jörg Lanz von Liebenfels (born Adolf Josef Lanz; 1874–1954) was a former Cistercian monk who later taught a racially based occult doctrine he called **Ariosophy**. Spread through his group Ordo Novi Templi (Order of the New Templars), Ariosophy was an esoteric ideology that pioneered many of the same ideas about superior and inferior races—and the religious implications of these differences—that were later adopted, mostly independently, by the Nazis. While Liebenfels's journal *Ostara* was known to have been read by some of the early members of the Nazi party, their interest was mainly in the racial ideas; after the Nazis came to power, both the Ordo Novi Templi and *Ostara* were suppressed along with the vast majority of other occult groups and publications.

†Helena Blavatsky (1831–1891) was a Russian spiritualist and occultist who founded the Theosophical Society. Amid claims—most likely fanciful—of travel to exotic locations where she was supposed to have received secret teachings from various ascended masters, Blavatsky taught that these masters have a grand plan to initiate those worthy of receiving their teachings into a new society that will overthrow the decadent current world religions and restore the original spirituality of mankind. Theosophy was a major vehicle in the spread of knowledge of Eastern religions to the West—these Eastern religions are supposed to have maintained closer ties to the original spirituality of mankind due to their physical proximity to its sources.

runic code, the Commandments of Gôt provide keys to the cosmology that underlies Wiligut's philosophy. The closest Wiligut came—at least in his few written sources; his methods of teaching were largely mouth-to-ear—to defining or explaining Gôt was through the analysis of its significance in his family seal. The runic formula identified with Gôt is broken down into the runes *gibor* (ᛉ), *os* (ᚪ), and *tyr* (ᛏ). Wiligut expands the formula into signifying "Hallowed All-Light of spiritual-material being in an eternal cycle in the circle of creation in the All."[8]

While this source was not known to Michael Aquino in 1971,* Wiligut's Commandments are nonetheless relevant to our historical survey of antecedents of the Nine Angles due to their recasting of Pythagorean ideas in a new form, much as Aquino himself did.

The Nine Commandments are:

1. Gôt is Al-unity!
2. Gôt is "Spirit and Matter," the dyad. He brings duality, and is nevertheless, unity and purity . . .
3. Gôt is a triad: Spirit, Energy and Matter. Gôt-Spirit, Gôt-Ur, Gôt-Being, or Sun-Light and Work, the dyad.
4. Gôt is eternal—as Time, Space, Energy and Matter in his circulating current.
5. Gôt is cause and effect. Therefore, out of Gôt flows right, might, duty and happiness.
6. Gôt is eternally generating. The Matter, Energy and Light of Gôt are that which carry this along.
7. Gôt—beyond the concepts of good and evil—is that which carries the seven epochs of human history.
8. Rulership in the circulation of cause-and-effect carries along the highness—the secret tribunal.

---

*Nor, would it seem—in light of the complete lack of mention in any contemporary sources—was it known to anyone else in the English-speaking world. Even in Germany, Wiligut's writings were extremely obscure until the publication of the Mund biography. Wiligut did not begin to assume his well-deserved place in the neo-mythology of "Nazi occultism" until the publication of Nicholas Goodrick-Clarke's *The Occult Roots of Nazism* (Aquarian, 1985).

9. Gôt is beginning without end—the Al. He is completion in Nothingness, and, nevertheless, Al in the three-times-three realization of all things. He closes the circle at N-yule, at Nothingness, out of the conscious into the unconscious, so that this may again become conscious.[9]

Now, let's look at the distinct Pythagorean influence on these Commandments. Note that Wiligut considers nine to be both the end of one cycle of creation and the seed from which a new one forms. This "seed of re-creation" role is fulfilled by ten in the Pythagorean **decad**, as a bridge between the **ennead** and the **monad**; to Wiligut, the bridge is contained **within** nine itself. This also creates a much closer correspondence to the geometrical and symbolic function of the Ninth Angle—whose central Mystery is that it is both end and beginning, both source and destination, and ultimately both subject and object.

1. Gôt is Al-unity!

The first Commandment of Gôt is a clear reference to the **monad**, the entire potential of existence contained in seed form.

2. Gôt is "Spirit and Matter," the dyad. He brings duality, and is nevertheless, unity and purity . . .

Again, the connection to Pythagorean number symbolism is plain. The basic dualism (after the manner of the Gnostic division between the "good" Spirit and the "evil" Matter), suggests the monad split into two, but with neither component meaningful without reference to each other—thus, in effect, it is a unity in two parts.

3. Gôt is a triad: Spirit, Energy and Matter. Gôt-Spirit, Gôt-Ur, Gôt-Being, or Sun-Light and Work, the dyad.

A third element—Energy, implying differentiation and motion—

is added to the dyad. The triad of Spirit, Energy, Matter is central to Wiligut's conception of the function of the cosmos and man's place within it. The prefix *Ur-* in German refers to the primal or archetypal form of something; the second sentence of this Commandment could be read as Gôt being the source of Spirit, primal creation/existence, and being.

> *4. Gôt is eternal—as Time, Space, Energy and Matter in his circulating current.*

To the three material dimensions, the fourth—time—is added. As master of these four dimensions, from which the universe can be constructed or deconstructed at will, Gôt is eternal because he has mastered Time itself. Those who have mastered the Space/Energy/Matter triad, and learned to perceive it in its proper relation to Time, can themselves become like Gôt through enlightened emulation.

> *5. Gôt is cause and effect. Therefore, out of Gôt flows right, might, duty and happiness.*

In the Pythagorean arithmology, the **pentad** is the symbol of Man as capable of developing his individual intelligence and spirit to godlike levels. Such an initiated person would, by virtue of his superior understanding of both himself and the world outside himself, command right, might, duty, and happiness, as he understands them.

> *6. Gôt is eternally generating. The Matter, Energy and Light of Gôt are that which carry this along.*

Here, a variation on the triad is given. Two figures emblematic of the triad—two triangles—combine to form the six-pointed figure of the hexagram. The eternally generating property of six is contained in its mathematical permutations: any two numbers ending in 6 multiplied by each other yield another number which **also** ends in 6.

*7. Gôt—beyond the concepts of good and evil—is that which carries
the seven epochs of human history.*

The "seven epochs of human history" are a reference to the teachings of Blavatsky and the Theosophists. The Pythagorean association
of the **heptad** with life, birth, and spiritual law is a natural analog for
Wiligut's identification of seven as "beyond the concepts of good and
evil." That is, Gôt is beholden, along with those who seek to become
like him, to no absolute moral code except that which arises from his
own higher purpose.

*8. Rulership in the circulation of cause-and-effect carries along the
highness—the secret tribunal.*

With eight, the property of five—mastery of cause and effect—is
repeated. This resonance between five and eight is also an integral concept in understanding the relationship between the Fifth and Eighth
Angles. Having gone beyond good and evil, Gôt—and those seeking to
arise on their own through developing his properties and actions within
themselves—has attained and manifested true Rulership.

*9. Gôt is beginning without end—the Al. He is completion in
Nothingness, and, nevertheless, Al in the three-times-three realization of all things. He closes the circle at N-yule, at Nothingness, out
of the conscious into the unconscious, so that this may again become
conscious.*

Spirit descends into matter, thus vivifying it. Gôt has become
both the subject and object of the wisdom and power won through
applications of these laws. The triad has been multiplied by itself,
amplifying all three of its components. *N-Yule* is the icy stillness
at Yule, the maximum extent of darkness in the coldest part of the
year in the Northern Hemisphere; through the power of nine, Gôt
has closed the circle of the seasons (and indeed any cycle unfolding

through his laws), only to begin it anew at the precise point where the previous was completed. Consciousness has passed nine tests, and can now remanifest at will.

SACRED GEOMETRY

Sacred Geometry ascribes symbolic meaning (often in a religious or sacred context) to particular geometric proportions, forms, and functions. Implicit in this study is the assertion that there is an underlying deliberate order to the cosmos, and that understanding the geometric manifestations of those designs and patterns leads to a deeper understanding of the workings of the cosmos and humanity's place within it.

While the study of sacred geometry is often associated with the Right-Hand Path religions (e.g., design principles in churches, temples, and mosques), it is certainly not limited to that context. In this book, we use the term **Infernal Geometry** to distinguish the Left-Hand Path approach to geometrical symbols as tools for self-directed change.

The Enneagram

Among the representations of nine-angled figures that preceded the Nine Angles as conceived by Michael Aquino, the **Enneagram** stands as a prominent example with both exoteric and esoteric significance.

Enneagram is a generic name for a nine-pointed geometric figure, typically resembling a star. The form in which the name most often appears in an occult context is that of the figure popularized (although

The Enneagram

multiplied = 48 · 12 = 3. E, so, 1-9 is this a relexitration (15)? the root (1) and stem (3) inherently contains the 5th — the completion

perhaps not quite invented, as we shall see) by G. I. Gurdjieff.* The same form, with a debt usually acknowledged to Gurdjieff, is used as a "personality mapping" tool in some modern methods of psychology. That is, each point is said to correspond to certain ingrained personality traits, and the geometric relationships to other points in the figure are supposed to provide a means of understanding how persons embodying the different types should interact with each other. Like all such systems, attempts to prove them as literally true will be futile, but their real value lies in the ability to which they may be used as a means of understanding your own tendencies. The map is not the territory.

The three fundamental shapes of this particular version are the circle, the triangle, and the irregular yet symmetrical six-pointed figure.

The question of whether Gurdjieff invented the particular form of the enneagram associated with him, or adapted it from earlier sources, is a bit unclear. James Webb argues persuasively in his 1980 book *The Harmonious Circle*† that Gurdjieff adopted the nine-pointed figure utilized by the medieval philosophers Athanasius Kircher‡ and Ramon Llull, and made minor changes both to conceal its origin and to encode other ideas from his own synthesis.

---

*George Ivanovich Gurdjieff (1877?–1949) was a mystic and philosopher who taught primarily in Russia and France. The cornerstone to Gurdjieff's philosophy and practices—which he called "The Work"—was that man was "asleep" in his natural state, and he must do strenuous mental and physical tasks under the direction of a qualified teacher in order to "awaken" to full consciousness. The collection of techniques referred to as **self-remembering** emphasize the continuing struggle for full self-awareness.

†Webb's study *The Harmonious Circle: The Lives and Works of G. I. Gurdjieff, P. D. Ouspensky, and Their Followers* (Shambhala, 1980) was the first major book to analyze The Work (and the people behind it) that was not written by Gurdjieff or his students. As such, this objectivity allowed Webb to dig deeper into areas where Gurdjieff's followers tended to take the master's explanations at face value. The most important section of the book in terms of studying predecessors to the Nine Angles is the lengthy appendix entitled "The Sources of the System."

‡Kircher (1601–1680) quantified the significance of the nine-pointed figure featured prominently on the frontispiece of his book *Arithmologia* (1665) as follows: "The ennead results from the triad multiplied by itself, and has all the more arcane significance because it thrice contains the triad. While making the square of the triad it contains within itself the greater mysteries."

Frontispiece to Anthanasius Kircher's *Arithmologia* (1665)
showing the ennead

Everything is process.

The Enneagram embodies Gurdjieff's Law of Octaves. That is, events unfold in a manner similar to other events of the same type, and discreet stages within such an octave—just as in a musical scale—provide a means of affecting the future outcome of those events. This is a vital idea in the meaning and use of the Nine Angles as both a reflective and operative system, and will be discussed in detail in chapter 5.

All three of the component figures of the Enneagram represent different types of octaves, with different effects and means of influence. The circle is readily understood as suggesting naturally recurring events; here, it is the background against which awakening must be continually won. The triangle, and the fact that there are three figures expressed as one, embodies the Law of Three (the doctrine that three causes are necessary for any given effect, harkening back to the significance of the number three in Indo-European cosmology). The remaining (six-pointed) figure embodies the Law of Seven (the law of octaves itself, and intended to be reminiscent of a Western musical scale, which has seven discreet notes before the first note—the beginning of the next octave—is repeated). The six-pointed figure is connected to the circle at the points identified as 1–4–2–8–5–7, which are the digits of the infinitely repeating decimal representation of the fraction 1/7 (.142857142857 . . .).

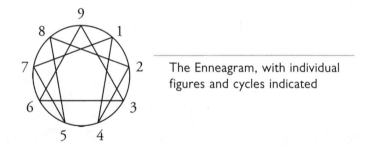

The Enneagram, with individual figures and cycles indicated

As Gurdjieff himself described it, "the triangle represented the presence of higher forces and the six-sided figure stood for man."[10] Gurdjieff was also said to have described his Enneagram as "an incomplete and theoretical form."[11] In this sense, it could easily be seen as a symbol that while having deep significance in and of itself, is nonetheless intended to be a hint toward further investigation into the roots of the form—which then reveal further mysteries. Understanding the triangle—these "higher forces"—would then be both the apex of the system being pursued by those who work with the Enneagram in this form, and the connection to the "purer" version of the Enneagram in the system described by Kircher as the gateway to the highest mysteries of existence.

THE INFLUENCE OF JOHN DEE

John Dee (1527–1608/9) was the foremost collector of books and astronomical instruments in Elizabethan England. Additionally, he was an alchemist, mathematician, cartographer (and cartomancer), court astrologer and general advisor to Elizabeth I, and both coined the phrase "British Empire" and taught navigational techniques to Britain's explorers to use in expanding that empire. The likely model for the magician Prospero in Shakespeare's *The Tempest*, Dee combined studies of magic, Hermetic philosophy, and astrology into a lifelong search for understanding—a worthy exemplar for those seeking beyond the mundane, toward knowledge of other realms. For these reasons, among many other plausible choices, Lovecraft named Dee as the most recent real historical personage who had possessed and translated the *Necronomicon*.*

Dee was especially interested in mathematics and cartography, along with their magical applications. Because of his renown as a mathematician, he was commissioned to write the lengthy introduction to the first English translation of Euclid's *Elements* (the foundational text in geometry and one of the most important and influential mathematical texts of all time). A key magical component of Dee's work as a cartographer and geometer was his use of those disciplines to create maps of the cosmos—as above, so below. The territory that is mapped out can

---

*Technically, Olaus Wormius (Ole Worm, a Danish natural philosopher; 1588–1654) would be a slightly more recent historical figure whom Lovecraft also credited with translating the *Necronomicon*. However, Lovecraft fictionalized Worm into a more sinister character than he really was and moved the time of his life several centuries earlier in his account.

Enochian; 48; Kabulla 4

KABBALAH

then be examined more thoroughly and systematically to study the relationships between different areas, thereby providing a key for greater knowledge of the territory itself. The precise use of symbols is important to cartography (and its magical application in cartomancy); the age of exploration provided a new dimension to the use of occult symbols and their role in cosmology, as mathematical and astronomical advances in cartography and navigation then began to be applied to other studies as well. This use of symbols as applied cosmological maps is a vital stepping stone in the development of a system like the Nine Angles.

On April 13, 1584, John Dee, along with a seer named Edward Kelley, began to record in his diary a series of incantations and other communications received from entities he referred to as Angels. These transmissions were in a language he dubbed "Enochian" or "Angelic," and English translations were provided through Kelley by these Angels.* Many years after Dee's death, his diaries were published (largely in order to discredit them and harm Dee's reputation) by Meric Casaubon as *A True and Faithful Relation of What Passed for Many Years between Dr. John Dee and Some Spirits* (1659). The incantations, forty-eight in number, derived from these communications are today commonly referred to as the Enochian Keys.

The Enochian Keys were adapted by the Hermetic Order of the Golden Dawn in the late nineteenth century and were reworked to more closely conform to the Golden Dawn's emphasis on the Kabbalah. The Order's leaders claimed fluency in the Enochian language and adapted it for use in their highly ornate and symbolic form of ceremonial magic. Following his schism with the Golden Dawn in 1898, Aleister Crowley further adopted Enochian in his Thelemic magical system under the auspices of his own magical order, the A∴ A∴, while also claiming fluency in the language.

The Keys were largely forgotten in the mid-twentieth century, until Anton LaVey adapted them for publication in *The Satanic Bible*

---

*The most comprehensive and well-informed study of the history of Enochian and its use by various magical groups (including the Church of Satan and Temple of Set) is Egil Asprem's *Arguing with Angels: Enochian Magic and Modern Occulture* (SUNY Press, 2013).

RELEXIFICATION
JARGON   Navajus

Word ut Set

(1969). LaVey's rendition drew heavily on that used by the Golden Dawn, but with many of the angelic and heavenly references altered to utilize Satanic imagery instead. The resulting outcry from those who still were familiar with the Casaubon and Golden Dawn versions was one factor that led to a revival of interest in Dee and Kelley's work. Among the outcomes of this revival, an important development was the new translation of the original Keys (from the text of the actual diaries that are in the collection of the British Museum) created by Michael Aquino and referred to as the "Word of Set."*

Despite the claims of the Golden Dawn—repeated uncritically by Aleister Crowley, Anton LaVey, and others—Enochian is not a true language (possessing rules for grammar, conjugation, etc.). Both Michael Aquino (using skills from his professional interest in cryptography) and Patrick Dunn† (a professor of linguistics and magician/author) concluded through applying their respective disciplines that Enochian is more akin to either a jargon or relexification. A *relexification* is a form of language manipulation that substitutes significant portions of the vocabulary from one language into the grammatical structure of another language. Essentially, it is a type of substitution code. A well-known example of this was the use of Navajo code talkers by the U.S. military in World War II; words from an obscure language were substituted for specific English words when transmitting secret or sensitive messages, while the underlying grammar of English remained unaltered. In case of Enochian, the roots of the words carry consistent meanings, but there are no identifiable regular rules for using the words as different parts of speech; the illusion of grammar (which has regularly fooled nonlinguists

WIND TALKERS

---

*In contrast to LaVey's approach, which while effective in ritual use was still beholden to the work of earlier translators, Aquino's translation was created "not as a historian seeking to reprint what Dee did, but as a magician seeking to operate the same 'magical machinery' that Dee did—and to operate it with greater care and precision than he did" (Aquino, *The Temple of Set*, 271). See appendices three and four of Aquino's *The Temple of Set* for more information and context.

†Dunn's *Magic, Power, Language, Symbol: A Magician's Exploration of Linguistics* (Llewellyn, 2008) is a highly recommended companion to this book for its treatment of language and semiotics in a magical context.

throughout the history of Enochian) can be achieved by altering the endings, but there are no consistent rules for doing so as a real language would possess. The claims also made by Israel Regardie, Anton LaVey and others that Enochian is a "language older than Sanskrit"[12] can thus be dismissed out of hand as well.

This approach to artificial language construction was a key influence on the creation and use of "Yuggothic" in *The Ceremony of the Nine Angles* and *The Call to Cthulhu*. Aquino writes (bracketed text in the original):

> It was the work of about two months to develop the jargon that became the "nameless language" [I called it "Yuggothic"] of *The Ceremony of the Nine Angles* and *The Call to Cthulhu*. A word that sounded properly "Lovecraftian" would be constructed arbitrarily: *El-aka* = world, *gryenn'h* = [of] horrors. Then the word would be used consistently throughout the text of both rituals. Slight modifications of endings would suffice for different sentence constructions, and there you have a "language" every bit as flexible as Enochian![13]

The other inspiration that the Enochian Keys provided to Anton LaVey's magical terminology were the references to **Angles**. Angles in Enochian magic are another name for the quadrants of the tables that are used in conjunction with the invocations and with sigil construction—by tracing out letters in certain configurations using these tables, the names of the different celestial and elemental beings associated with Enochian magic can be derived.

As with the recasting of the "Angelic" rendering of Enochian into more Satanic terms, LaVey also made connections between these "strange angles" illuminated in the text with his own theories of the Law of the Trapezoid. This connection was reinforced by the fact that the tables as used in the Golden Dawn system of Enochian magic had the individual squares designed as truncated pyramids.

For example, LaVey's rendition of the Sixth Key in *The Satanic*

Bible is slightly altered to begin: "The spirits of the fourth angle are Nine, mighty in the trapezoid . . ."[14]

Between the evocative magical form and tone of the English versions of the Keys, and the mysterious and primal-sounding Enochian vernacular itself, the blueprint for the construction of *The Ceremony of the Nine Angles* had already been created centuries prior to its realization. The missing piece was a suitably enigmatic metaphysical framework, which was to be inspired by the fiction of H. P. Lovecraft.

THE INFLUENCE OF HOWARD PHILLIPS LOVECRAFT

Much more will be said about the profound influence of Lovecraft on the development of the Nine Angles in chapter 3. For the moment, the important aspect to be aware of is Lovecraft's obsession with cycles— especially those expressed through astronomical phenomena. This seems to be an area where Lovecraft's deep respect for Friedrich Nietzsche's ideas—particularly the **eternal return**, in which events in a purely mechanistic universe repeat forever in self-similar forms—intersected with his love of astronomy to leave a noticeable impression on his writings.

Lovecraft's descriptive phrase for this obsession with patterns in the night sky is **Starry Wisdom**. The name comes from the short story "The Haunter of the Dark"; in this story the "disliked and unorthodox" Starry Wisdom Sect uses a strangely angled scrying stone to contact an entity who fears the light and originates from beyond the visible stars.

Starry Wisdom is the study of the night sky's effect on individuals, from the deep past and the formation of uniquely human intelligence and self-awareness, to the present where symbolism related to the movements of the heavens is implicit in much of religion, philosophy, and other concerns about humanity's place within the cosmos.

Many assume the Left-Hand Path attraction to darkness to be merely aversion to daylight and to ordinary socialization. In contrast, think about the incredible courage it took to go off by oneself and just

→ CONSIDER THIS

"Every man and woman is a "star" – Crowley

PRISM

antinomianism

gaze at the stars instead of remaining in the safety of light, shelter, and other humans. Further, consider the idea that much could be learned by the study of patterns in the sky and their reflection in human thought and behavior; this shows something critical about the individual, self-aware psyche and its cultivation. This takes the Left-Hand Path beyond merely being contrarian and into the realm of the transcendent.

In the Right-Hand Path religions—the "religions of the day side"— all creation is considered to spring from a single cosmic figure often represented by or closely associated with the Sun.

A critical distinction between the Paths of the Right and the Left is mirrored in this solar/stellar dichotomy.

The Right-Hand Path takes its cues from the Sun, which defines the times, orders human life, dominates agriculture, and functions as the prototype for cosmic order in its regularity.

The Left-Hand Path, by contrast, is stellar. The night sky becomes an entrance not a barrier, allowing the observer to see multiple points of light—and to be aware of others present but hidden due to ever increasing distance. Many of these points of light are themselves suns, scattered throughout the sky, many if not most with entire planetary systems orbiting them. This provides a potent symbol for the individual—after all, as Crowley remarked, "every man and every woman is a star." The Self is a gravitational center of worlds—not one, like our sun, but many. Such a worldview encompassing this plurality grants liberty to its fellow beings that cannot exist in a solar worldview.

The individual, self-aware, self-evolving psyche functions as a prism: these experiences of the objective world are transformed and reshaped into a diverse range of structures of understanding, such as scientific thought, myth, religion. The study of this in turn leads to thinking of the night sky as a mirror in which the psyche sees itself. The stars are not only "out there," but interior reflection allows us to see ourselves in them.

The study of astronomy and its metaphysical connections played a major role in the development of modern science. In the late sixteenth century, astronomy becomes a tool of antinomianism, used in fighting against prevailing norms and assumptions. The challenges to the

centuries-old dominance of the Church—by the work of those such as
Copernicus, Kepler, and Galileo—brought about a new understanding
of the workings of the cosmos and humanity's place within it. For those
who broke free of the yoke of the Church, a new model for personal
attainment was provided.

Lovecraft was an avid amateur astronomer. Obsession with the night
sky is prominent in many of his stories, with some of the more vivid
examples being "Polaris," "What the Moon Brings," and "Azathoth."
One of the central themes is that the stars will one day "come right
again." A repeated bit of verse in "Polaris"—beginning with "Slumber,
watcher, till the spheres / Six and twenty thousand years / Have
revolv'd"[15]—refers to the mystical significance he attaches to the precession of the equinoxes. Lovecraft's obsession with this concept invokes
Nietzsche's concept of eternal return and the challenges of breaking free
from the imprisoning cycles of time.

Axial precession is caused by the earth's slight wobble on its axis,
as the precise orientation of the poles in relation to the earth's rotation
gradually moves in cycles covering some 26,000 years. This phenomenon causes the periodic change in the star that most closely aligns with
the North or South Pole (currently the star known as Polaris, or Alpha
Ursae Minoris). Lovecraft saw in this precession a fundamental truth
about the background against which individuals must either suffer an
inescapable fate, or step outside the constant recurrence of the same in
order to chart their own destiny with the stars as their inspiration.

The eternal recurrence, which can either be transcended or har-
nessed by those who know, is a deep idea in Indo-European lore, most
vividly illustrated by Norse mythological events of Ragnarök, which
leads the world into new cycles of existence. Concepts of the eternal
return profoundly influenced Anton LaVey as well. In the concluding essay to *The Satanic Rituals,* entitled "The Unknown Known,"
LaVey writes of his theory that nine is the most magical of all numbers,
because it always returns to itself, and that humans and their institutions adhere to cyclical behavior patterns based on periods of nine years.

In "The Haunter of the Dark," the disliked and unorthodox

Parzifal; Lucifer; Grail Stone falls from Heaven

(Dark Crystal? LoL)

Starry Wisdom Sect use a multifaceted, alien stone called the Shining Trapezohedron to contact an entity from beyond the stars (later revealed to be an avatar of Nyarlathotep). This object is likely a transfigured representation of the lens of a telescope, which also has the ability to bring the stars closer so that much more can be learned of them. Another directly stellar interpretation of the Shining Trapezohedron could be a parallel to the Grail stone from Wolfram von Eschenbach's epic poem *Parzifal,* where the Grail was an ornate gemstone that fell from Lucifer's crown during the war in heaven, and which bore certain "heathen writing" that enabled those who knew how to read it to learn much of the realms beyond the Earth.

"Heathen Writing"

The fiction of Lovecraft is an important influence, often subtle and implied, on the aesthetics of the Left-Hand Path in the twentieth century and beyond. His stories contain preciously few descriptions of actual rites, and any descriptions that are found typically come from the perspective of disbelieving onlookers ignorant of their true purpose. This, however, leaves a great deal of flexibility in adapting the aesthetics implied by the magical and fantastical into actual rituals.

It is from this foundation that the use of angular magic in the Church of Satan and Temple of Set was to grow far beyond anything Lovecraft might have imagined.

3

ANGULAR MAGIC WITHIN THE CHURCH OF SATAN AND THE TEMPLE OF SET

Despite others' attempts to identify a certain number with Satan, it will be known that Nine is His number. Nine is the number of the Ego, for it always returns to itself. No matter what is done through the most complex multiplication of Nine by any other number, in the final equation Nine alone will stand forth.[1]

ANTON LAVEY, "THE UNKNOWN KNOWN"

IN *THE SATANIC RITUALS*

While the philosophies and practices of the Church of Satan from 1966–1975 were not especially concerned with numerology,* the mysterious nature of the number nine does play a major role. The idea that nine "always returns to itself" refers to the properties of multiples of nine: when the individual digits of such numbers are added together, they always add up to (or can be further reduced to) nine. For example,

---

*For an in-depth (and exhaustively documented) history and analysis of the Church of Satan from 1966 to 1975, see Michael A. Aquino's *The Church of Satan*, 2013.

$9 \times 3 = 27$ and $2 + 7 = 9$; $9 \times 123 = 1107$ and $1 + 1 + 7 = 9$.*

In this chapter, we'll take a close look at the influences behind the synthesis of Anton LaVey's ideas on cycles in his "The Unknown Known" essay that concludes *The Satanic Rituals*. The Law of the Trapezoid will be examined in detail, including its formative ideas derived from German Expressionist films, the works of H. P. Lovecraft, and William Mortensen's theories for making compelling photographs. We'll also discuss the theories and forms of the rites in *The Satanic Rituals,* and go much deeper into the Lovecraftian cosmology and its applicability to black magic. To conclude the chapter, we will explore the work of Stephen Flowers in developing the Nine Angles from its original conception into a fully formed magical system, along with accounts of some additional contributions and experiments with the Angles within the Temple of Set.

FIRE AND ICE

LaVey's theories on cycles drew from the Austrian engineer Hanns Hörbiger (1860–1931). Hörbiger had gained quite a substantial following in interwar Germany for his **Welteislehre** or "World Ice Doctrine," which characterized all change in the world as resulting from alternating ages of fire and ice. In 1894 Hörbiger invented a new type of valve for the compressors in blast furnaces, which greatly increased their power and reliability; his valve design is still used to this day. Also in 1894, curiously, at the height of his inspiration and creativity, he had the series of visions that led to the formulation of the *Welteislehre.*

Hörbiger's cosmology expresses the notion that the cosmos unfolds according to the interactions between fire (the sun) and ice (most solid bodies in the solar system, other than the Earth itself). All sig-

---

*Nine is the number with these properties in our Western base-10 number system. In fact, it is easy to prove that in any number system base-N, the number N-1 will always exhibit these same properties. But since the base-10 system is the one we use for most purposes in Western cultures, nine is for the "magic" number that returns to itself.

nificant geological events on Earth result from the movements and relationship between fire and ice, and the cosmology also specifically contradicts Newton's laws of motion and Einstein's theory of relativity in its explanations for how large bodies in the solar system interact. The *Welteislehre* was exceedingly popular in interwar Germany, largely because of the perception that it was a "German" physics that refuted the "Jewish" physics of Einstein.

LaVey most likely came to be introduced to Hörbiger's ideas by way of the book *Le Matin des Magiciens* (1960) by Louis Pauwels and Jacques Bergier, which was published in the United States in 1964 as *The Morning of the Magicians*. This book had a profound influence on the advent of the "New Age" movement in the United States, and reintroduced such occult figures as Madame Blavatsky and G. I. Gurdjieff to popular awareness. While presented as a factual account of the strange and mysterious, there were nonetheless some serious shortcomings with the book as reliable history. Like many other popular accounts of mysterious things—for example, Trevor Ravenscroft's book *The Spear of Destiny* (1973), or the late-1970s-era television series *In Search Of* . . .—its value lies more in its ability to awaken in certain readers and viewers the sense of mystery that compels them to dig deeper and to separate fact from fiction. *The Morning of the Magicians* is one of the most effective examples of the magical value of spinning a good tale, embellishments and all.*

The writings of Gurdjieff—who had been largely forgotten in the English-speaking world until *The Morning of the Magicians* stirred a renewed interest in his work—refer often to his idea of "octaves," which describe the development and unfolding of processes. These may be

---

*The Morning of the Magicians also introduced one of the early popularizations of the "ancient aliens" mythos, with a focus on the Nazca lines in Peru, thus paving the way for authors like Erich von Däniken, Zecharia Sitchin, and their numerous imitators. Its account of Gurdjieff was especially effective since Pauwels had been one of his students and was thus able to give first-hand interpretations of his teachings. It's not a stretch to say that many of the stranger occult ideas that became prevalent in the 1960s and 1970s can be blamed on this book.

on a scale as large as a person's entire life, or applied to more discrete processes of creation such as writing an essay or composing a piece of music. This is related to the musical concept of an octave, where a note can be the same as another—for example, F—but at a higher frequency (precisely double to be exact) and therefore different, even while being perceived as deriving from the same note. Gurdjieff also referred to his Law of the Octave as the Law of Seven, as his octaves had seven discrete stages (just like most occidental musical scales). These stages refer to points in the process of the evolving octave where the outcome can be affected, both for the object (what is being brought into being) and the subject (the one who is enacting the process).

This approach to octaves was important to the Pythagoreans as well. Their musical scales (ordered successions of distinct notes) had seven notes, with the eighth again being the same as the first as the cycle begins anew. The word *scale* in fact comes from a Latin word meaning "ladder," another instance of a physical object being the inspiration for a rich metaphor (the ladder as representation of the individual notes along the scale as it subdivides the octave).

The connection to the Pythagoreans is important as it combines their ideas about cycles with their number mysticism, also a critical influence on the conception of the Nine Angles as created by Michael Aquino.

THE LAW OF THE TRAPEZOID

Anton LaVey had long been fascinated with the aesthetic of German Expressionist films and their visual successor, the film-noir dramas of 1940s Hollywood. He was also an admirer of the works of H. P. Lovecraft, particularly their emphasis on the pre-rational horrors of the human psyche given form as gods not of this Earth, and the atmosphere of dread that forced Lovecraft's protagonists (and sometimes even his readers!) to face their deepest, most primal fears.

LaVey also saw connections between the "strange angles" of human and alien architecture in the stories of authors like Lovecraft* and Frank Belknap Long,† which functioned as gateways into other realms of existence and awareness; he connected those strange angles with the visceral, angular sets of such films such as *The Cabinet of Dr. Caligari* (1919) and *Metropolis* (1927), as well as the photography of William Mortensen.‡

The film *The Seventh Victim* (1941) provided an important inspiration as well. Produced by the influential horror impresario Val Lewton, the story follows a young woman as she tries to understand her older sister's involvement with a Satanic cult in New York City. Along with the striking portrayal of the diabolists as seemingly normal, everyday people (which was similarly shocking in *Rosemary's Baby* a quarter-century later), the Satanists were shown to use a parallelogram—a special form of the trapezoid—as a symbol and focus of meditation.

These influences came together to form what LaVey called the **Law of the Trapezoid**, which proposed that certain angles perceived as harmful to those unaware of their significance would be beneficial and inspirational to those who were properly initiated into their mysteries.

All of these ideas were formative on the rituals and aesthetics of the early Church of Satan, as can be seen in the various rites in LaVey's 1972 book *The Satanic Rituals*. A discussion of the Law of the Trapezoid is

---

*In particular, Lovecraft's stories "The Haunter of the Dark" and "The Dreams in the Witch-House" refer to strange angles and their properties, which are integral to the plots. The magical and/or interdimensional properties of strange angles are also hinted at in "The Call of Cthulhu," "The Silver Key," "Through the Gates of the Silver Key," and others. See also Charles Hinton's *The Fourth Dimension* (1904) and Rudy Rucker's book of the same title (1984).

†In "The Hounds of Tindalos" (1929).

‡A well-known photographer in the U.S. in the 1930s, William Mortensen was notorious for his photos depicting witches and fetish scenes; Ansel Adams referred to him as "The Antichrist" (Alinder, *Seeing Straight*, 47). After many years of being out of print and quite rare, Mortensen's definitive 1937 book on photography theory *The Command to Look* was recently reprinted by Feral House (2014); it includes an essay by Michael Moynihan, "Infernal Impact: *The Command to Look* as a Formula for Satanic Success," which delves into the influence of Mortensen on LaVey. Also recently published by Feral House is a collection of Mortensen photos called *American Grotesque: The Life and Art of William Mortensen* (2014), edited by Larry Lytle and Michael Moynihan.

given as an introduction to *Die Elektrischen Vorspiele* in that volume, and also in an article for a 1976 issue of *The Cloven Hoof* (reprinted in *The Devil's Notebook* [Feral House, 1992], a collection of LaVey's essays).

THE PSYCHODRAMA

Before discussing the three rites in *The Satanic Rituals* that utilize angular magic, it is necessary to introduce the particular type of ritual called the psychodrama. A further discussion of this can be found in chapter 22 of Michael Aquino's two-volume history, *The Church of Satan.*

Magical rituals generally take the form of two categories: the *operative* (intended to set a particular change in motion, whether observable in the objective universe or merely to change the magician herself) and the *reflective* or *illustrative* (intended to aid the magician in gaining some insight or inspiration).

The psychodrama is a particular type of reflective ritual, designed to illustrate to its participants imagery and action that will help with breaking down specific barriers to their understanding. (An illustrative albeit fictionalized example can be found in George Orwell's novel *1984*, where the interactions between O'Brien and Winston Smith in the Ministry of Love have all the hallmarks of a psychodrama: O'Brien creates situations for Smith that challenge him to confront dearly held notions about the nature of himself and society, leads him through alternate views of reality, and ultimately creates a framework in which Smith can't help but transform *himself*.) The line between "reflective" and "operative" is sometimes blurry, as a reflective ritual will very often inspire or instigate operative work; insights and changes of perspective are only truly useful when they lead to action and discernible change.

The most provocative example of the technology of the psychodrama is the Black Mass. Stereotypically, this is conceived of as a parody or reversal of the Roman Catholic Mass, although the imagery that is most useful to the individual will vary depending on what belief system they are moving away from (e.g., someone who was raised as a Muslim or in predominantly Muslim culture, or raised as an atheist, would probably not find the Roman Catholic aesthetic to be particularly effective for this purpose of liberation). The intent of the Black Mass is to lay bare the contradictions, oppressiveness, or absurdity of a particular attitude or belief system (religious or not) so that it can never again be seen with the same degree of reverence or respect by the participant. Think of it as a ritual technique for showing beyond a doubt that the emperor has no clothes.

The use of the psychodrama need not be limited to clearing out emotional or philosophical debris that is preventing the personal fulfillment of the magician, however. Another use of the psychodrama, as expertly conceived in *The Ceremony of the Nine Angles* and *The Call to Cthulhu* in a form blended with operative elements as well, is to immerse the practitioner in imagery designed to open her eyes to a new way of looking at and manipulating reality. This is where the crucial step of moving from simply reading about a ritual to actually performing it must be taken; magical rituals don't truly make sense until experienced in the flesh.

Die Elektrischen Vorspiele is not a psychodrama but rather an operative ritual. To show some of the earliest and most powerful applications of operative angular magic, we must now turn to the Electrical Preludes.

DIE ELEKTRISCHEN VORSPIELE

In this chapter, the discussion of *Die Elektrischen Vorspiele* will focus on the historical and quasi-historical background given in its introduction.

The ritual had been part of the inventory of the Church of Satan since the late 1960s. Like the other rituals in *The Satanic Rituals,* its description and introduction function on three levels:

1. It claims to be accurate history.
2. Upon closer examination and research, the reader may discover that history to be mostly just a good yarn, but with glimmers of truth and hints of resources to suggest further study.
3. Finally, those who actually **perform** the ritual will find that its effectiveness transcends the shortcomings in its claimed history.

This multi-level interpretation falls in line with LaVey's comments in the book's introduction, where he points out that application of the underlying principles is the only way to truly understand the function and effectiveness of a ritual. The effectiveness of magic depends on the magician's will, applied toward creating and defining the phenomena he or she experiences. Put another way, the background as given for any of the rituals in *The Satanic Rituals* is made as real as it needs to be in the context of the ritual chamber.

One of the first things to be aware of when approaching *Die Elektrischen Vorspiele* is the unlikelihood of it being the genuine German magical rite that LaVey claims it to be. This doubt begins with the title, which he erroneously translated into the plural (thus, the literal title in German is "The Electrical Preludes," not "Prelude" as LaVey refers to it).[2] Furthermore, there are other issues with word choices and grammar in the German text that suggest an English-language origin of the ritual.

A distinct set of literary influences feed into the aesthetic and form of *Die Elektrischen Vorspiele*. Let us examine these in turn.

"Einstein and John Dee are strange bedfellows"

The 1929 short story "The Hounds of Tindalos" by Frank Belknap Long introduced the concepts of *curved time* and *angular time*. These loosely parallel the ideas of the objective universe (curved time being experienced within the material universe, governed by physical laws that may not ever be completely discovered and described) and the subjective universe (angular time being perceived through the awareness and experience of a particular sentient creature within the objective universe).

Long was familiar with the then-new ideas of general relativity, where gravity is envisioned as acting as if guided by curvatures in space-time. According to this view, objects possessing more mass create greater distortions in their local space, and gravity behaves as if it is following these resulting curves. Long's conception of angular time works in contrast to this, suggesting shortcuts through the constraints of these natural curved pathways.

In the story, the author and occultist Halpin Chalmers invites the skeptical narrator to witness and chronicle his attempts to apprehend time as a multidimensional illusion. Chalmers pursues this by a combination of an obscure, ancient drug and deep contemplation of geometric and mathematical concepts designed to open the mind to otherwise unattainable visions.

Based on his initial explorations, Chalmers explains his new understanding of time:

> Time and motion are both illusions. Everything that has existed from the beginning of the world exists now. Events that occurred centuries ago on this planet continue to exist in another dimension of space. Events that will occur centuries from now exist already. We cannot perceive their existence because we cannot enter the dimension of space that contains them. Human beings as we know them are merely fractions, infinitesimally small fractions of one enormous whole.[3]

As he penetrates further back into the reaches of time, accessed by pathways opened by strange angles in his physical surroundings, he encounters the Hounds. The Hounds are artifacts of the most primal hinting of consciousness—they can be either protectors or predators depending on the extent to which the one who encounters them has developed or shunned this essential Gift. Those who, like the Hounds, know the angles will find guardians; those whose existence is primarily governed by their relationship with curved space will find their tormentors. Having been "scented" by the Hounds, the ultimately unprepared Chalmers is relentlessly pursued by them amid desperate attempts to remove all angles from his environment to block their access to our world of curved space.

The Hounds became part of the Cthulhu mythos, and the power of studying geometric principles to open gateways to other dimensions also plays a critical role in Lovecraft's "The Dreams in the Witch-House."

An Atlantean Detour

In a strange twist, LaVey may not have learned of these concepts and imagery directly from Long's story. In the December 1970 *Cloven*

Hoof article announcing and describing the Order of the Trapezoid, he recommends "a thorough study of the Eighth Tablet of the Book of Thoth." This at first appears to be a possible reference to the eighth precept of the well-known *Emerald Tablet of Hermes* (source of the "As Above, So Below" axiom). LaVey also mentions in the prologue to *Die Elektrischen Vorspiele* that the litany spoken by the celebrant is a paraphrase of the same work.[4]

The imagery of "The Hounds of Tindalos" deeply influenced the American occultist and founder of the Brotherhood of the White Temple, Maurice Doreal.* Central to his group, which is still active some eighty years later, is a supposedly 38,000-year-old text called "The Emerald Tablets of Thoth-the-Atlantean." Doreal claimed to have retrieved it himself from beneath the Great Pyramid. Nevertheless, it is clear from the descriptions and language of the text that it borrows phrases and imagery from Long's story for its descriptions of the purpose, perils, and salvation of mankind.

In an analysis first brought to light by Don Webb,[†] a side-by-side comparison of Doreal's text and *Die Elektrischen Vorspiele* shows the extent of the adaptation that LaVey made from the former work. In a twist of intent reminiscent of LaVey's rendering of the Enochian Keys in a Satanic rather than Angelic idiom, the wisdom being dispensed by Thoth the Atlantean "showing the way of attainment when ye shall be One with the Light"[5] is turned toward the decidedly Left-Hand Path angle of the *Vorspiele*.

---

*Born Claude Dodgin (or Doggins), Doreal was also one of the prime sources of the alien-reptiles-masquerading-as-humans neo-mythology beginning in the 1940s, expanding on ideas from the stories of Robert E. Howard a decade earlier. With his borrowing and adaptation of "The Hounds of Tindalos," Doreal is very likely the first author to expand on the Cthulhu mythos who was not a personal correspondent of Lovecraft.

†Webb is a former High Priest of the Temple of Set, and a prolific author of fiction and esoteric works; his books most relevant to the current study are *Uncle Setnakt's Essential Guide to the Left Hand Path* (Rûna-Raven, 1999), *Mysteries of the Temple of Set* (Rûna-Raven, 2011), and *Uncle Setnakt's Nightbook* (Lodestar, 2016).

Set and Die Elektrischen Vorspiele

The two mentions of "Set" in *Die Elektrischen Vorspiele* are likely references to the works of Robert E. Howard,* more so than to Egyptian mythology. Howard's Set borrowed attributes of both the Egyptian Set and the Apep serpent (who, ironically, was Set's traditional enemy, signifying stasis). Howard then cast this god as a reptilian figure who walked upright like a man. The worshippers of Set were the enemies of the great hero Conan in Howard's fiction.

LaVey's reference to the Children of Set probably refers to this passage in Howard's "The God in the Bowl" (not published until 1952, sixteen years after Howard's suicide):

> The thought of Set was like a nightmare, and the children of Set who once ruled the earth now slept in their nighted caverns below the black pyramids.[6]

This quote is also indicative of other connections LaVey would have drawn between Set and the magical frame of reference underlying *Die Elektrischen Vorspiele*. The Egyptian Set was known as a god of storms, which aligns with both the general "storm" references in the tactics and imagery of the National Socialists,† and the quote from Nazi Party cofounder Dietrich Eckart that opens the rite's introduction. Additionally, LaVey's interest in "pyramid-ology" is well known in the context of his Law of the Trapezoid. Two of the literary influences listed in his introduction of the Order of the Trapezoid are directly related to this obsession (Louis McCarty's *The Great Pyramid Jeezeh*

---

*Robert E. Howard (1906–1936) was one of the pioneers of the "sword-and-sorcery" genre of fantasy literature (his 1928 story "Red Shadows" is generally considered the first published work in the genre). Howard is most famous for his character Conan the Barbarian and was a major contributor to the Cthulhu mythos as a member of the Lovecraft circle.

†For example, the *Sturmabteilung* ("Storm Detachment," often referred to as the *SA*) was the original paramilitary wing of the Nazi party; and *blitzkrieg* (lightning warfare) as the short and forceful attack methodology utilized by the German military in World War II.

[1907], and Chapter 27 of Ostrander and Schroeder's *Psychic Discoveries Behind the Iron Curtain* [1970]).[7]

Ultima Futura

The scene in the 1927 film *Metropolis* showing the animation of the robotrix Ultima Futura provided a key bit of imagery for *Die Elektrischen Vorspiele* as well. Ultima Futura is given life in the chamber of the magician/scientist Rotwang, using a vast array of electrical equipment beneath a prominent inverted pentagram. The visual and symbolic effect is stunning and a prime example of the "mad-labs" form of magic where technology is used as a key component in the effectiveness of the ritual.

The archetype of the mad scientist runs deep, revealed in various other settings whose imagery can be used in magical contexts by those who find it stimulating. A few additional film examples, which derive directly or indirectly from *Metropolis* in their portrayal, include *Frankenstein* (1931), *The Black Cat* (1934), *Forbidden Planet* (1956), and *The Fly* (1958).

Magical experimentation involving electronic gadgetry had been used by some German occultists (both in fact and in legend) since the mid-nineteenth century. The phenomenon of **Winkelmauerei** ("quasi-Masonry") refers to the various lodge traditions that imitated some of the forms of masonry but were not in any sense "regular." The most infamous of these is the Freemasonic Order of the Golden Centurium (FOGC), supposedly founded in 1840 by rich industrialists, but which may have never existed except in legend. The FOGC was rumored to possess a machine called the **Tepaphon**, which, powered solely by the will of the magician using it, could kill at a distance.*

A contemporary German lodge continuing the tradition of the

---

*The Tepaphon was used by the FOGC as part of fulfilling the meaning of the "Centurium" in its name: the lodge was limited to 99 members (with the hundredth being the lodge egregore itself), and each year a new member was to be initiated. In the event that no members had died or resigned in the previous year, one was randomly chosen to be sacrificed. If the chosen sacrifice would not voluntarily comply with this edict, the Tepaphon was used to accomplish the task anyway. The primary source for information about the Tepaphon and the Freemasonic Order of the Golden Centurium is *Frabato,* the magical autobiography of the Czech occultist Franz Bardon.

"mad lab" is the Fraternitas Saturni (founded in 1926).* The Fraternitas Saturni utilize such technologies as Tesla coils, high-frequency sound, ionization of the atmosphere, and ultraviolet lights. All of these are used to enhance the ritual chamber in various ways to add to the successful performance of their rites.

The Electric Pentacle

Also related to the "mad labs" aesthetic and magical techniques utilized by *Die Elektrischen Vorspiele* is the "occult detective" character Thomas Carnacki, created by the early twentieth-century writer Charles Hope Hodgson. Curiously, in the December 1970 announcement introducing the Order of the Trapezoid, when listing the various literary influences on the conception of the Order, LaVey misidentifies Hodgson as the author of "The Hounds of Tindalos." Whether this was intentional (dropping a subtle hint about another author to explore), or merely a misremembering, is impossible to say at this point. In any event, the importance of the Carnacki character to LaVey is clear (he even included a Hodgson reference in the name of his only son, Satan Xerxes Carnacki LaVey).

The occult detective was typically a doctor who had an interest in the supernatural and kept an open but skeptical mind when investigating unusual goings-on (the most famous example is Dr. Abraham van Helsing from Bram Stoker's *Dracula*). Like many occult detectives, Carnacki was well versed in the cutting-edge technology of his day (ca. 1910). His most effective tool was a series of wires and vacuum tubes, which glowed with an eerie blue light, called the Electric Pentacle. This device was a five-pointed star-shaped structure, approximately 21 feet across, and provided a protective environment that malevolent spirits and "vibrations" could not penetrate, and from which Carnacki, as a skilled operator of the Pentacle, could project his will on his immediate environment. This was clearly a direct influence on the aesthetic and working method of *Die Elektrischen Vorspiele*.

---

*The only book-length study of this group in English is Stephen E. Flowers's *The Fraternitas Saturni: History, Doctrine, and Rituals of the Magical Order of the Brotherhood of Saturn* (Inner Traditions, 2018).

Hodgson was well aware of the effects of strange geometric environments and objects on people. For example, in the first Carnacki story, "The Gateway of the Monster" (1910), a ring in the shape of a pentagon functioned as a portal to other dimensions, allowing a creature suggestive of a Hound of Tindalos to enter this world and wreak havoc on anyone unfortunate enough to be without appropriate protection such as the Electric Pentacle.

The Strange Story of Wilhelm Reich

Not all of the influences on *Die Elektrischen Vorspiele* were fictional. The theories of the Austrian American psychoanalyst Wilhelm Reich concerning the buildup, blockage, and release of sexual energy are crucial to the magical mechanism of the ritual. This is reflected in the title: the German word *Vorspiel* could be translated literally as "foreplay" (indeed, the progressively intense excitation and then cathartic release on the part of the chief celebrant is highly suggestive of the orgasm). The use of sexual energy as a magical tool, in the context of the work of the Ordo Templi Orientis (O.T.O.), is alluded to in the introduction. Taking the recommendation from the introduction that the celebrant should be male, he literally seeds the future via the magical orgasm experienced within the rite itself.

LOVECRAFTIAN IDEAS IN MAGIC

Despite the adaptability of Lovecraft's fiction to esoteric purposes, his own views on magic and the supernatural were very unsympathetic. As an ardent materialist, Lovecraft rejected out of hand the idea of magic as a means of affecting the objective universe. This was reinforced by his dim view of those in his day who did hold such attitudes; his association with Harry Houdini, who spent quite a bit of effort debunking the claims of Spiritualists, no doubt contributed to this. His apparent disdain for Aleister Crowley, who was the most well-known self-identified magician during Lovecraft's lifetime, also colored his perception— although he seemed unaware of the actual practices of Crowley's A∴A∴

or the O.T.O., which might have shown him the serious legitimacy of some of the magical work being done at that time.

In the essay "The Metaphysics of Lovecraft" in *The Satanic Rituals,* Michael Aquino puts forth the idea that the primary contribution of Lovecraft to magical practice is the study of the effects of physical and geometrical laws on the psyche.[8] Aquino also points out that if Lovecraft had a strong aversion to conventional religion (citing his comments in *The Silver Key*), he was even more critical of those who turned to the magical and diabolical.[9] In a 1935 letter to Emil Petaja (a young admirer of Lovecraft's who later became a well-regarded author in his own right), Lovecraft wrote:

> In the 1890s the fashionable decadents liked to pretend that they belonged to all sorts of diabolic Black Mass cults, & possessed all sorts of frightful occult information. The only specimen of this group still active is the rather over-advertised Aleister Crowley.[10]

In the version published in *The Satanic Rituals,* LaVey augmented Aquino's essay to include claims that Lovecraft was in fact aware of genuine nameless rites that were hinted at in his stories. While this does fit in with the "second interpretation" aspect of *The Satanic Rituals* (as evocative history that often falls apart on closer examination), Lovecraft's own correspondence simply does not substantiate this suggestion.

Lovecraft's focus was on communicating his subjective, inner imagination where such things **were** possible and as real as they needed to be, in order to bring about the desired effect on himself (and hopefully in his readers). Recall from the prelude that our definition of black magic utilizes the primary intent of making a change within the subjective universe, which may or may not (depending on the need and skill of the magician) result in a corresponding change in the objective universe. From this point of view, there is a clear compatibility between Lovecraft's approach and the type of magic covered in this book.

Desiring to avoid the familiarity that would come from using classical mythology in his stories, Lovecraft instead chose to create his own pantheon and mythos. This mythos was expanded on by his various fellow corresponding authors (the "Lovecraft Circle"), and he would incorporate their additions into his own stories. It was, in effect, an "open source" neo-mythology, and one that is still being expanded today (by authors such as Thomas Ligotti and S. T. Joshi). Aquino's contributions in the magical realm are also prime examples of this neo-mythology, working within a different medium than "weird fiction."

Despite the avoidance of classical mythology, Lovecraft's work does bear its influence (and he was certainly well read in it). In the world of his stories, he even hints in places that classical mythology may be a corruption of his own "true" mythos! References to ancient Egypt and its *neteru** hold special significance in his tales.

One particular recurring connection is the inclusion of "Thot[h]" in the names of the primary deities of Azathoth, Yog-Sothoth, and Nyarlathotep.[†] Thoth, as messenger and scribe of the Egyptian gods (and patron of communication), has a close analog to the function of Nyarlathotep in the Mythos. Given the importance of communication within Lovecraft's stories (via dreams, the stars, the *Necronomicon* and other books, folklore, etc.), Thoth is clearly a significant influence.

In the Hermetic school of magic, the influence of Egypt is readily apparent. Hermeticism originated in the collection of second- and third-century-CE texts known as the *Corpus Hermeticum,* which featured the teachings of Hermes Trismegistus—as a Hellenized form of the Egyptian god Thoth—instructing a disciple in the nature of

---

*The Egyptian word *neter* (plural: *neteru*) is often translated as "god"; however, even a cursory examination of the actual function of these so-called gods reveals them to be causal principles rather than merely persons-writ-large in the Greek and Roman mode. For example, Ma'at is the principle of justice/balance, Thoth is the archetypal form of communication and preservation, Set is the source of isolate intelligence (and the *neter* against the *neteru*), Apep embodies delusion and stasis, and so on.

†The suffix -**hotep** is a common one in Egyptian names. Ironically, at least in terms of its usage in the name Nyarlathotep, it is typically translated as "to be at peace." With the name of this particular deity, Lovecraft both reinforces the Egyptian connection **and** manages to work in another implied reference to Thoth.

the cosmos, the mind, and the divine. The experimental nature of Hermeticism, and attempts by its practitioners to apply its philosophies to real-world models of the universe, made it an influential area of study in the fourteenth to seventeenth centuries. Scientists, philosophers, and mathematicians of the time who drew heavily on its influence include Isaac Newton, John Dee, Giordano Bruno, and Paracelsus. The Greek Hermes (namesake patron of the Hermeticists) and the Egyptian Thoth both represented the magic and mystery of the written word in an era when literacy was reserved to an elite few.

As Don Webb relates:

> The plots of [Lovecraft's] stories often came to him in dreams. Particularly noteworthy was the dream that lead to the production of the prose-poem "Nyarlathotep" in which he found the Hermes of his pantheon. This particular communicator from the other side, with his swarthy Egyptian skin, resembles both the figure of Hermes-Thoth and the preternatural entity that Crowley contacted in 1904.
>
> Lovecraft knew his need for the cosmic feeling his stories brought him, and throughout his letters and critical writings we see that need to evoke a mood repeated time and time again. In fact, Lovecraft was sensitive enough to this process (despite the fact his materialist attitude kept him from ever consciously expressing it) that many of his stories are about the desired result of receiving communication from the other side.[11]

Azathoth

Azathoth is the oblivious, chaotic creator god—the other Outer Gods are his descendants. The first mention of Azathoth was in a note dated 1919, where Lovecraft merely referred to it as a "hideous name."[12] Later that year, he hinted of a dream described as "a terrible pilgrimage to seek the nighted throne of the far daemon-sultan Azathoth."[13]

While Lovecraft did not describe the origin of the name, it is possible that it was a reference to *Azoth*—an alchemical term for the universe medication/solvent sought by certain operations. This substance is associated with Ain Soph (ultimate substance) of the Kabbalah, and the element mercury (the god of the same name being the Roman equivalent of Thoth).

In *The Dream-Quest of Unknown Kadath,* Azathoth "gnaws hungrily in inconceivable, unlighted chambers beyond time and space amidst the muffled, maddening beating of vile drums and the thin monotonous whine of accursed flutes."[14] In *The Whisperer in Darkness,* he is described as the "monstrous nuclear chaos beyond angled space"[15] ("nuclear" in this case meaning "central," since the story predates the atomic age when the term took on an additional popular connotation). The reference to "chaos" (in the sense of the unmanifest void, or the seed form holding all that is yet to be) will also be important when discussing *The Ceremony of the Nine Angles.*

As already mentioned, the two most significant Lovecraft works with direct bearing on the practice of angular magic are "The Dreams in the Witch-House" and "The Haunter of the Dark." Further along the "ultimate chaos" theme, "The Dreams in the Witch-House" refers to Azathoth's "the throne of Chaos where the thin flutes pipe mindlessly."[16] "The Haunter of the Dark" describes "the ancient legends of Ultimate Chaos, at whose center sprawls the blind idiot god Azathoth, Lord of All Things, encircled by his flopping horde of mindless and amorphous dancers, and lulled by the thin monotonous piping of a demonic flute held in nameless paws."[17]

Yog-Sothoth

Yog-Sothoth first appears in *The Case of Charles Dexter Ward* (1927). The most significant references are in "The Dunwich Horror," which describe him as the "key" and the "guardian of the gate."[18] The door or gate is a familiar theme in the occult and also the stories of Lovecraft, acting as links between conventional reality—as recognized by the 'normal' and the oblivious—and other realms of possibility. Gates must be transcended, often at great cost, in order to gain access to knowledge not available in any other way.

In "Through the Gates of the Silver Key," there are mentions of an avatar of Yog-Sothoth: 'Umr at-Tawil, whose name is said to mean "the most ancient and prolonged of life."[19]

Nyarlathotep

Nyarlathotep represents the bridge between the cosmic and the earth-bound in the Mythos; as the true identity of the Haunter of the Dark, the Starry Wisdom Sect summon him from the stars via the Shining Trapezohedron. As the story says, suggestive of the trio of meanings of the Egyptian word **s'ba***: "These people say the Shining Trapezohedron shows them heaven & other worlds, & that the Haunter of the Dark tells them secrets in some way."[20]

The first mention of Nyarlathotep was in a dream,[21] which Lovecraft followed with the prose poem of the same name. This Outer God is unique in that he can walk as a man upon the earth. As the messenger of the other gods, he acts as a bridge between the objective universe and the pre-rational horrors of the human psyche still affecting "evolved" mankind.

Humans can make pacts with Nyarlathotep, and one of his many forms is highly suggestive of traditional depictions of Satan (see "The Dreams in the Witch-House"). In addition to appearing of his own will (or at least, the will of the other gods), he can be summoned to manifestation as recounted in "The Haunter of the Dark." Two of his primary tools for influencing humans are mad science—a reference to the work of Nicola Tesla?—and propaganda (including mass hypnosis).

And it was then that Nyarlathotep came out of Egypt. Who he was, none could tell, but he was of the old native blood and looked like a Pharaoh. The fellahin knelt when they saw him, yet could not say why. He said he had risen up out of the blackness of twenty-seven centuries, and that he had heard messages from places not on this planet.[22]

---

*The Egyptian word **s'ba** has three meanings: "star," "door," and "teach." This is a key to the concept of Starry Wisdom explored in "The Haunter of the Dark," and all three meanings are encompassed by the role and attributes of Nyarlathotep within the Lovecraft mythos.

Shub-Niggurath

Lovecraft generally referred to Shub-Niggurath as female, but also as male as the black goat of the woods with a thousand young. This suggests a hermaphroditic entity akin to the traditional representation of Baphomet. A key influence on the description of Shub-Niggurath's activities and properties is the Greek god Pan, especially given Lovecraft's well-known affection for Arthur Machen's novella *The Great God Pan*.

There is very little description of Shub-Niggurath in Lovecraft's own stories, but he elaborated on this entity stories he ghostwrote for others. In this expanded mythos, he/she is identified with life and the state of being via association with the figure of the "great mother" and often invoked along with the other entities.

Cthulhu

Cthulhu, while by far the most well known, does not appear in Lovecraft's fiction nearly as much the Outer Gods. In "The Call of Cthulhu" he is a "monster of vaguely anthropoid outline, but with an octopus-like head whose face was a mass of feelers, a scaly, rubbery-looking body, prodigious claws on hind and fore feet, and long, narrow wings behind."[23] He serves as the High Priest of the Great Old Ones, charged with waiting until the time is right to summon them forth to overrun the Earth.

He hibernates in an unfathomably ancient city beneath the Pacific called R'lyeh. Lovecraft based R'lyeh in part on the ruins of Nan Madol adjacent to the island of Pohnpei (Ponape) in the Federated States of Micronesia. These ruins lay abandoned from the early seventeenth century after serving as the isolated home of the nobility of Pohnpei from approximately the twelfth century. Today, the ruins are shrouded in mystery and shunned by the islanders as remnants of a decadent culture rumored to have utilized "black magic" in constructing them; the origins of the stone used to create the ancient city, or the building techniques used to realize the unique structures, have not been conclusively determined.

The famous phrase describing Cthulhu's state of "dead but dreaming," which was a significant key for Michael Aquino in creating the

"Yuggothic" language used in the Lovecraftian rites in *The Satanic Rituals*, is:

Ph'nglui mglw'nafh Cthulhu R'lyeh wgah'nagl fhtagn ("In his house at R'lyeh, dead Cthulhu waits dreaming.")[24]

Cthulhu's potential return to the surface world is suggested to be a source of constant subconscious anxiety in humanity (perhaps manifesting as fear of water, earthquakes, and tsunamis).

While there are various references to other gods and supernatural entities haunting Lovecraft's dreams and fiction, these five are the ones that appear as more than merely brief or isolated mentions.

THE LOVECRAFTIAN RITES IN
THE SATANIC RITUALS

In late 1971, Anton LaVey was preparing the sequel to *The Satanic Bible*. Taking the suggestion of his friend, science fiction writer Mike Resnick, LaVey asked Michael Aquino to contribute a ritual based on Lovecraft's fiction and style; when *The Ceremony of the Nine Angles* was completed, LaVey requested a second "water" rite to balance the "fire" of the Nine Angles ceremony. At the same time, Aquino also wrote an introductory essay about the elements of Lovecraft's work that could be adapted into genuine black magical rituals.

While today it is trendy in the darker corners of the occult world to draw upon Lovecraft as an influence, the rituals published in *The Satanic Rituals* represent the first publicly revealed adaptations by actual practitioners. Lovecraft's work was experiencing a minor resurgence at that time, from the psychedelic band named after him (active from 1967–1969), to the film adaptation of *The Dunwich Horror* (1970) and the inclusion of his stories on Rod Serling's television series *Night Gallery* (1971), to *Nyctalops* (a magazine published in the early- to mid-1970s containing articles about Lovecraft and related writers).

None of these instances, however, had the same effect as the inclusion of the rites in *The Satanic Rituals*. The significance of these rituals was not lost on those in the nascent field of Lovecraft scholarship; in *Nyctalops #10* (1975), Rob Hollis Miller's article "Lovecraft and Satanism" offered a quite perceptive analysis of the subject while drawing on the publication of these rituals as a significant (and unsettling) occurrence.

Nyarlathotep alone was said to be able to communicate with humans in human languages. Having originally written *The Ceremony of the Nine Angles* in English only, Aquino realized that a rite intended to be performed in connection with these entities not of this Earth would also need an appropriately challenging language to accompany it. Drawing on the handful of phrases of this language he dubbed "Yuggothic" (primarily from *The Call of Cthulhu* and *The Case of Charles Dexter Ward*), Aquino expanded on them while creating new vocabulary and usage patterns in the same style. The intention when performing these two rituals is that the English would be read first by the participants in order to begin to understand what they were saying, but the actual performance would use the Yuggothic exclusively. The desired effect is not unlike that of a Catholic mass conducted entirely in Latin or an Enochian ritual, both of which leverage the sense of mystery (and detachment from the "everyday" world) that the ceremonial use of unknown languages awakens in the participants.

Strange Angles in Lovecraft's Works

A central aspect of both *The Ceremony of the Nine Angles* and *The Call to Cthulhu* is that of **strange angles**. As the Law of the Trapezoid states, these oblique angles can be beneficial for those attuned to them or harmful for those unaware or apprehensive of them.

"The Haunter of the Dark" contains one of the most vivid descriptions of a mysterious set of objects that both attract and repel with their strangely angled design:

In the centre of the dust-laden floor rose a curiously angled stone pillar some four feet in height and two in average diameter, covered on each side with bizarre, crudely incised and wholly unrecognizable hieroglyphs. On this pillar rested a metal box of peculiarly asymmetrical form; its hinged lid thrown back, and its interior holding what looked beneath the decade-deep dust to be an egg-shaped or irregularly spherical object some four inches through. [. . .]

The four-inch seeming sphere turned out to be a nearly black, red-striated polyhedron with many irregular flat surfaces; either a very remarkable crystal of some sort or an artificial object of carved and highly polished mineral matter. It did not touch the bottom of the box, but was held suspended by means of a metal band around its centre, with seven queerly designed supports extending horizontally to angles of the box's inner wall near the top.[25]

In "The Haunter of the Dark," the strange angles of these objects have a profound psychological effect on the protagonist Robert Blake.* The sense of mystery they convey draws him in and compels him to confront great danger in his quest to understand their significance.

The multifaceted Shining Trapezohedron acts as a gateway for Nyarlathotep, in the form of the Haunter of the Dark, to manifest on earth for unknown purposes. The object is likely a transfigured representation of the lens of a telescope, which likewise has the ability to bring the stars closer so that much more can be learned of them. As mentioned earlier it can also be seen as a parallel to the Grail stone from Wolfram von Eschenbach's epic poem *Parzifal.*

In "The Dreams in the Witch-House," the witch Keziah Mason draws strangely angled sigils on the walls to create gates that allow her to transport herself physically between dimensions (thus taking shortcuts to move between different places in this dimension). Recall from chapter 1 the difference in tracing the Nine Angles in curved time as opposed to angular time, as shown on page 82. These diagrams give a visual

---

*Blake is based on Lovecraft's friend, the horror and science fiction writer Robert Bloch, best known for having written the novel *Psycho* and several of the more atmospheric episodes of the original *Star Trek* television series. Bloch's short story "Shambler from the Stars" (1935) included a character based on Lovecraft who was killed; here Lovecraft returns the favor.

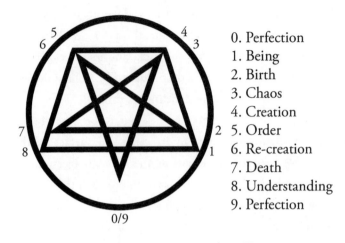

0. Perfection
1. Being
2. Birth
3. Chaos
4. Creation
5. Order
6. Re-creation
7. Death
8. Understanding
9. Perfection

The Angles through circular time

0. Perfection
1. Chaos
2. Order
3. Understanding
4. Being
5. Creation
6. Sleep/Death
7. Awakening/Birth
8. Re-creation
9. Perfection

The Angles through angular time

representation of the same type of "short cut" via the Angles as used by Keziah Mason in the story. In angular time, much like the human thought process, ideas and awareness unfold in ways that are out of sync with the predictable processes of nature.

In the story, Walter Gilman's obsession encompasses the intense study of higher dimensions and abstract geometry, combined with the local folklore concerning the witch's exploits:

As time wore along, his absorption in the irregular wall and ceiling of his room increased; for he began to read into the odd angles a mathematical significance which seemed to offer vague clues regarding their purpose. Old Keziah, he reflected, might have had excellent reasons for living in a room with peculiar angles; for was it not through certain angles that she claimed to have gone outside the boundaries of the world of space we know? His interest gradually veered away from the unplumbed voids beyond the slanting surfaces, since it now appeared that the purpose of those surfaces concerned the side he was on.[26]

The significance of a gate itself is represented in the Mythos by Yog-Sothoth, but the one most associated with **utilizing** gates is Nyarlathotep (who appears in the story as the mysterious Black Man: the object of the quest and recipient of the oath binding this knowledge in secrecy when traversing the angled gates).

Having established some of the vivid descriptions of "strange angles" in Lovecraft's fiction, we can now turn to a few key concepts that are central to *The Ceremony of the Nine Angles* and *The Call to Cthulhu*. These are: the Angles and their connections to Lovecraftian deities, the concept of the World of Horrors, and the language constructed for use in these rites.

The Individual Angles and Their Lovecraft Connections
The first four of the Angles, those comprising the trapezoid, are associated with (in order) Azathoth, Yog-Sothoth, Nyarlathotep, and

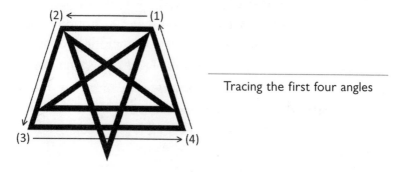

Tracing the first four angles

Shub-Niggurath. The descriptions are given as part of the Bond of the Nine Angles, and each of the nine stanzas of the Bond describes the essence and significance of that Angle both individually and as part of the continuum of the recurring sequence.

> From the First Angle is the infinite, wherein the laughing one doth cry and the flutes wail until the ending of time.[27]

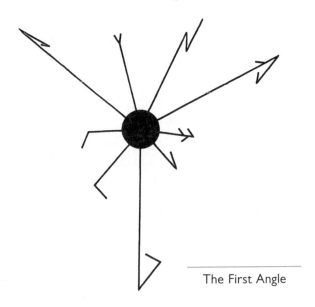

The First Angle

Lovecraft's "The Dreams in the Witch-House" refers to Azathoth's throne "at the center of ultimate Chaos [. . .] where the thin flutes pipe mindlessly."[28] Azathoth represents the unmanifest void, the ultimate source of all the other Outer Gods and the objective universe itself as a knowable phenomenon. Aquino's description of "the laughing one [who] doth cry" lays bare the contradictions and lack of order or logic in this state (logic is itself an intellectual manifestation of order, and requires a rational being to perceive it). Stephen Flowers would later correlate this state with that of *Ginnungagap* in the northern Germanic cosmology; that is, the unmanifest void from which the objective universe is created by Ymir after he arises from it as a result of spontaneously organizing order.

From the Second Angle is the master, who doth order the planes and the angles and who hath conceived the World of Horrors in its terror and glory.[29]

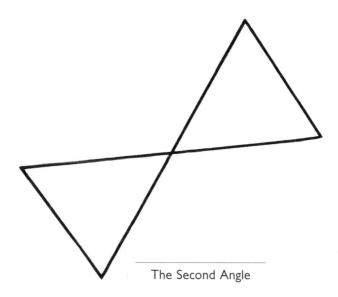

The Second Angle

Yog-Sothoth, the avatar of the Second Angle, represents the unconscious, spontaneously arising order from the unmanifest void of Azathoth. Yog-Sothoth is both the key to and guardian of gates, and the one who would transgress them must bargain with Yog-Sothoth in order to gain entry. These gates, including perhaps most importantly the one guarding the transition between nonexistence and existence, are a result of this emergent order. Yog-Sothoth governs order and cycles: it is because of Yog-Sothoth that the stars will one day "come right again" (due to axial precession), and those transformed by the slowly evolving cycles of existence will gradually learn to perceive them for their own ends and to chart their destiny with the stars as their inspiration.

From the Third Angle is the messenger, who hath created the power to behold the master of the World of Horrors, and who giveth to thee substance of being and the knowledge of the Nine Angles.[30]

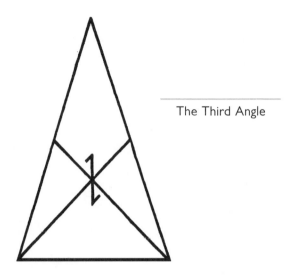

The Third Angle

In the Mythos, Nyarlathotep (the Third Angle) is the messenger of the Outer Gods on Earth, interacting with mankind in forms and communication patterns they are able to comprehend while opening their eyes to wonders beyond the visible world. He enlightens them to previously unimagined orderings within the cosmos (or frightens them with the same, as appropriate). In the form of the Nine Angles known as the Seal of Rûna (symbolic of the pursuit of the Mysterious in understanding the relationship between the subjective universe [the pentagram] and the objective universe [the untouched circle]), the Third Angle is the first of two connections between the subjective and objective. In other words, the study of Nyarlathotep and of the Third Angle is the study of this relationship and of how the subjective and objective universes affect each other.

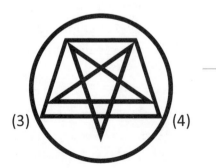

The Seal of Rûna, with Third and Fourth Angles indicated

Nyarlathotep illustrates these pursuits via alchemical work, mad science, and the power of the moving picture to reveal new ways of understanding the world and yourself. There is a deep danger in losing the sense of self and individuality in his visions—the "substance of being" he provides comes at a steep price for those unable to retain their awareness and identity.

What Nyarlathotep teaches is not containable or explainable by the ordinary physical laws—his transgression of those laws gives us a way to more deeply understand them, embodied by Yog-Sothoth as the "master who doth order the planes and angles."[31]

> From the Fourth Angle is the ram of the Sun, who brought thy selves to be, and who proclaimeth the time that was, the time that is, and the time that shall be, and whose name is the brilliance of the Nine Angles.[32]

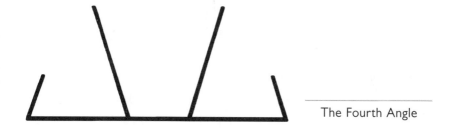

The Fourth Angle

Shub-Niggurath—the Fourth Angle—is nowhere described by Lovecraft himself in very much detail, although the depiction was expanded on somewhat by other members of the Lovecraft circle and in various of his collaborations with other authors.

The function of Shub-Niggurath in the Mythos is somewhat akin to that of the figure of Baphomet—goatlike, both male and female, representing the past and the future, creation (as the "goat of a thousand young," thus similar to a "great mother" deity) and destruction (the tendencies of her offspring). Shub-Niggurath is the womb of chaos that can give rise to any abomination, and is the wellspring of nightmares.

Michael Aquino also identified Shub-Niggurath with the Egyptian *neter* Amon (the ram-headed sphinx who was one of many *neteru* associated with different aspects of the Sun, a natural obsession in a culture based in the desert sands). As such, Shub-Niggurath and the Fourth Angle are identified with transitions and thresholds; these are times when change is afoot, and when matter, space, and consciousness have the potential to transform. Energy from the Sun provides fuel for material transformations on Earth—yet in a sense we are part of the same substance, consisting in part of elements that are only created in stars.

Along with the Third Angle—signified by Nyarlathotep—the Fourth Angle is one of only two that directly link the subjective and objective universes. The study of the interplay between them is vital to understanding the workings of magic as a practical pursuit capable of creating real change in the world (and in the Self informed by its presence within the world). Otherwise magic is an ineffective, purely intellectual curiosity and hobby instead of a means of bringing about change in accordance with will and desire.

These four entities are different facets of the pre-rational component of the human consciousness, not fully within the realm of conscious awareness but nonetheless accessible by working outside of the intellectual apprehension of the self, the body, and the objective universe. These could be seen as manifestations of the so-called reptilian brain that exert influence on our conscious, rational awareness. Knowing the aspects of the intellect, and its biological foundations, is a vital component of actualizing all aspects of the body-self complex. In other words, magicians ignore the nonintellectual aspects of themselves at their peril.

The World of Horrors

The World of Horrors conceived of by Yog-Sothoth is a rich concept that has its origins by that name in *The Ceremony of the Nine Angles*. The phrase is not intended in a negative sense, but rather describes the complexities of existence while explicitly stating that there is potential for both terror and glory—subject to the interplay between personal choices and chance. The terror comes from the realization that ultimately the individual must be the final arbiter of how his or her existence unfolds, and that to fully take on this responsibility can be truly horrifying in its implications. On the other hand, great treasures await those who embrace this mandate and fulfill its terrifying potential.

Magicians tend to project a great deal of pessimism onto the world in its present form. After all, if they were already satisfied with things as they are, they would have no need to seek out a means for escaping the world (via fantasy) or transforming it (via magic). Nonetheless, it is necessary to have an understanding and acceptance of the world *as it is* in order to know **how** to effectively transform it (and your place in it). This realization that the world is complex, governed by the forces of stupidity and ignorance, yet full of wonder that can be sought or created, is vital.

The World of Horrors only appears in *The Ceremony of the Nine Angles* in connection with the trapezoid—the first four Angles and their corresponding Lovecraftian principles. The brutal dichotomy of the World of Horrors—capable of both terror and glory—is laid bare throughout the *Ceremony* and in some ways this is the crucial realization that the psychodrama intends to illustrate.

A Constructed Magical Language

The use of a liturgical tongue not known to the participants has a hypnotic effect that magnifies its importance. The focus shifts from the meaning of the words to the emotion and drama of the delivery of the words. A magnificent example of this technique is the "Satanic ritual" scene in the 1934 film *The Black Cat,* where Boris Karloff's austere and dramatic delivery of such random but profound sounding Latin phrases as Cum grano salis ("with a grain of salt") and Fructu, non foliis arborem aestima ("by fruit, not by leaves, judge a tree") creates an atmosphere of utmost power and sincerity in the ritual chamber.

One of the characteristic features of Yuggothic is the prevalence of glottal stops* (signified by the apostrophe '), as in the phrase *N'kgnath*

---

*A glottal stop is a sharp sound created by sudden obstruction of the air flow in the vocal tract. The variant of the sound suggested for use as a glottal stop in Yuggothic is the abrupt *k* sound that follows a drawn-out vowel at the end of a word; for example, the final sound in *hawk.*

ki'q Az-Athoth r' jyarh wh'fagh zhasa phr-tga nyena phrag-n'glu ("Let us do honor to Azathoth, without whose laughter this world should not be."). The use of glottal stops suggests a voiceless language (that is, one that doesn't rely on the vibration of vocal cords for creating many of its sounds), and this in turn contributes to the nonhuman sound of Yuggothic.

In the early 1990s, the Yuggothic language inspired by Lovecraft and created by Aquino was expanded for use in the Order of the Trapezoid by one of its members, Timothy McGranahan. Along with expanding the vocabulary, he also created a lexicon and a set of alphabetic symbols called **R'lyehian** (both in written form and as a typesetting font) that provide a striking visual component to the presentation of Yuggothic text. (The full set of symbols from the R'lyeh font is given in Appendix F.)

Example of the R'lyehian font

This addition to the richness of the magical language used in *The Ceremony of the Nine Angles* and *The Call to Cthulhu* allows them to be used as part of a living magical neo-tradition—instead of relegating them to historical relics of the early 1970s.

NEO-TRADITIONALISM, NEO-MYTHOLOGY, AND SEMIOTICS

The Nine Angles as a magical system is a living, still-evolving example of neo-traditionalism—building a new paradigm with roots in other established traditions. The Angles build on elements of other traditional systems, such as Pythagorean number mysticism and the significance of collections of threes and nines in Germanic cosmology. These are, however, cast in an entirely new light and built into a new system that is part unique synthesis, and part previously unimagined aesthetic and symbolic speculation. The neo-mythology of H. P. Lovecraft—itself built in subtle ways on mythological forms of the deep past—provides the background through which the metaphysical foundation of the Nine Angles is expressed.

Those who would work with the Nine Angles must be equally at home exploring the deep past and drawing on the neo-mythologies that will shape the legends of the future.

The Tradition of the runes, as understood today and practiced in organizations dedicated to their authentic study such as the Rune-Gild, has a rich history and body of practice that is being continually rediscovered (and recast in forms relevant to the needs of today's practitioner). This illustrates a contrast to the system of the Nine Angles, which while perhaps in the process of being encoded as a system that may stand the test of time, is at its core being innovated instead of re-created.

The primary strength of neo-traditionalism also leads to its greatest challenge: the freedom to create the new tradition in whatever form it may need to take can easily result in a loss of coherence since "anything goes." This is the inherent problem of postmodernism: as the old traditions and patterns of thought come to be seen as arbitrary and interchangeable, creating something capable of retaining validity and coherence is necessary. That which is true becomes more dependent on the integrity and focus of the individual; there is no absolute authority on what is valid, but a consensus on what is meaningful and worthy of preservation can be built by those who have done the work to build true foundations in the ever-shifting sands.

RÛNA AND THE INFLUENCE OF STEPHEN EDRED FLOWERS

In 1984, the runologist Stephen Flowers made contact with the Temple of Set due to his interest in its Order of the Trapezoid. He had been a member of the Church of Satan around 1972–73, and a self-described "occultizoid nincompoop"[33] engaged in various aspects of the "New Age" and popular occultism in the early 1970s. After an experience in 1974 where he was introduced to the concept of *Rûna* under appropriately mysterious circumstances, he embarked on an academic and practical study of the runes and their cultural-linguistic matrices that culminated in earning a Ph.D. in Germanic Languages and Medieval Studies from the University of Texas at Austin in 1984.[34]

Rûna is the ultimate Mystery, the sense of the hidden that draws forth those receptive to its call in a never-ending quest to explore and understand the mysteries of existence. Far from being another form of mysticism, the pursuit of *Rûna* is the path toward *clarity:* as one mystery is comprehended, another lurks just beyond, but what has been uncovered is now made part of the pursuer's subjective universe. Line 143 the *Hávamál* ("The Sayings of the High One [= Óðinn]," an Old Norse poem dating from the Viking age) embodies this: "One word led me on from a word to another word, one work led me on from a work to another work."[35]

Rûna, meaning "mystery" or "something concealed," is an early form of the same Germanic word that provided the name for the runes. While often reduced in popular understanding today to the "letters" or signs themselves, in their traditional usage the runes explicitly facilitated magical acts. Additionally, they were also worked with as reflective symbols (and linguistic maps) for understanding the mysteries of existence.

In the mid-1980s, Flowers founded a Pylon—or geographically focused group within the Temple of Set—in Austin, Texas called the Bull of Ombos. One of the activities that the Pylon engaged in was the regular performance of *Die Elektrischen Vorspiele,* and this led to the renewal of interest in some of the other aspects of the philosophies and practices of the Church of Satan. Much of Flowers's work in this area was published as articles in *Runes,* the private journal of the Order of the Trapezoid; a selection of his work from this period was later reprinted in a 1995 anthology, *Black Rûna.* Among these articles, the essays relating to Satanic topics included "The Command to Look," "The Trapezoidal

Cinema," *"Magie und Manipulation,"* and "On the Choice of a Human Sacrifice" (an analysis of the infamous—yet not intended to be taken literally—section of the same name in *The Satanic Bible*). Articles written during this time but not republished in *Black Rûna* include "The Nine Angles of the Seal" (see appendix C) and "V'Yn'khe Rohz: The Cycle of Nine," both of which are key components to the expansion of the philosophy and practice of angular magic beyond Michael Aquino's original formulation in *The Ceremony of the Nine Angles*.

This was a curious time to be revisiting such roots that had long been neglected. For one thing, the late 1980s in the United States was the height of the so-called "Satanic Panic," where popular hysteria held that Satanists were lurking everywhere and waiting to kidnap, molest, and sacrifice children (along with various other unfounded—and ultimately disproven—fears). That the "blood libels" attributed to Satanists had in earlier eras been directed at Muslims, Jews, and even Christians, with the same level of fervent belief but equally absent proof, did not deter those who were bent on fear-mongering (and profiteering in many cases, by filing lawsuits alleging heinous "Satanic" acts).*

In 1994 Flowers wrote the article "The Alchemy of Yggdrasill" (see appendix E), which formed a vital bridge between the neo-traditionalism of the work of the Order of the Trapezoid and that of the northern Germanic tradition. This article traces the alchemical formulas underlying the cosmology in the *Eddas* as combinations of **forms** and **energies**; the form/energy pairs described in this cosmology are: (1) water/fire, (2) ice/air, (3) iron/yeast, and (4) salt/venom. Flowers elaborates:

> The first two pairs (1–2) manifest the concrete order of the cosmos, while the second two pairs (3–4) constitute the manifestation of living information in the natural cosmic order. Most of the cosmic ordering is made up of substances and processes restricted to the first two pairs. The living information (genetic code) dynamically,

---

*For more info on the phenomenon and its effects on innocent people, see Michael Aquino's *Extreme Prejudice: The Presidio "Satanic Abuse" Scam* (self-published, 2014).

but still from our perspective unconsciously, evolves to a point where enough information (from *Ginnung*) has been cross-referenced to make a mutation into a semi-conscious being possible. This is the first of the Æsir: Óðinn–Vili–Vé—the first reunification of the spectrum of all the qualities present in *Ginnung*.[36]

Recall from our earlier discussion of the first four Angles (the trapezoid), that the First and Second Angles represent the transition from chaos (unformed potential) to order (the rules and laws of manifestation coming arising from their own interactions). In other words, before life can arise, a sufficiently stable yet non-static order must be in place, and this arising must be spontaneous as there is not yet any consciousness capable of directing it. Similarly, the Third and Fourth Angles signify the transition (based on the ordering already in place) to understanding (the capability of perceiving your own existence) and then to being (the full realization of this perception through temporal awareness).

Continuing with Flowers's explanation of the Nine Angles through this process of alchemical evolution, the Æsir (gods capable of full consciousness) overthrow the established order to create it (the Fifth Angle) in an image of their own choosing. With the Sixth Angle, the Æsir have focused their attention elsewhere and left the process of creation to their subconscious agents (the dwarves) who continue to create based

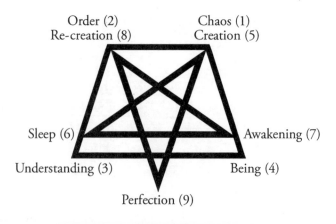

The Nine Angles with keywords

on the rules and desires that have already been established. Óðinn, as chief of the Æsir (i.e., the source of consciousness itself), has undergone his ordeal of sacrificing himself to himself over nine long nights hung from the tree Yggdrasill; he reawakens (the Seventh Angle) with a fully formed vision of what direction creation must take. He is now conscious and self-aware in a way that is accessible to other conscious beings by emulating his example, and he applies this newfound clarity of purpose to reconfiguring the cosmos itself (the Eighth Angle) to realize his vision. At this point, Óðinn fully comprehends *Rúna*, as this clarity and knowledge of his own limitations gives him the ability to know with precision where the boundaries of his awareness end—and the mysteries beyond the Self begin. With the cyclical process now complete (the Ninth Angle), it can begin anew (a refined version of the First Angle informed by all the previous cycles of the Angles).[37]

OTHER EXPLORATIONS OF ANGULAR MAGIC IN THE TEMPLE OF SET

Inspired by the work of Stephen Flowers (and others like Don Webb), various experiments with angular magic were undertaken in the Temple of Set from the late 1980s onward. These experiments, workings, and workshops have usually been conducted under the leadership of the Order of the Trapezoid, although it is certainly not necessary to be a member of the Order (or even of the Temple of Set) to work with these ideas. The following is a summary of some of the more notable undertakings that can be publicly discussed; many more opportunities are available to those whose drive to understand leads them to a suitable school.

At two of the Temple of Set's annual International Conclaves in the early 1990s, a ritual known as the Shub-Niggurath Working took place. The focus of this magical act was on the sending of a message to a past conception of the participants' selves; this was done by concluding the Working and **receiving** the message at one Conclave, while opening the Working and **sending** the message at the **next** year's Conclave. Remember that the focus of the Fourth Angle, associated with Shub-Niggurath, is among other things concerned with the magical use of time. ("From the Fourth Angle is the ram of the Sun, who brought thy selves to be; who proclaimeth the time that was, the time that is, and the time that shall be, and whose name is the brilliance of the Nine Angles."[38]) By engaging in work of this type, and accurately recording its results (or failures), the magician can learn to be a more effective student of his own timeline, and to send back signs to an earlier manifestation of that timeline, which will ensure that personal existence unfolds in accordance with individual desire and will.

In conjunction with the Shub-Niggurath Working, Flowers revealed and discussed the image of the Seal of Rûna, thus providing another tool for comprehending and affecting the unfolding of one's individual path to the Grail. Recall that the Seal of Rûna illustrates the connection between the Nine Angles and the objective universe (represented by the surrounding circle).

The Seal of Rûna

The fourth Grandmaster of the Order of the Trapezoid, referred to here as Sir Rudra, introduced the concept of **angular rites of passage** around 1995. While this approach was not fully realized during his time as Grandmaster, it forms the basis of some of the practical magical work suggested in chapter 8. In contrast to the ethnographer Arnold van Gennep's threefold model of rites of passage,* Rudra suggests a

---

*See Arnold van Gennep, *The Rites of Passage* (Routledge & Kegan Paul, 1960). Gennep's model includes stages of *separation, transition/liminality,* and *(re)incorporation.*

four-stage model of *desire, redefinition, transgression,* and *realization.* Later experiments with this idea have shown that this sequence can be mapped onto the first four Angles, and thus form the basis for a specifically angular type of operative magic. The Angles thus function as a geometric metaphor for the relationships between the elements of self-transformative magical experiences, and also provide a guide for methods of breaking those experiences into their appropriate stages in order that they may be enacted more precisely.

Also around 1995, a project to compile an Order of the Trapezoid–specific version of Lovecraft's fabled *Necronomicon* was begun. The intent behind this was to compile the various writings on magical theory and practice inspired by the work of Lovecraft. In addition to the rites created by Michael Aquino in *The Satanic Rituals,* other aspects of the neo-mythological pursuits of the Order were included in the book—such as a Lovecraftian Grail Mass, a Mythos-inspired rendition of the *Rite of the Headless One,** accounts of the previously mentioned Shub-Niggurath Working, and commentary and analysis of the previous two decades of practice of these ideas within the Church of Satan and Temple of Set. Eighteen years later (a magically appropriate period of time to have allowed the ideas to work within the world, now to be cast into a new form), the original *Necronomicon* was revised and expanded.

Over a period of nine years, beginning in 2008, the Order of the Trapezoid engaged in an in-depth review of the material behind the Nine Angles and the work that has been done with it since its introduction in *The Ceremony of the Nine Angles* in 1972. Each of these years in the fall, at the Temple of Set's annual International Conclave, the Order presented the results of that year's exploration of the Angle at hand in the form of

---

*Also known as the "Bornless" ritual after the opening line of Aleister Crowley's version of it called *Liber Samekh* ("Thee I invoke, the Bornless one"; "Bornless" was actually a mistranslation in the sources consulted by Crowley). The rite allows the practitioner to enter a state of being that allows conversation with their Holy Guardian Angel or, alternately, to raise the practitioner to a higher level of divinity and magical power through the use of certain sigils and "barbarous" names.

a magical working open to all in the Temple. As the Angles are best seen as individual markers that are nonetheless part of a coherent whole,* this series of workings was also considered to be a single nine-year working. The value in this work was in the revisiting of the roots behind these ideas, uncovering the meaning and interpretations that were there from the beginning but not yet evident; as understanding and practice unfold in a living, evolving system there will always be new nuances to uncover and explore. This book is one of the fruits of that labor, revealing to the wider world much that has previously lain hidden.

---

*Much as the runes can be seen as 24 (or 16 or 18 or 33, depending on the particular system used) aspects of one all-encompassing Mystery.

4

THE FOUNDATIONS OF
GEOMETRY IN MAGICAL
PRACTICES

This chapter bridges the gap between the theoretical and the practical, exploring how the mathematical study of geometry can be applied to the metaphorical use of geometry in magic. To do this, we'll examine the linguistic significance of the concept of metaphor, then return to the very basics of geometry to provide the reader with a firm foundation for translating mathematics into magic. The differences between *sacred* and *infernal* geometry will be explained. No serious discussion of sacred geometry is complete without taking a close look at the Golden Ratio, and as there is a lot of confusion and misinformation surrounding the Golden Ratio in esoteric literature, it is necessary for this chapter to differentiate between fact and fiction regarding this most interesting of numbers. Following from the idea that a metaphor must be lived in order to provide the most accurate and effective usefulness, the chapter includes demonstration of a technique for constructing a pentagram using only the traditional tools of a compass and straight edge.

MAKING METAPHOR INTO REALITY

Metaphor is a common feature in magical traditions—the actions undertaken by the magician often manifest as rarefied versions of nonmagical acts. Metaphor in its mundane sense is a figure of speech that equates one thing with another; for example, "That movie was the bee's knees." Metaphors are never **literally** true—not only do bees not possess knees, a movie is a very different thing from any part of an insect's body. Metaphors do, however, symbolically evoke sensations and associations, and at one level or another form the basis for virtually all ritual and magical behavior. Linguistically, it is not at all clear how metaphors work in terms of symbol processing, nor is it well understood how we distinguish metaphors—which are in fact untruths in the strictest sense—from deliberate attempts to deceive or mislead. Nonetheless, their use appears to be a fundamental feature of human intelligence expressed through our capacity for highly nuanced language.

A few examples of mundane activities expressed metaphorically in various magical traditions are in order, leading up to the practice and metaphor of geometry used in the magic of the Nine Angles.

The Egyptian god Khnum (or Xnum) was said to have gifted self-awareness and consciousness to mankind—somewhat akin to Prometheus, but without the resulting punishment for his supposed transgression. Khnum shaped mankind on a potter's wheel, leading to the metaphor of the magician—the one who uses this gift of self-awareness to shape her own subjective universe—as a pot waiting to be fired. That is, as the magician develops in herself this capacity for self-awareness and consciously directed existence, she tests herself against and overcomes ordeals that have a transformative effect—much like a pot that has been shaped and then fired in a kiln to add greater permanence to its form, but which will burst apart if too many imperfections remain in its constituent components.

To fully appreciate this metaphor and its applicability to this process of self-development, the magician would learn the actual skills of pot making. Like any skill that takes focused study to master, the nuances and difficulty of perfecting the different parts of the process will both be more challenging than they may at first appear, and will also provide great insight into the necessity of patience and submitting yourself to a learning process.

In his highly symbolic work *The Vision and the Voice,* Aleister Crowley explores in the thirteenth part the state of being called Magister Templi (or Master of the Temple). This set of visions equates the Magister Templi with a master gardener, and explains his task and method of working through gardening metaphors. That is, the Magister Templi calls to himself students that resonate with the method and paradigm that he teaches. In this garden of students, he nurtures their development as he would a seed he has planted: providing what the student needs to grow, but knowing that he is more a caretaker of the process of growth rather than being the sole cause of it.

This metaphor—the Teacher as gardener—is wonderfully illustrated in Arthur C. Clarke's novel *2001: A Space Odyssey* (originally published in 1968), where it is said of the unnamed intelligent beings that cultivate consciousness where it has emerged on the planets they have explored:

And because, in all the galaxy, they had found nothing more precious than Mind, they encouraged its dawning everywhere. They became farmers in the fields of stars; they sowed, and sometimes they reaped. And sometimes, dispassionately, they had to weed.[1]

As with the example of Khnum and the potter's wheel, using such a metaphor in the abstract ultimately limits its effectiveness unless combined with the experience of the actual physical process. Kenneth Grant referred to this experience as "the physical nature of the gnosis."[2]

You can study in minute detail the physics and mechanics of riding a bicycle, along with the physiological aspects used and experienced by the rider. However, these alone cannot create the actual work that is needed to learn to ride a bicycle comfortably and efficiently. That can only come from having had the physical experience and developing the skills, balance, and muscle memory that are needed to ride effectively. Once those are in place, these skills are used with actual understanding of the true nature of the experience—rather than just relying on incomplete and untested assumptions about what riding a bike "must" be like.

A third example of physical (and also mathematical) experience used metaphorically in a rich magical tradition—one also very relevant to our study of angular magic—is that of Freemasonry.

Although the precise beginnings of Freemasonry are shrouded in legend and speculation (plus a good deal of intentional misdirection), we know for certain it was being practiced in something akin to its present form by the early eighteenth century.

The central metaphor of Freemasonry is the construction of a temple (specifically, Solomon's Temple as known from the book 1 Kings in the Old Testament, and other related Judaic sources) and this metaphor is expressed in the ritual setting through the study and application of sacred geometry. Originally an outgrowth of medieval masonry guilds, where the specialized knowledge passed on as part of the guild teaching process took on a more symbolic and metaphysical meaning, the lodge requirement of admitting only properly trained stonemasons was eventually relaxed. This relaxation is the origin of lodges of "Free and Accepted Masons"; that is, professional masons who have experienced the physical nature of the gnosis, doing lodge work alongside those who are taught the symbolic and metaphysical aspects of it (but who probably have never actually laid a brick in real life).

In the article introducing the Order of the Trapezoid in the December 1970 issue of *The Cloven Hoof,* Anton LaVey mentioned that "it might also be added that the 'G' in Masonic tradition does **not** stand for 'God', as American Masons would like to believe!"[3]

LaVey is referring here to the Masonic symbol of the ruler and compass with the stylized *G* in the center, arranged to form a symbol suggestive of the unicursal hexagram found in Golden Dawn and Thelemic magical traditions.

The Masonic ruler and compass

The true meaning LaVey alludes to is that the *G* stands for "Geometry"—with the identification of "God" as the Grand Geometer of the universe (the master who doth order the planes and the angles?). The study of geometry in Freemasonry extends to the orientation and proportions within a lodge, as well as to the precise positioning of the different officers during the various ritual activities.

The magician and author Frater U∴D∴ includes the elaborate and very precise rituals of Freemasonry in what he calls the **angular tradition** of magic.[4] Although this particular use of the term *angular* has little in common with the theory and techniques described in the present book, it does refer generally to magical forms where the magician is working within a highly symbolic framework that is based on a particular cosmology or "map" of the macrocosm. The power and effectiveness of this form of angular magic derive from how precisely the rituals are performed, more so than the skill and intent of the individuals performing them.

ORIGINS OF GEOMETRY

The earliest hints of geometrical knowledge and practice can be traced to circa 3000 BCE in the Indus river valley and ancient Babylonia. A millennium later, it was the cultures of Egypt and Mesopotamia that began to document their insight into ever more complex geometric problems. Even then, their methods were almost strictly empirical, relying on trial and error rather than applying mathematical abstractions.

The Greek historian Herodotus (ca. fifth century BCE) suggested that geometry arose in Egypt as a necessity caused by the annual flooding of the Nile river—the need for surveying of property boundaries required a knowledge of plane geometry. Egypt was, however, not the only ancient civilization built around a river valley that was prone to flooding, and in any event the documented evidence of geometric understanding in other places contemporary with (or perhaps even predating) the knowledge in Egypt makes it difficult to accept Herodotus's claim. It is more likely that Herodotus—given the Greeks' status as the most

○ And perhaps "60t," pp 47-43

thoroughly accomplished geometers to that point in history—was following the general trend toward claiming greater prestige for the work of his culture by casting it as the successor to the work of the Egyptians.

One of the earliest geometry texts is the so-called "Moscow" papyrus,* created in Egypt circa 1850 BCE. Among the notable problems in this papyrus is a formula for calculating the volume of a frustum (or truncated pyramid); a frustum has four trapezoids as faces, and its magical properties are discussed in detail in Anton LaVey's article "The Law of the Trapezoid" (reprinted in *The Devil's Notebook*).

The introduction of deductive reasoning to the solving of geometric problems is credited to Thales of Miletus (635–543 BCE), who applied this new approach to tasks such as calculating the height of pyramids. Deductive reasoning starts from premises that are accepted as true within the context of the particular argument, then develops conclusions whose correctness can be traced directly back to the original premises. The combination of deductive reasoning and geometry was one of the pair of developments that set the stage for Euclid, whose *Elements* is widely considered to be the most important and influential mathematical text of all time. The other development came from someone who was not himself a mathematician.

Geometry was considered such an important study by Plato's time that legend has it the warning "Let none ignorant of geometry enter here" was inscribed above the entrance to his school, the Academy. Plato was not a mathematician, but his views on mathematics were nonetheless very influential along with the rest of his profound effect on philosophy. He is credited with introducing the precept that the "true" geometer only uses a compass and straight edge; measuring instruments like rulers were considered workmen's tools and thus not worthy of a scholar.

Euclid—who was likely a student of Plato's academy although Plato himself was no longer living by then—composed his famous text *The Elements* circa 300 BCE. *The Elements* did not introduce much that

---

*The common name for the Golenishchev Mathematical Papyrus, named after the Egyptologist Vladimir Golenishchev, who was the first to possess it following its removal from Egypt.

was new in terms of theory; however, Euclid's vital contribution was the mathematical rigor he brought to the overall organization of the geometric knowledge known at the time. Geometry texts in use prior to *The Elements* were no longer used once it was widely available and are now generally lost or forgotten. Most importantly, Euclid drew on and formalized the Greek innovation (by Plato) that geometry is the study of Forms and abstractions, of which physical objects are only approximations.

The shift toward study of abstractions (paired with real-world applications) is an important precursor to the study of semiotics—the manipulation of symbols (**signifiers**) facilitates the manipulations of things and ideas that partake of those symbols (**signifieds**). The human capacity for abstract thought and pattern-recognition thus gained an important new tool from geometry. See chapter 5 for more information about semiotics and symbols and their use in magic.

Like any ancient science that was only understood by an elite class of scholars and/or magicians, geometry would have from its very beginning carried associations with various cultic practices. There are hints of this throughout the early history of geometry, from its uses in celestial calculations to mundane acts that bridge the gap between earth and the heavens.

For example, there are records as far back as the Second Dynasty in Egypt (beginning ca. 2900 BCE) that refer to a foundation-laying ceremony called the Stretching of the Cord. The pharaoh, assisted by Seshat, the goddess of temple records, brings the cosmic order governing the stars down to earth where the orientation of the new temple reflects this order. Depictions of Seshat normally showed her wearing a leopard hide, the spots of which represented the stars of the night sky.

By the medieval period in Western Europe, the study of geometry coincided with the study of the divine (perhaps as part of the continued influence of Aristotle that pervaded much of medieval philosophy). This identification of "God" as a geometer is of course central to the symbolism in Freemasonry, and this is the time period when the beginnings of the practices that were later formalized as Freemasonry began to take shape.

Geometry was treated as a mostly static science in Europe in the medieval period, however; there was little mathematical innovation occurring there until the beginnings of the Renaissance in Florence (which then spread to other Italian city-states and eventually into all of Western Europe). Interestingly, the Renaissance was largely seeded by the rediscovery of various Greek texts that had only survived in Arabic translations; thus, in many ways, the geometric thinkers of the day merely picked up where the Greeks had left off.

CORE GEOMETRIC CONCEPTS

The study of geometry arises from a group of principles—varying in number depending on the type of geometry being discussed—called **primitive notions**. These primitive notions can only be defined, not derived from other geometric concepts; rather, they are expressed as **axioms** that are the starting point for further definitions.

Axioms cannot be proven; they are accepted as true in the context of their use, and confirm their validity and applicability by the more complex geometric theorems they help to prove. In the geometry of Euclid (the starting point for all other types of geometry), he famously includes five axioms that form the basis for all the theory and practice in *The Elements*. (A discussion of these axioms is beyond the scope of this book; however, any competent text on geometry includes them by necessity and discusses how they are integral components of proving geometric theorems.)

A **point**, represented by a dot (.), is a single, unique location in space. A point does not possess any length, area, or volume, and other figures (lines, curves, polygons, etc.) are said to consist of an infinite number of points. On a two-dimensional grid, points are usually expressed in terms of their position on the horizontal axis (traditionally called the **X** axis or coordinate) paired with their position on the vertical axis (**Y**). There can by definition be only one such point at any given **x,y** pair of coordinates. (With the addition of the **Z** axis, that of height/depth, points can be located in three-dimensional space as well; the same holds for the higher dimensions, *ad infinitum*.)

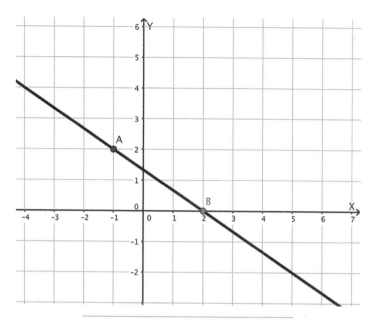

A line plotted on a cartesian grid

A **straight line** connects two points via the shortest path between them, and extends infinitely in both directions. There are an infinite number of points on a line, and any two are sufficient to define the line. Since points themselves have no width, a line has no width as well. If two points on a line are described as x_a,y_a and x_b,y_b, then the **slope**—the rate of change in the line's height (or **y** coordinate) relative to the increase in its **x** (horizontal) coordinate—is $(y_b - y_a) / (x_b - x_a)$.

In the preceding line graph, x_a,y_a is **-1,2** and x_b,y_b is **2,0** (places where the line precisely crosses the intersections on the grid). The slope of this line is therefore **(0 - 2) / (2 - -1) == -2 / 3**. Note: A positive slope indicates that the line **rises** as it moves toward the right of the grid, and a negative slope (as in this case) indicates that the line **falls** as it moves toward the right.

Planes and Angles

The geometric ideas of planes and angles—imbued with magical significance—are central to the study of the Nine Angles. This is explicitly referenced in *The Ceremony of the Nine Angles:* "From the Second Angle is the master who doth order the planes and the angles, and who hath conceived the World of Horrors in its terror and glory."[5]

A **plane** is a flat, two-dimensional space that extends infinitely in both directions. A plane is an extension of a zero-dimensional point (with no length, width, nor depth) into a one-dimensional line (infinite length, but no width or depth), and further into a two-dimensional representation with infinite length and width but no depth.

An **angle** is formed by the intersection of two lines, at a single point that is referred to as the **vertex** of the angle. These lines, terminating at the vertex, are called the **rays** of the angle. An angle can also be the intersection of two planes (where it is then called a **dihedral** angle). The English word *angle* comes by way of both Latin and Greek roots, ultimately derived from the Proto-Indo-European word **ank* (corner).

Angle can also refer to the measurement of the portion of a circle (with its center at the vertex of the angle) traced by intersection of the two raws on the circle. For example, a complete circle is divided into 360°; an angle of 72° thus covers 72/360 or 1/5 of the circumference of a circle. The number of degrees measured in an angle is thus a proportion—an expression of value built on its relationship to another value rather than being an absolute measurement in and of itself.

A **curve** is similar to a line, and continually changes its direction as

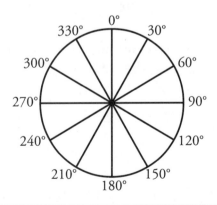

Circle with degrees shown as portions of the whole

a point on the curve moves along the x and y axis. Strictly speaking, a line is a special case of curve, with no curvature—continuous change in direction—as it moves along the x and/or y axis.

THE PENTAGRAM AND THE GOLDEN RATIO

The Golden Ratio (also called the Golden Section or the Divine Proportion) results from dividing a line into two unequal parts such that the length of the shorter compared to the longer is in the same proportion as the longer is to the original line (see below). Approximately equal to 1.618..., the Golden Ratio is a recurring theme in sacred geometry and has applications within such diverse fields as architecture, visual perspective in art, botany, and music.

The first published reference to the Golden Ratio by that name was in Martin Ohm's *Die Reine Elementar-Mathematik* (*The Pure Elementary Mathematics*; second edition 1835). Other claims that the name goes back as far as the fifteenth century are not universally accepted. The "divine proportion" derives from the book *De Divina Proportione* (1509) by the Italian mathematician Luca de Pacioli (1477–1517). Pacioli was a collaborator with Leonardo da Vinci, and in this book he first published some of Leonardo's famous drawings that illustrate or otherwise employ the Golden Ratio.

There has been a lot of nonsense spread around, usually with good intentions, about the properties and occurrences of the Golden Ratio in natural and man-made forms. The Greek letter *phi* (Φ) typically represents the Golden Ratio in nonspecialist mathematical literature. Much like the "23 Enigma" cited by William Burroughs, once you think you've seen Φ anywhere suddenly you see it everywhere. Among other aspects of Φ's history, Mario Livio in his highly recommended

The Golden Section

book *The Golden Ratio** spills a lot of ink poking holes in a wide variety of claimed occurrences of Φ. The notion that the concept of Φ exists anywhere in nature itself is a fallacy—the actual number is nowhere in nature; what we respond to as the Golden Ratio is an abstraction that consciousness is using to know about itself and its relationship to the objective universe.

The Golden Rectangle has the lengths of its sides related to each other by the Golden Ratio. This special rectangle is perpetually self-generating: removing a square with sides equal to the shorter side of the rectangle, or adding a square with sides equal to the longer side, results in a new Golden Rectangle. This is related to the peculiar and unique mathematical property of the Divine Proportion that Φ multiplied by itself is equal to Φ + 1.

Drawing diagonals in any two successive pairs of reduced Golden Rectangles results in an intersection in the same point in the overall structure. This point is the center on which the rectangles will perpetually converge, but never actually reach. And of course, the crossed

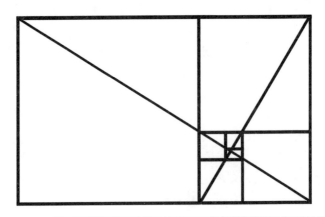

The convergence of repeatedly reduced Golden Rectangles

*Livio's *The Golden Ratio: The Story of PHI, the World's Most Astonishing Number* is absolutely essential to any study of the symbolism and application of the Golden Ratio in sacred geometry and magic. Far from being merely a debunking of mystical claims, by eliminating the erroneous ideas about the Golden Ratio and its manifestations, Livio's book gives the deeper mystery of the concept an uncluttered platform through which he reveals more of its true nature. The pursuit of *Rûna* always leads to clarity.

diagonals are divided at precisely the Golden Ratio. This recurring self-similarity is both the essence of the symbology of the Golden Ratio—the supreme metaphor for self-directed, self-aware change—and the reason why many natural processes can be analyzed in terms of Φ. A well-known example of such a natural process is the arrangement of leaves on plants, called *phyllotaxis,* that maximizes the amount of sunlight available to the lower leaves.

The Pentagram

The pentagram is a very ancient symbol, with documented occurrences (with and without an enclosing circle) as early as 3500 BCE. All the angles and subdivisions of lines within a pentagram are precisely keyed to Φ—even though its use as a symbol predates the geometric understanding that forever coupled it to the Golden Ratio, this discovery only enhanced the already intuitive significance associated with the pentagram (and its closely related figure, the pentagon).

The pentagram was used—always inverse—as a symbol and sign of recognition by the Pythagoreans. There is a significant amount of circumstantial evidence that the Pythagoreans were also aware of the Golden Ratio and some of its properties, and thus likely used the pentagram to encode this secret and sacred knowledge. The theoretical basis behind the system of magic revealed in this book specifically utilizes the pentagram with one point down. This symbolism is not employed solely because of its common association with Satanism and black magic in general—although that certainly is an added bonus and entirely appropriate in a symbolic sense—but because of that represented by the inverse pentagram inside a circle.

The pentagram itself represents the self-aware, self-evolving, and self-perpetuating psyche distinguishing itself from the objective universe (the enclosing circle). One point is down (instead of the often-seen two) to indicate the necessity of continual dynamic balance; two points down are stable enough to balance themselves with very little effort. With one point down, the constant effort must be utilized to ensure balance, just as the psyche must nourish itself and constantly

The pentagram representing the Self as distinct from the objective universe

reinforce its own stability. The circle—a function of *pi* (π), another peculiar irrational number that pops up in sorts of interesting and unexpected places—does not touch the pentagram to indicate that the psyche doesn't depend on or originate from the objective universe.

Analogously to the endless transformations of the Golden Rectangle by adding/subtracting a square, the relationship between the pentagon and the pentagram forms a similar pattern of perpetual self-similarity. All three of these figures have proportions based entirely on Φ, and as a consequence of this also benefit from Φ's self-regenerative features. Thus, the figure of the pentagram, self-similar and self-regenerative throughout infinite iterations, is an ideal symbol for the evolving psyche, which also retains yet refines its essence throughout successive transformations.

Nested construction of pentagons and pentagrams

The Greek interest in the Golden Ratio was a natural outgrowth of their fascination with the Platonic solids and the construction of such figures as the pentagram and pentagon, and their knowledge of it at least in this context (and with basic understanding of its applications) is well documented. Claims that the Greeks were "obsessed" with the Golden Ratio are a bit harder to substantiate, however, especially as they pertain to instances commonly cited in books about the Divine Proportion. While the goal of this book is not to promote or debunk the various claims about the Golden Ratio (other than as they directly pertain to our topic of angular magic), it is worth taking a slight detour to address a couple of the more commonly held misconceptions in order to clear the way to the deeper mysteries that lurk behind this number.

OCCURRENCES OF THE GOLDEN RATIO: FACT AND FICTION

One of the most widely cited examples of the Golden Ratio being used as an essential architectural design element is that of the ancient Greek temple known as the Parthenon. The temple was build circa 440 BCE on the Acropolis in Athens, and dedicated to *Athena Parthenos* (Athena the Virgin). Even though it was heavily damaged in 1687 during an attack by the Turks, it is still widely held to be a brilliant example of beauty expressed through architectural simplicity and cohesion.

The claims about the deliberate use of the Golden Ratio in its design usually refer to its overall proportion of length to height, and sometimes also include assertions about the triangular façade (now heavily damaged) in relation to itself and to the whole.

An unfortunate tendency in sacred geometry literature—especially in books written for nonspecialists in mathematics or architecture— is to repeat such claims uncritically, and to use measurements that are massaged to fit the numbers (or conveniently ignore features like steps and pedestals, which break the proportions). Often, instead of working from absolute and verifiable measures and deriving Φ, they **start** with Φ and look for places to measure it (sometimes very arbitrarily).

In the case of the Parthenon (as with many other ancient structures), the measurements will vary widely depending on the source and what parts of the structure are (or are not) included. Textbooks and reference books written by **architects**, on the other hand, generally cite detailed and repeatable measurements that agree with other sources in the discipline, and which are not especially close to any reasonable approximation of *phi*. Finally, there is little widely accepted documentation of the Golden Ratio (especially in the context of it being pleasing to the senses) prior to the temple's construction. All of these facts make it difficult to accept the common claim that the proportions of the Parthenon were designed according to the Golden Ratio.

For another widely cited example of the Golden Ratio in ancient architecture that falls apart on critical review, we now turn to the most abused structure in the history of esoteric literature and mystical speculation: the Great Pyramid.

The most common claim is that the height and area of the triangular sides of the Great Pyramid incorporate the Golden Ratio as a fundamental design principle. This assertion is typically attributed to an original source of the Greek historian Herodotus. The first major problem is that Herodotus made no such claim, but was instead misleadingly misquoted by English publisher John Taylor (1781–1864) in his book *The Great Pyramid: Why Was It Built and Who Built It?* (1859). Lest the reader think this was an innocent mistake on Taylor's part, it is also worth noting that he embellished the original quote to suggest other numeric gyrations that he used to "prove" the mathematical connections. Taylor's book was a major influence on Piazzi Smyth (1819–1900), the Astronomer Royal for Scotland who essentially launched the pyramid craze with his fanciful theories and questionable measurements used to support his various claims about the geometric properties of the pyramids.

The second major problem with the claims of Taylor and Smyth is the inaccuracy in the measurements they relied on, which multiply into larger errors when using those numbers as a basis for further calculations. Modern measurements, even when allowing for variations from the original dimensions due to the decay of long years, simply do not substantiate any clear connection between the Golden Ratio and the construction of the pyramids.

There is no end to the claims about the profound secrets symbolized by, or encoded in, the pyramids. Whether such claims are ultimately useful in symbolic pursuits is dependent on the extent to which they are understood to be idealized rather than absolute. To that end, it is worth noting that a later contribution to the ever-expanding pyramid mania was an important influence on Anton LaVey and his Law of the Trapezoid: Louis McCarty's *The Great Pyramid Jeezeh* (1907), cited in his article introducing the Order of the Trapezoid in the December 1970 edition of *The Cloven Hoof.*

These two famous examples illustrate the necessity for applying skepticism and independent verification to supposed instances of the Golden Ratio. It is all too easy to cherry-pick—or massage—the data to match predetermined conclusions, whether or not the claimant is intending to deliberately deceive.

Now that we've ruined a bit of the traditional fun, where else does this magical number, the Golden Ratio, **actually** appear and how does this relate to the theory and practice of angular magic?

CONSTRUCTING THE PENTAGRAM

The Golden Section is essential to the construction of the pentagon (and thus the pentagram as well, by extending the lines crossing adjacent vertices until they meet in the familiar points). Indeed, it has often been conjectured—not at all unreasonably—that the reason the Pythagoreans used the pentagram as their symbol was precisely because it encoded this great secret.

Continuing with the principle of experiencing the physical nature of the gnosis, we will now examine a method for constructing the pentagram in the traditional style of using only a compass and a straight edge. It is highly recommended that the reader experiment with this technique until it can be reliably and efficiently repeated—metaphors must resonate with your lived experience in order to be at their most effective.

Determine the length you want to use for the sides of the pentagon inside the pentagram; the length of a line in the completed pentagram will be Φ cubed (Φ x Φ x Φ, or approximately 4.236) times the length of the interior pentagon side. Note that once you set your compass to the length of the initial line segment, you will keep it set to that same distance for the remainder of the construction.

1. Draw a horizontal line segment of the desired pentagon side length. Call the endpoints of this line **A** and **B**, and the line segment **AB**.

2. Set your compass to the length of segment **AB**, and draw *two* circles with radius **AB** using **A** and **B** as the centers.

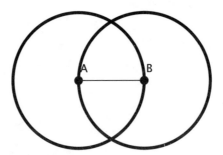

3. Draw a vertical line segment that connects the points where the circles intersect (note also that this line *bisects*, or cuts in half, the original line segment **AB**).

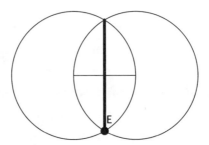

4. Using the bottom point (labeled **E**) of intersection between these two circles as the center, draw a third circle. Note that this circle intersects the original circles precisely at points **A** and **B**, and as well as at two other points labeled **C** and **D** in the diagram.

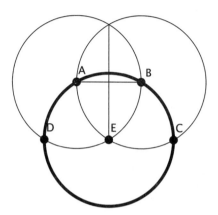

5. The third circle intersects the vertical line at one point, labeled **F**. Draw two line segments from points **C** and **D** *through* point **F** until they intersect at the tops of the two original circles. These new points of intersection are labeled **M** and **N**.

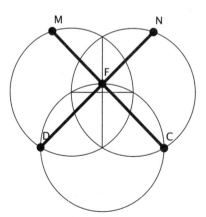

6. Using points **M** and **N** as the centers, draw two more circles. The top point where they intersect is labeled **P**. Note also the intersections with the points **A** and **B**. (See page 118.)

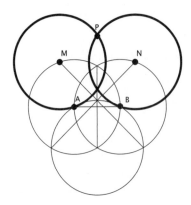

7. To complete the pentagon, connect the points **A** and **M**, **M** and **P**, **P** and **N**, and **N** and **B** (**A** and **B**, being the original line segment that determined the measurements for the rest of the figure, are already connected).

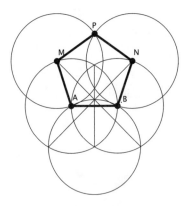

8. To extend the pentagon into the pentagram, extend the sides of the pentagon until they meet.

SACRED AND INFERNAL GEOMETRY

Books on sacred geometry have an unfortunate tendency to repeat many questionable claims about the Golden Ratio (including some of those already examined in this chapter). They also tend to obscure the factual aspects of the subject behind unnecessarily cryptic mysticism rather than focus on an approach to the mysterious that allows the reader to advance her own understanding. (As we have noted earlier, *Rûna*—the draw of the Mysterious—works best as a transformative tool when it leads to clarity rather than obscurity for obscurity's sake.) While it is not without its flaws, a generally recommended work on both the mysterious and practical facets of sacred geometry is Robert Lawlor's *Sacred Geometry: Philosophy and Practice.*

Geometry is the study of **spatial** order and relationships. Contrast this with astronomy, which is the study of **temporal** order expressed through cyclical movement.[6] Thus the Starry Wisdom of H. P. Lovecraft is as much about geometry as it is about astronomy. The relationship between astronomy and geometry is a close one: the angles between stars, the forms of the constellations, the representations of the heavens arranged onto a spherical grid; these are all based in the same geometrical concepts discussed in this chapter and form the conceptual map that minds use to understand themselves in their reflections on the ordering of the heavens.

Plato taught that reality is based on archetypal ideas—Forms—that are phenomena we perceive as pale reflections of their true transcendent reality. He further taught that geometry was the purest, most ideal philosophical language. In effect, immersing oneself in geometric study was considered a perfected form of philosophical contemplation, leading to apprehension of the Forms: the more closely your personal relational map of the cosmos matches the idealized relationships behind these forms, the more precisely you can attain an understanding of the underlying pure Forms. These ideas from Plato drew from the teaching of Pythagoras that "all is arranged according to number."[7]

Observational astronomy is expressed in angular terms; the

proportions of the night sky traversed relative to other objects (or an object's previous position[s]) are represented as an angle forming a portion of the complete 360° of the "spherical" sky.[8] Even this representation—the night sky as a sphere surrounding the observer's vantage point of his position on Earth—is an idealized form; the Earth is not a perfect sphere, and the spherical appearance of the vault of the night sky is an illusion.

Sacred geometry is the study of universal order—the objective universe (the physical universe and the laws that shape its existence)—through geometrical metaphor. This is the traditional use of the phrase *sacred geometry* cast into a form that focuses on externally created phenomena; for example, natural occurrences (such as the ever-shifting arrangement of the night sky), or objects and structures created by others representing their own attempts to capture their understanding of themselves or the world in symbolic, geometric forms.

In contrast, I use the term **infernal geometry** in this book to denote the study of order created within the subjective universe (the self-awareness of each sentient being within the objective universe). This is a new understanding of the application of geometry to the psyche, requiring the precise definitions of magical, symbolic, and esoteric practices discussed in detail in chapter 5. **Infernal** is used to indicate this inversion of reflection toward the inner world; order within the Self rises up from the Black Flame that kindles each individual's unique, self-evolving essence.

> But the entities outside the Gates command all angles, and
> view the myriad parts of the cosmos in terms of fragmentary
> change-involving perspective, or of the changeless totality
> beyond perspective, in accordance with their will.[9]
>
> H. P. LOVECRAFT AND E. HOFFMANN PRICE,
> "THROUGH THE GATES OF THE SILVER KEY"

5

A Theory of Magic

This chapter provides a theoretical foundation for the practices in this book. This will begin with a survey of historical theories of magic, then moving on to later developments based on a shift in attitudes about magic among anthropologists and scholars of religion. We'll define *magic* and the *Left-Hand Path*, and frame them in a further discussion of the concepts supporting the theory of magic used in this book. To turn toward practice, we'll examine the Nine Angles themselves and the Law of the Trapezoid in terms of these theoretical concepts. With the philosophical basis for angular magic established, we'll revisit the ideas of *angular* vs. *curved* time and William Mortensen's photography manual *The Command to Look*. The Germanic view of time, expressed through the meaning and significance of the Norns, provides another way of exploring the magical significance of nine-angled figures. The chapter concludes with a discussion of various types of ritual magic, including both their theoretical and practical underpinnings that make them effective.

HISTORICAL THEORIES OF MAGIC

Before discussing the theory of magic that underlies the practices in this book, it is necessary to give a bit of related background and history. Most historical theories of magic attempt to explain (a) why the magician **thinks** that magic works, and/or (b) what effect magical thinking has on the practitioner or on the society in which it is practiced. That is, magic is treated as a form of social control or self-delusion used by so-called "primitive" man, who acts without benefit of our modern understanding of the world gained through psychology, sociology, and the physical sciences. Anthropologists began to codify theories of magic in the late nineteenth century in Europe as part of a broader attempt to understand the relationships between modern, industrial Western cultures and those regarded as less developed (and thus seen as necessarily inferior).[1]

A common feature of older theories of magic and mythology is the assumption that magical thinking results from ignorance of science; that is, magic purportedly began as a flawed attempt to explain natural processes by a culture that did not have the benefit of the scientific knowledge available to more modern cultures. Twentieth-century mythologists and religious historians, such as Joseph Campbell and Mircea Eliade, have superseded this assumption by contextualizing the role of myth in terms of how it reflects the cosmology, ethics, and social structure of its host society.

Another theory, put forth by anthropologist Claude Lévi-Strauss, suggests that magic fulfills a purely symbolic role: when someone is otherwise helpless to deal with a situation or need, or needs to feel in control of the phenomena arising from it, magic provides a form of placebo that relieves the anxiety of being unable to act (or reinforces the belief that the magician was the active force in the phenomena that were out of his control). Again, the implicit assumption—that magic is ineffective and borne of ignorance—serves to discount other possible functions and mechanisms by which magic produces results.

The sympathetic theory of magic was a central idea in Sir James Frazer's *The Golden Bough* (1889). As this was the predominant theory prior to the advent of the semiotic theory of magic, it is worth a bit more explanation so that the semiotic theory can be discussed in its proper context.

While Frazer may not have been the first to put forth the sympathetic theory, he was the anthropologist who popularized it in the English language. Frazer's work was exceedingly popular at a time in

Victorian England when the British Empire was nearing its height in terms of reach and prosperity; his ideas became an essential component of the desire of the educated English public to understand their own culture's relationship to that of their colonies, and to reinforce their belief in their own cultural superiority (largely resulting from the notion that the more technologically advanced culture was necessarily the superior one).

The sympathetic theory holds that the interplay between the **law of similarity** and the **law of contagion** is responsible for the belief in magic among "primitive" cultures. The law of similarity is that "like influences like"; that is, the magician creates effects by imitating or acting out what he wants to happen. The law of contagion relates how magic can be transferred by touch; once an object has been touched in a magical act, any other object or person that comes into contact with the object can be a recipient of the magical intent. This is a key feature in fictional treatments of magic, such as M. R. James's classic short story "Casting the Runes" (1911) and Fritz Leiber's *Our Lady of Darkness* (1977), where a curse is transferred by means of a parchment that has been suitably inscribed.

While the sympathetic theory can no longer be seen as a comprehensive explanation of the mechanism and significance of magic, it is still in widespread use as an effective means of behavioral suggestion, particularly in the realm of mass advertising. Any time there is an ad for a fancy car that is directed at heterosexual men and includes a beautiful, scantily clad woman leaning up against it, or a commercial showing people you can relate to attributing their happiness or success to a particular item they possess, you're seeing a modern use of the sympathetic theory. Whether or not it is an adequate explanation of magic, it's still effective psychology.

Introducing the Semiotic Theory of Magic

Instead of the sympathetic theory of magic, the basis of practice for this book is the **semiotic theory**. According to this theory, the magician utilizes signs and symbols as part of a communication process with the phenomena she wishes to understand or affect and assigns meaning to the phenomena that become known to her. Previous historical theories of magic are generally predicated on the idea that magic **does not work**, and explain magic through the effects it has on the psychology of the individual or on the individual's host culture. The semiotic theory proceeds from the assumption that magic **does** work and then attempts to explain why; this approach is an outgrowth from the postmodern field of semiotics— the study of communication through systems of signs and symbols. This becomes a theory of magic when applied to the ways that the magician manipulates her own internal perceptions (i.e., affects the subjective universe), or brings about change in the observable world (i.e., affects the objective universe or the behavior or thoughts of those within it).

A THEORY OF ANGULAR MAGIC

The Objective and Subjective Universes

In order to perceive and affect the complexities of reality, we first require definitions for framing these pursuits.

Magic is the process by which perceptual changes are created and made permanent within the inner world (the magician must first transform herself), and these changes may, when needed, create observable change in the phenomena of the outer world (as the portion of the world that the magician has the power to influence is reconfigured to more closely match her desired form).

The Nine Angles as a magical system have a theoretical basis in the distinctions between the **objective** and **subjective universes**, and between **angular** and **curved space/time**. It will be seen that angular magic is at its core a Left-Hand Path practice; the Left-Hand Path, as used in this book, is the assertion of absolute personal responsibility for enhancing and perpetuating the individual's self-aware, psyche-centric existence. This is done through refining and actualizing your Will and desires and by doing so becoming the active force in your existence. The transformations that result from this practice will often also be seen by their effects on the world outside the Self.

The objective universe is what in common usage might be called the physical universe: matter (animate or inanimate), energy, time, and space—and the laws that govern their existence (whether discovered and described, or not). Our physical bodies are a function of this same objective universe—made primarily of elements that can only be created in the deep infernos of stars and destined to be scattered across the ever-expanding physical universe. Yet, in conscious and self-aware beings, there is Something that cannot be adequately explained as merely a function of matter, energy, and their governing laws; this leads us to the concept of the subjective universe.

The subjective universe is the self-awareness of each sentient being within the objective universe. This self-awareness creates and enables the individual's knowledge, experiences, and attitudes, and acts as the mediator and interpreter of the objective universe. This subjective universe is largely modeled on the objective universe, since as an incarnate being interacting with the objective universe the individual is subject to its laws. The subjective universe can be seen as the ability of consciousness to perceive, reflect on, and change itself; this also leads to understanding, categorizing, and distinguishing itself against the objective universe.

It is important to understand the precision behind the usage of subjective and objective in this context. Contrary to colloquial usage, where *objective* is usually taken to mean "correct" or "provable," and *subjective* to mean "based on opinion or preference" rather than fact, the terms are used in this book in a specific linguistic sense. In linguistics—the study of language and its effects on the thought processes of humans—the **subject** is the doer of an action, and the **object** is the thing acted upon. In the sentence *I apprehend the universe,* "I" is the subject while "universe" is the object (or the thing apprehended).

From the subjective universe arises the desire to create or act, as well as the means to bring the appropriate symbols to bear in order to make that creation or action "real" (observable in the objective universe). The subjective universe can also be the object of its **own** actions, and, in fact, all magic first arises as an act of self-transformation—the world as known internally to the magician must be reconfigured before the objective universe can be remodeled on that change. Thus, the more accurate of an understanding you have of the objective universe, the more accurately and effectively the model of it in the subjective universe can be modified.

It is also important to note that this distinction between the subjective and objective universes is not intended as a form of matter/spirit dualism (such as we find in Gnostic thought). Neither is there any moral implication to the contrast between the two—that is, an assumption that one of these must necessarily be "good" or "desirable," and the other therefore "evil" or "undesirable." This description attempts to group aspects of existence according to the most effective means of studying, interacting with, and altering them. The subjective and objective universes are each facets of one universe, defined here as the totality of existence whether known or unknown. (Whether there is more than one universe as used in that sense is beyond the scope of this book.)

Angles and Curves

Another key aspect of the theory of angular magic is the distinction between **curved** and **angular** time. Angular time is that experienced within the subjective universe; curved time is the phenomenon of time that arises from the orderly workings of the objective universe.

Curved time is what we experience as physical inhabitants of the orderly cosmos (i.e., the objective universe). Curved time can be **linear**—a one-way path that events appear to follow. It can also be **cyclical**, such as in recurring processes like the progression of the seasons as the tilted Earth marks its positions in its elliptical path around the sun; each season is largely similar to its previous occurrence, even though it may vary slightly in its particulars. *Curved* can be most readily understood as a reference to the cosmology of Plato, in which the cosmos—the physical universe—was conceived of as a sphere.

Angular time in contrast is subjective—the subject or "doer" makes of time what he will and is able to conceive of it in ways that are not possible in the objective universe. In angular time awareness and thoughts unfold in ways that are not completely beholden to the predictable processes of nature—inspiration and insight arise seemingly from nowhere, but those aware of the angular properties of these experiences can have greater awareness and control over them.

By learning to perceive and cultivate angular time, the magician can master the ability to transform the perception of his own past and possess profound influence over the ways individual existence unfolds as observed within the objective universe.

Any examination of the patterns apparent in life will reveal their cyclical nature; they can't always be perceived while you are immersed in such a pattern, but by increasing awareness of how the cycles of curved time operate in a mostly non-conscious manner, you can change their trajectory by learning to make the right thoughts and actions at the right time. The alternate perspective of angular time, known only to those aware of the workings of the subjective universe, provides a key to unlocking the mystery of where effort is most effectively applied when affecting angular **or** curved time. For example, while struggling with deciding the details of a painting you are creating, you realize that you are at the point in the artistic process where it is more productive to *cease* direct action for a time; the Sixth Angle—*Sleep* or *Incubation*—suggests that moving the question about the direction of the creation away from your active attention will allow it to reemerge later (i.e, the Seventh Angle) when the insight develops that gives you inspiration to complete the work of art.

THE SEMIOTIC THEORY OF MAGIC

The final key to the theory behind magic using the Nine Angles is the direct influence of late twentieth-century theories of magic. In particular, angular magic reflects the semiotic theory of magic as developed from work by anthropologists and linguists such as Jan van Baal,[*] Stanley Tambiah,[†] and Stephen E. Flowers.[‡]

---

[*]In *Symbols for Communication: An Introduction to the Anthropological Study of Religion* (Van Gorcum, 1971)
[†]In his essays "The Magical Power of Words" (1968) and "Form and Meaning of Magical Acts: A Point of View" (1973)
[‡]In *Runes and Magic: Magical Formulaic Elements in the Older Runic Tradition* (Lang, 1986; third revised and expanded edition, Rûna-Raven, 2010)

The semiotic theory of magic suggests that the use of symbol systems—and the mechanisms by which symbol systems are encoded, communicated, and decoded—is the key to understanding how magic functions. The hidden meaning of phenomena the magician encounters and desires must be uncovered, and in this process the phenomena become partners in the communication with the magician. In the case of the Nine Angles, the various Lovecraftian entities—and the symbolism of their roles in the creation and evolution of the cosmos—provide a framework for constructing magical intent that communicates via these signs and symbols. This cosmic evolution is macrocosmic as a description of the unfolding of the physical and metaphysical universes, and the evolution of mankind as a whole; and microcosmic in the sense of the paths of individuals and their specific magical acts.

Grammatical Subjects and Objects

The grammatical terms **subject**, **direct object**, and **indirect object** are necessary to review as part of explaining the semiotic theory. The **subject** is the doer of an action, while the **direct object** is the thing acted upon. For example, in the sentence *Michael wrote the ritual,* "Michael" is the subject while "ritual" is the direct object. An **indirect object** is affected by the action on the direct object, but is not the primary recipient of the action. For example, in the sentence *Michael wrote Anton a letter,* "Anton" is the indirect object (and "letter" is the direct object, or the thing being acted on).

Stephen Flowers described the function of subject, direct object, and indirect object in the semiotic theory of magic as follows:[2]

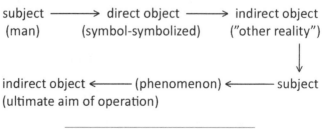

subject ———→ direct object ———→ indirect object
(man)   (symbol-symbolized)   ("other reality")

indirect object ←——— (phenomenon) ←——— subject
(ultimate aim of operation)

The semiotic magical process

In this model, the magician (the *subject*) encodes her desire via the *frame of reference* (the *object*, or the symbolism and meaning that represent what she wishes to create or affect through magic). Through finding this effective *mode of address*, she communicates with the hidden realm of the unmanifest in order to induce the desired response (the effect or creation she wants to bring about). This response is the *subject* in a communication back to her, with the desired phenomenon (the results she seeks) being the indirect object. The magician, the intended phenomenon, and the unmanifest become equal partners in the communication and participate as equals through the *law of similarity* (i.e., communicants understand each other most effectively when they have similar understanding and goals; see below for more information on this concept).

In an influential passage in the development of the semiotic theory of magic, Jan van Baal writes of this communication formula for the fulfillment of desire:

> In this discourse Man feels addressed or singled out by his universe and he endeavors to address it in turn trying to discover the kind of address to which his universe will be willing to answer; that is, willing to show itself communicable. The formula he finally discovers in answer to his quest is not really Man's discovery but a gift— a revelation bestowed upon him by the universe. The formula is the outcome of an act of communication in which Man's universe reveals to him the secret of how it should be addressed in this or that circumstance, a secret which is at the same time a revelation of its hidden essence in that particular field.[3]

The magic is in the communication.

Performative Utterances, Similarity, and Frames of Reference

Also integral to the semiotic theory of magic are the concepts of **performative utterances**, **the law of similarity**, and the **frame of reference**. Let's look at each of these in turn.

Performative utterances were identified and described by the philosopher of language J. L. Austin in his set of seminal lectures published as *How to Do Things with Words* (1962). These are words and phrases that create action or changes in state (e.g., a judge pronouncing a sentence, where the words themselves cause something to happen by being spoken correctly and in the right context). In order to be effective, performative utterances must be done by someone with the correct authority and frame of reference and with the correct attitude toward the effectiveness of their speech. The correct authority is necessary for an utterance to qualify as *performative;* for example, a phrase such as *This court is now in session* does not have any effect unless uttered by a judge (or their recognized representative). Similarly, even a judge uttering the same phrase in jest at a party does not bring about the same performative result because it is not done with the necessary attitude toward the effectiveness of that speech act.

In terms of performative utterances as magical acts, the magician must use the appropriate set of signs and symbols in the right circumstances and with sufficient intent toward the desired outcome (relative to its likelihood of coming into being).

Two other important components of the semiotic theory of magic are similarity and the frame of reference. **Similarity** is the principle that the more alike the subject (doer) and indirect object (recipient) of the communication are, the more likely the communication is to be successfully transmitted and understood. In a mundane example, the concepts in this book are being encoded in the English language, which you as the reader then decode; the more similar my and your understanding of English are, the more likely it is that my ideas are communicated clearly and correctly understood by you, the reader. Similarly, two experienced technicians who both work with the same type of technology will be able to communicate with each other about their area of expertise in ways that someone unfamiliar with the subject could not.

The **frame of reference** is the combination of objective and subjective factors that form the background and execution of the magical act. This includes such factors as the knowledge and experience of the magician, the effectiveness and suitability of the signs and symbols the magician uses, and the proper execution of techniques and ideas within the context that they are called upon. The meaning and significance ascribed to this frame of reference becomes a partner in the communication at the core of the magical act, first as the indirect object but then as the agent (or subject) of actions that, in turn, affect the magician as a response to her initial magical act.

APPLYING THE SEMIOTIC THEORY TO THE NINE ANGLES

Now that we've more fully defined the objective and subjective universes, and the relationship between the two, we can take a closer look at the Seal of Rûna. As mentioned before, the Seal is symbolic of the pursuit of the Mysterious in understanding the relationship between the subjective universe (the pentagram) and the objective universe (the circle), with the trapezoid as the connection (or magical link) between the two. The Seal is an important addition to the Nine Angles themselves, presenting a map of how the Angles—a particular viewpoint on how the psyche, or subjective universe, becomes aware of and transforms itself—interact with the objective universe and thus providing a means for each to affect each other. The mysterious aspect of this, *Rûna* itself, is that your knowledge and understanding are always limited in some way, and there is always more to discover or comprehend beyond that; as you become able to see past your current horizon, more knowledge and understanding are available to pursue. William Shakespeare expressed this masterfully in *Hamlet:* "There are more things in heaven and Earth, Horatio, than are dreamt of in your philosophy." As your

The Seal of Rûna

philosophy—your understanding—expands, you find that there is *more* which is undreamt of, not less.

In terms of the Nine Angles, all of the Angles are accessible from within the subjective universe, but only the third (**Understanding**, symbolized by Nyarlathotep) and fourth (**Being**, represented as Shub-Niggurath) touch the circle of the objective universe. In other words, those signify the two places where the subjective universe—all of an individual's knowledge, experience, and capacity for self-awareness and self-directed change—can impress its desires and transformations on the objective universe. Conversely, these two Angles also indicate stages in the unfolding of a process where information, stress, and Mystery from the objective universe—and its *doppelgänger,* the World of Horrors (see chapter 3)—can affect the subjective universe.

The trapezoid is not the objective universe, as might be assumed from the Angle keywords of **Chaos, Order, Understanding,** and **Being,** and the description of those Angles as representing (in a macro-cosmic sense) the initial stages of a cosmological process of creation. Rather, the trapezoid is the subjective internalization of those features of the objective universe. Without a consciousness to perceive and assign meaning to these phenomena, there is no purpose or direction to their existence. The trapezoid symbolizes the perception of the role these natural, physical processes held in creating the foundation for awakening that consciousness was then able to animate.

In terms of the symbol system and frame of reference that enable the semiotic effectiveness of the Nine Angles, the Lovecraftian entities associated with the first four Angles provide much of the necessary imagery and qualities.

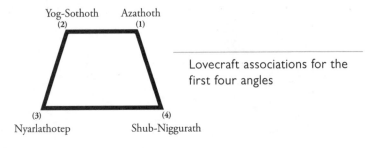

Lovecraft associations for the first four angles

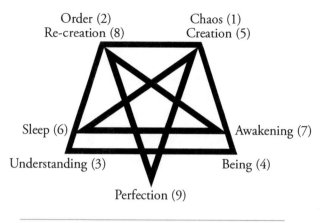

The original set of keywords for the angles

Another key aspect of the semiotic nature of the Nine Angles—introduced in the early 1990s by Stephen E. Flowers—is the association of keywords with each of the Angles. These keywords both capture an essential aspect of the meaning and significance of each Angle and also provide a means of address when working with the Angles.

The keyword—or unifying concept—for the First Angle is **Chaos**. This is a state of unity, but which holds all possibilities. In terms of Lovecraft's pantheon, the First Angle corresponds to Azathoth. The Second Angle—associated with Yog-Sothoth—refers to **Order**. Here, the possibilities implicit within the Chaos of the First Angle begin to be glimpsed. **Understanding** is the keyword of the Third Angle. Here, perspective is possible; a vantage point outside the simple, binary dualism of the first two Angles allows for intentional differentiation between the two. As the one who brings Understanding and is the messenger of the Outer Gods, Nyarlathotep is the essence of the Third Angle. The Fourth Angle has **Being** as its keyword. The perception possible through the Understanding of the Third Angle expands to include temporal awareness, with Shub-Niggurath as the Outer God who represents this Angle.

The neo-mythology created by Lovecraft—still living as a continually created cosmology for those influenced by his stories—can assume whatever level of reality is necessary for effective use by the magician. This frame of reference provides a richly symbolic and mysterious means of addressing the other reality that the magician desires to affect, which in turn addresses the magician having become a partner in the communication (and in the change that the magician desires to come into being).

Whether you "believe" in the Outer Gods is irrelevant in terms of working with them; the capacity of human intelligence to create "gods" in response to need also aids in their effectiveness in magical acts. In other words, they are as real as they need to be for the operation at hand. It is important to distinguish the causal principles (the significance, purpose, and relationships behind the Outer Gods) from the subtle deity forms (the appearance and other symbolism that we use to relate to them). For example, Nyarlathotep may be a personification of the principle of communication between the macrocosm and microcosm, but other forms with the same underlying essence—for example, Thoth and Hermes—would work just as well; it just happens that when working with the Nine Angles one of the primary frames of reference is that of the imagery attached to these principles by Lovecraft.

THE SEMIOTIC THEORY AND
THE LAW OF THE TRAPEZOID

Recall from the earlier discussions of the Law of the Trapezoid that while Anton LaVey never gave a formal, succinct definition for the Law, Michael Aquino summed it up as:

> All obtuse angles are magically harmful to those unaware of this property. The same angles are beneficial, stimulating, and energizing to those who are magically sensitive to them.[4]

As might be expected, a Law that contains its symbol in the name itself also has implications for the semiotic theory of magic. In this case, the signs and symbols used—the visual representations of the Law—are nonverbal. What is it that gives this symbol potency as a magical tool?

Throughout Anton LaVey's writings on the visual aspects of magic, there are references to trapezoids, pyramids, and other "dominant masses." This comes in part from his fascination with William Mortensen's photography manual *The Command to Look* (1937). Mortensen identifies three aspects of his **Command to Look** formula for creating a compelling and memorable photograph: (1) Impact (the irresistible draw to the picture),[5] (2) Subject Interest (the significance of what is being represented),[6] and (3) Participation (identification with the subject matter, whether in terms of reality or fantasy).[7] It is Impact that concerns us here, as that aspect of the Command to Look formula is central to the Law of the Trapezoid.

According to Mortensen, Impact derives primarily from instinctive feelings of danger when confronted with certain visual stimuli.[8] It is this factor that subconsciously causes the viewer to take notice, and to differentiate the imagery from the background. Mortensen categorizes these visual archetypes that create Impact into four types that induce the biological reaction of fear (via sensing the potential for danger).

1. The *diagonal,* something that moves across the field of vision with "swiftness and determination."[9] The lightning flash symbolizes this as a primitive source of terror (emphasizing that reactions to these visual archetypes arise from instinctive behaviors left over from earlier points in our evolution).
2. The *S-curve,* something that approaches in a slithering or curved manner. This is the predator moving through the savanna, the stealthy serpent moving nearby—or even the curves of the female form (the connections were no doubt intuited by the creators of the Garden of Eden myth and its infamous temptation).
3. Threatening *sharpness,* "whether in tooth or blade."[10] The triangle—composed entirely of acute angles—signifies dangerous edges and points. If the dangers of the **S-curve** are not heeded, sharp claws or teeth await.
4. A compact *dominant mass,* presenting an imposing obstacle

that restricts the ability to move freely and implies weakness on the part of the person unable to move it. This could be a large, immovable object (a tree, a pyramid) or an animal that is intimidating due to its size. In terms of the impact of the visual environment, the dominant mass shows its effect through:

a. *Unity*—objects of more manageable size gain strength through being connected

b. *Cohesion*—compact, dense masses are more dominating

c. *Isolation*—a large mass is more dominating if it stands alone, its impact coming only from itself

d. *Contrast*—a lightly colored mass is more domineering against a dark background, and vice versa[11]

These symbols form the basis of the semiotic foundation of the Command to Look, and in turn that of the Law of the Trapezoid as well. They can also provide clues for how to construct an effective ritual chamber, by using imagery that evokes these archetypal, biologically based symbols that can provide stimulation and inspiration to those aware of their significance—or for drawing forth the most basic visual instincts of those who are unaware of their implications.

Within the Law of the Trapezoid, the dominant mass in the form of the trapezoid and the threat of sharpness are the two elements directly present from Mortensen's theory of Impact. The intimidating aspect of the diagonal is implied, but largely shadowed by the other elements of

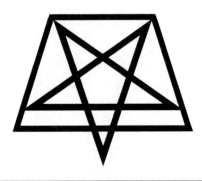

The dominant mass and sharpness of the Nine Angles

the Command to Look formula. While seven of the nine angles are acute (less than 90°), the two that are most significant for their perilous sharpness are that of the third and fourth—not coincidentally the two places where the subjective universe and its mysterious laws meet the perfect curve of the objective universe.

THE SIGNIFICANCE OF OTHER OCCURRENCES OF NINE-ANGLED FIGURES

The Nine Angles in its configuration of trapezoid-plus-pentagram has precedents in other similar figures. It can be useful to examine some of these predecessors as illustrative of other instances of the symbolism of the number nine in geometric form. Whether directly influential on the creation of this manifestation of the Nine Angles or not, they are part of the legacy of ideas that coalesced in this modern—and explicitly Left-Hand Path—rendition of the concept.

This examination of different configurations of the Nine Angles seen from alternate temporal perspectives is based on a suggestion by Don Webb concerning these relationships. To frame this properly, it is necessary to describe a few key features of the Germanic view of time. Bear in mind that Germanic cosmology is also a significant influence on the work of Stephen Flowers, who is the figure most responsible for expanding the magical system of the Nine Angles beyond its roots in *The Ceremony of the Nine Angles.*

In Germanic cosmology the three Norns rule the destinies of individuals. While they are sometimes known as the Fates, "weavers of destiny" is a more appropriate description of their role, as destiny arises from the deeds of the individual, while fate originates outside the individual and is fixed and inescapable. In other words, *destiny* is largely directed by the individual who must then take responsibility for its unfolding, and is thus a Left-Hand Path concept. In contrast, a completely fixed *fate* condemns the individual to a predetermined path where her actions have no significance except as they lead toward this preordained state; thus, fate is a concept of the Right-Hand Path.

The names of the Norns in Old Norse are *Urðr, Verðandi,* and *Skuld.* They are said to be female beings (likely of the race of giants) who spin the threads of the destiny of Men; they reside at the base of the World Tree Yggdrasill near Urðr's Well (from which they nourish the roots of the tree). It would be inaccurate to reduce them—as in some popular accounts—to simple personifications of the past, present, and future, especially since in the Germanic languages the "future" is a nebulous concept that can only be approximated in words.*

Urðr is that which has turned, happened, or occurred. Linguistically, the name derives from the past participle of the Old Norse verb *verða* (to become). *Urðr* sets the path along which Becoming unfolds. The same word, with analogous meaning and significance, is the more familiar *Wyrd* in Old English.

Verðandi is that which is turning, or happening or becoming, right now. It is a single moment in time, the present participle of the verb *verða.* What *Urðr* has wrought is the key to what *Verðandi* can turn— the present moment only exists in the form that the past allows it to take. *Verðandi* is the active component of the story told by *Urðr,* and is the destiny the individual is weaving from their actions and desires.

Skuld is different. To begin with, it is from a different verb, and is expressing a different relationship. The verb that *skuld* derives from is *skulla,* meaning "ought to be, need to be." *Skuld* means "should"; it is the auxiliary word that helps to form the future tense, but is it not by itself the future. What *Urðr* has wrought, and what *Verðandi* can then turn, are the keys to providing shape to what then *should* be.

The future according to the Germanic view is unshaped, amorphous, and imprecise. The past, on the other hand, is fully formed, and has a

---

*Germanic languages (a group that includes English) lack a true future tense. The past and present can be expressed by conjugating a verb directly, but the future requires additional words to convey the shifting of time. For example, with the phrase *I write,* the present and past tenses are expressed by *I write* and *I wrote,* respectively. To convey that the action of *write* is to occur later than now, additional words are required such as *I will write* or *I am going to write* (note that the verb itself generally retains its present-tense form in such constructs). Thus, it can be claimed that the Germanic languages do not have a natural concept of the future, and it can only be created synthetically.

definite "shape" resulting from what has occurred. This is a very Left-Hand Path idea. In the Right-Hand Path, the future is fixed; that is, any mindful evolution by the individual guides her toward this fixed state, at which point Becoming stops. Goals like nirvana and heaven are the end of the line, but the Left-Hand Path empowers the magician to imprint self-determination on whatever arises through *Urðr* remanifested as *Skuld*.

THE *VALKNÚTR*

That which has turned—has already become—is tightly intertwined, and inseparably knotted. It is not going anywhere, and can no longer be reconfigured *except* within the context of the shape it has already taken. Notice also that this shape cannot be drawn unicursally. Geometrically, it is stuck and is composed of three identical shapes. Looking at what has already occurred, the Nine Angles can be seen as the *Valknútr*.*

The *Valknútr*

In the moment when something is unfolding—*Verðandi*—there are fixed parts of that moment (what has already occurred, and led to things as they are) and there are flexible parts (what can be influenced to create things as they may yet become). Geometrically, this can be represented as three different, but independently cyclical, figures. From this perspective the Nine Angles can be seen as the Enneagram.

---

*Keep in mind that there is very little historically attested explanation of what the symbol of the *Valknútr* may have signified; even the name is a modern coinage. This description of the *Valknútr* in terms of the Nine Angles is highly speculative, although it certainly is supported in the context of the geometric significance ascribed to it here.

THE ENNEAGRAM

The three fundamental shapes within the enneagram are the circle (symbolizing the objective universe as in the Seal of Rûna), the triangle, and the irregular yet symmetrical six-pointed figure. All three of these figures can move in perpetual cycles and can be drawn unicursally.

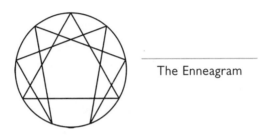

The Enneagram

The first thing to observe about the enneagram is that there are nine points where the circle—the objective universe—intersects with the angular figures. They are all evenly distributed along the circle though, implying that they are all equally valid to the objective universe, but ultimately each the same. There is no consciousness in the objective universe itself to distinguish or make value judgments about what is done to it.

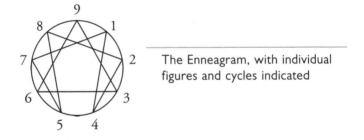

The Enneagram, with individual figures and cycles indicated

Next, notice that the enneagram includes the essential shape from the *Valknútr*—the triangle—stuck in its own cycle in perpetuity. This is the aspect of what has already turned that still impinges directly on the now.

There is a third figure, also cyclical but irregular. There is no way to connect the two angular, subjective figures except through the objective universe. They have no way to be integrated and self-contained.

What is turning—what is happening right now—is malleable but heavily influenced along the pathways implied by this shape. In angular terms, we'd say the initial conditions, the initial parameters, set in motion by the First Angle are the dominant force. But, since this shape is not irrevocably intertwined as in the point of view of *Urðr* (the *Valknútr*), consciousness has the ability evolve it further through forward-thinking acts in the here and now.

THE SEAL OF RÛNA REVISITED

In *Skuld*—what **should** be—the full Seal is revealed and can be seen in one sense as a symbolic expansion and reconfiguration of the enneagram. The figure of the Seal is unified, and since it can be drawn unicursally all its possibilities are accessible in angled space. It shows, definitively, that most action occurs in the subjective realm— the Angles—with a well-defined but precisely limited interface to the objective universe (the circle).

The Seal of Rûna

The Nine Angles are a bridge from Pythagorean and Platonic notions of number and measurement, to the Germanic expression of how ideas and mindful evolution unfold through time. Just as the trapezoid acts as a mediator, or means of willfully harmonizing, the subjective and objective universes in the Seal of Rûna, the dynamic *Verðandi* is the point in space-time where the fixed, limited, unchangeable *Urðr* meets the malleable, unlimited, and changeable *Skuld*. Linguistically, two otherwise unconnected verbs are made part of a continuum, and those who know the roots of these mysteries can affect the unfolding of this continuum.

THE MECHANICS OF RITUAL MAGIC

Before explaining the main two types of ritual magic explored in this book, we must answer the question: Why do a magical ritual at all? This is closely related to the question: Is it necessary to actually perform rituals for them to be effective, or is merely reading and/or speaking the words enough?

The most important reason to designate a space as being (at least for a time) dedicated to the performance of magic is to isolate the magician from influences outside of herself. By deliberately and mindfully setting herself apart from the everyday world, and entering into a chosen place that is made sacred to the task at hand, she can then create and interact with the frame of reference for the ritual in any way that is necessary. By interacting with her thoughts and desires in a deliberately constructed environment, the magician reinforces that she is the ultimate arbiter of her actions and perceptions.

The chamber thus provides a self-contained environment that enables the intense focus—and awareness of the malleability of reality within the magician's subjective universe—necessary for the effective practice of ritual magic. In day-to-day life, the mind is accustomed to working with and perceiving external phenomena generally in objective terms; after all, this life takes place in the objective universe and you are most often interacting with others who act in ways heavily influenced by their lack of awareness of the subjective universe. That is, most people's actions occur as if only the objective universe exists because they are unaware (or at least skeptical) of any other possibilities.

The ritual process of turning thought in on itself, in order to reshape your perception of reality, is best done in the dedicated environment of the ritual chamber. Thus, there is value in having a place set aside for such purposes; if the chamber contains too many things unrelated to the ritual, it has the potential to distract from its focus and to interrupt the mind-set necessary for an effective ritual. Michael Aquino characterizes this as: "A ritual chamber keeps the ritual atmosphere in and the non-ritual environment out."[12]

Another reason that ritual magic is effective, and especially desirable when working with the Angles, is the visual bias of the human neocortex. Spatial awareness, depth perception, and superior hand-eye coordination were vital to humanity's emergence as the unique species it has become. Also for these reasons, the effects that come from interacting with geometric forms in a focused environment (especially when the meaning behind these forms is at least partially known) work well with the underlying mental mechanisms for visualizing new configurations of reality. Because we are able to conceive of things as they do not yet exist, we are able to reconfigure our awareness and our environment to bring them into being in the desired form and to utilize symbolic behavior as an essential component of this practice.

How then does ritual magic work?

The chamber is a deliberately constructed environment containing objects, imagery, and purpose to which the magician attributes significance—**Significance** is, in fact, another appropriate keyword for the Third Angle, which in the original Bond of the Nine Angles is conceived of as the "power to behold." The chamber facilitates magic because it is an interface between the subjective universe of the magician and the objective universe on which he will impress his will. The imagery associated with magic is part of its long tradition, but in the end the imagery has no more power or significance than what the magician is willing to grant it. The film *The Wizard of Oz* (1939) memorably illustrates this: after a long quest to find the Wizard who can hopefully send her back home to Kansas, Dorothy learns that the power to do so was within her the entire time. She was unable to utilize it until she was able to understand and articulate it for herself; even though she still uses the magical object of the Ruby Slippers, she has learned to use them as a means to focus the ability that she already possessed.

Giving the objects and imagery within the chamber the necessary significance within the subjective universe also suggests another important principle behind the mechanism of ritual magic: a ritual can be just as effective using a personally created mythology (such as that of Lovecraft) as it is using imagery and forms from a more traditional or historical perspective. Authenticity is a malleable concept in the ritual chamber, limited only by the effectiveness and conviction derived from it.

In normal daily interactions with the environments and phenomena that we participate in, the subjective universe mediates and categorizes the input it receives from the objective universe through the body's senses. The way we perceive the form, structure, and behaviors of the objective universe (and its other sentient occupants) is reinforced through this sensory input. Ritual magic depends on a realignment of this sense data to more closely match the intended effects of the magical act. The creation and preparation of the chamber—in whatever form you intend to express the frame of reference of the magical act—is itself part of the ritual and forms a key component of the momentum driving forward the task at hand.

It can also be beneficial to create specialized environments for certain kinds of magical operations. One of the most potent examples of this is the chamber devoted to the practice of *Die Elektrischen Vorspiele*. Anton LaVey's instructions are fairly specific (and as previously discussed, draw on such sources as the "Thomas Carnacki" stories of William Hope Hodgson and the 1927 film *Metropolis* for visual inspiration). Included in the setup of the chamber, which is recommended by LaVey to be a small room in order to enhance the effects of these tools, are:

- high-output electrical devices such as Tesla coils, Jacob's ladders, and Van de Graaff generators. In addition to the primal fear from being in close proximity to such dangerous objects, they also ionize the air in the chamber, which modifies the participants' physiological reactions to the rite
- lighting via argon/neon tubes, contributing to the futuristic aesthetic of the rite (and suggestive of the Art Deco style prevalent during the time of the ritual's supposed origin in the 1920s)
- a sound source that can generate pure sounds ranging in frequency from 60hz to 11,000hz, with a background sound of white or black noise, intended to enhance the increase and dispersal of the collected energy and intent of the participants and celebrant

- a simple altar with a human skull flanked by two black candles (in defiance of the inevitability of death), along with other Satanic ritual tools used with LaVey's style of magic
- a mirrored pentagon in which the celebrant stays for most of the rite
- a glowing trapezoid suspended above the pentagon
- a strobe light

As you can see, this is both fairly detailed and a bit different from what the average person might expect in the ritual chamber. LaVey was a master at crafting evocative and stimulating environments to accompany his rituals, and the chamber design for *Die Elektrischen Vorspiele* is one of the most potent and visually striking examples of that skill. Other examples are given throughout *The Satanic Rituals*.

One final reason to support the necessity of ritual magic is that doing so connects the practitioner to the magical traditions that have come before. In a neo-traditional system such as the Nine Angles, it is highly recommended that the practitioner have a firm grounding in the actual traditions that inspire the system. Ideas do not develop in a vacuum, and understanding the context of what has been effective before is important for bringing forth the best features of that into the neo-tradition being actively created. Aleister Crowley hinted of this brilliantly when he suggested that the aspiring magician study works of William Shakespeare such as *Macbeth, The Tempest,* and *A Midsummer's Night Dream* for the traditions revealed within. While the actual traditional basis for the magical scenes in these works is unlikely, they nonetheless have shaped popular ideas of what magic "looks like" and thus by virtue of their ability to evoke visions of a mysterious and magical past can provide much inspiration for the magician looking to produce a similar effect.* Furthermore, these are an excellent example of

---

*One of the more effective representations of this technique during the early years of the Church of Satan was a second season episode of the original *Star Trek* series titled "Catspaw." In this episode (written by Robert Bloch, who among other things was fictionalized as the protagonist of Lovecraft's "The Haunter of the Dark"), the crew of the Enterprise are drawn to an eerie castle on an otherwise uninhabitable planet. They find

why you must actually perform magical rituals in order for them to be effective; a play is likewise just words on a page until it is made to come alive as something that can be experienced.

One of the key practices to engage in when working with ritual magic is that of the magical diary. This is an important tool for keeping accurate records of what types of rituals are done, and under what circumstances—time; location; purpose; signs, symbols, and words utilized; sensations and insights arising during and after the ritual. When looking both within and beyond the Self to determine when the ritual seems to have brought the desired results, this record will prove very useful. Ideally, you would use the magical diary to record all aspects of your work with the Angles, from insights and information uncovered while studying the system and its sources, to copying in your own hand both the exercises suggested by this book and others that you create for yourself. The keeping of a diary is another connection to the traditional forms of magical practice,* cast into a postmodern form as a key part of the foundation of neo-tradition.

Given these definitions and frames of reference, let us now look at the distinction between **operative** and **illustrative** rituals. The characterizations here are influenced by the discussion in *The Satanic Rituals,* along with other insights and clarifications that have resulted from over fifty years of practice of these by the pre-1975 Church of Satan and later the Temple of Set (1975–present).

Operative Rituals

An **operative ritual** is one intended to set a particular change in motion. This change could be observable in the objective universe, or it

---

[**cont. from p. 145**] themselves immersed in an environment reminiscent of the castle in *Macbeth,* complete with witches and dungeons, that ultimately proves to have been created as an illusion based on their primal fears of cats, darkness, and death. It appeared magical and frightening, because it manifested what they expected a magical and frightening environment to be.

*See Stephen Flowers's book *Icelandic Magic: Practical Secrets of the Northern Grimoires* (Inner Traditions, 2016), an update of his previous translation and analysis of the early seventeenth-century Icelandic magical book called the *Galdrabók.*

could be effective merely within the subjective universe of the magician. *The ritual itself does not create the change, but lays bare to the magician what must be done in order to accomplish it and externalizes the desire to begin acting in accord with the frame of reference used to articulate it.* The primary purpose of an operative ritual is thus to begin (or continue) a discernible change within the subjective universe of the magician. This in turn affects her perception of the objective universe in terms of the corresponding change within the magician herself.

The effectiveness of the ritual depends on a variety of factors, the results of which will rarely be immediately known. Such details as the imagery and frame of reference used, the intensity of focus, and the sincerity and feasibility of the desire, all contribute to a successful ritual.

It is vital to follow up ritual magic with appropriate nonritual action to reinforce its likelihood of producing the desired effects. Contrary to popular depictions of magic, saying the right words and making the right gestures is not what produces the results; rather, the change in the attitude and attentiveness of the magician causes her to make both conscious and subconscious actions toward the fulfillment of the magical goal. As mentioned before, this is one of the reasons why the keeping of a magical diary is critical for successful magic.

Illustrative Rituals

Another name for an **illustrative ritual** is a reflective ritual: the "mind-mirror" aspect of ritual magic is focused on the subjective universe itself, with an aim to gain inspiration, insight, or understanding.

Illustrative magic is not necessarily a form of meditation, although if undertaken in a ritualistic frame of reference, meditation could be used as one component of an illustrative ritual. Effective magic begins by calming the mind and focusing it inward, both of which are necessary to form the basis of a ritual—these same foundations are key components of an effective meditation practice as well.

Other magical techniques such as divination are best thought of as forms of illustrative ritual; the act of divination reveals to you possibilities around which the psyche might reconfigure itself, and thus you construct a new view of the possibilities within the unmanifest. As divination within a Left-Hand Path context requires an unknown and unmanifest future, these possibilities are best understood as arising from the trajectory of what has already occurred, combined with the actions of the magician in the present moment; working with the principles embodied by the Norns is a key aspect of this practice.

The **psychodrama** is a special form of illustrative ritual. The psychodrama utilizes vivid imagery and action designed to break down barriers to understanding, or to open the participants' eyes to new ways of viewing or manipulating reality. As previously discussed, the most well-known example of this technique is the Black Mass. The method of the Black Mass is not limited to the parody or blasphemy of the Roman Catholic liturgy, however. The same underlying principles are at work when exposure to the true nature of a person, idea, or institution—perhaps by glimpsing aspects of their behavior or beliefs that are not normally revealed—leads to being unable to see them with the same trust, respect, or reverence ever again.

As with the operative type of ritual, the importance of the magical diary for recording the circumstances and results of illustrative rituals cannot be overstated. Just as a record of the magical acts undertaken (and their context) provides a framework for determining what has been effective, this record also provides a means of preserving the insights gained from reflective rituals. It is often the case that you can then utilize the results of a reflective ritual, now that its echos are seen clearly within the subjective universe, to form the basis of a later act of operative ritual.

Having established some definitions and background, we can now fully examine the original rites from *The Satanic Rituals* with connections to the Nine Angles and angular magic in general—these are *Die Elektrischen Vorspiele, The Ceremony of the Nine Angles,* and *The Call to Cthulhu.*

6

THE THREE RITES OF ANGULAR MAGIC ANALYZED

In addition to the historical analysis in chapter 3 of the foundational rites of angular magic practiced in the Church of Satan and later in the Temple of Set, we have now also established the theoretical background that permits us to discuss the magical method and meaning of these rites as well. The reader should be familiar with the following to gain the most from the insights and analysis in this chapter:

- H. P. Lovecraft—"The Haunter of the Dark," "The Dreams in the Witch-House," and "The Call of Cthulhu"
- Frank Belknap Long—"The Hounds of Tindalos"

Major portions of the aesthetic background behind the rites derive from these works (and they may also stimulate dreams and speculations on other applications of the same fictional suggestions to actual magical practice).

Additionally, the following primary source material (all found in *The Satanic Rituals*) forms the basis for this chapter:

- Anton LaVey—*Die Elektrischen Vorspiele*
- Michael A. Aquino—"The Metaphysics of Lovecraft," *The Ceremony of the Nine Angles,* and *The Call to Cthulhu*

With *Die Elektrischen Vorspiele,* we'll explore more of the ritual's background and suggestions for performance. Following the foundation, there is a magical analysis of its structure and *why* it works as effectively as it does; this includes a look at the hidden sexual component of the rite's conception and performance. The examination of the rite concludes with extensive commentary and analysis of its litany and proclamation.

Our look at *The Ceremony of the Nine Angles* begins with a review of Lovecraft's cosmology and its relationship to the Angles. This is followed with a detailed look at the gestures and construction of the universe within the context of the ritual, then continuing on to further explanation of the significance of the individual Angles in self-development and as tools for facilitating magical acts.

A study of the third of the foundational angular rites, *The Call to Cthulhu,* concludes the chapter. We'll compare the structure and purpose of this ritual to that of *The Ceremony of the Nine Angles.* The purpose of the ritual—experiencing the transition of humanity from mere animals to fully self-aware beings—is analyzed in terms of the meaning and significance of Cthulhu in Lovecraft's mythos.

DIE ELEKTRISCHEN VORSPIELE

Further Background

The magical underpinnings of *Die Elektrischen Vorspiele* warrant further discussion, despite the protestations of LaVey himself (and many of his followers and fans) from the mid-1970s onward that his work was always only metaphorical and that he never had any literal belief in Satan or magic.

As Anton LaVey constantly reinvented himself and modified his backstory at will throughout his life,* many of his own statements

---

*Starting with his name: he was born Howard Stanton Levey, first using the name Anton Szandor LaVey around the late 1950s (although variations on it, such as performing music as The Great Szandor, possibly date back to the late 1940s).

about his background and experiences must be taken with a grain of salt. Nevertheless, there are three categories of supporting information that persuasively suggest his writings and practices from at least the late 1950s through 1975 are those of a legitimate, practicing magician and Satanist. The reader is referred to Michael Aquino's *The Church of Satan* for extensive documentation and interpretations of LaVey's writings and practices during this time period, as well as the documentary film *Satanis: The Devil's Mass* (1970).

Satanis: The Devil's Mass includes interviews with LaVey, his wife, oldest daughter, neighbors, and early participants in the Church of Satan. Statements from both LaVey and others confirm he then regarded himself as "in league with the devil, as much as any mortal can possibly be."[1] LaVey consistently presented this stance until the mid-1970s in a variety of print* and TV interviews.†

Among the various writings from LaVey prior to the publication of *The Satanic Bible* in 1969,‡ much can be found regarding his magical theory and Satanic theology. Throughout these writings, as he developed their topics over time, there are references to Satanism as a religion and speculations on the nature of Satan as a real entity, all going to great pains to convey sincerity.

Finally, there are a number of comments and letters by LaVey to others associated with the Church of Satan during the late 1960s through the mid-1970s. One of the important recurring themes to point out is the seriousness and respect with which LaVey treated the Satanic

---

*Examples include interviews published in *Time* (June 19, 1972), *Newsweek* (April 13, 1970), *McCalls* (March 1970), and many other regional and national publications.

†Including an infamous appearance (ca. 1970) on the *Joe Pyne Show* where LaVey was adamant that he was sincere about his beliefs despite constant ridicule from the host. Pyne, who pioneered the exaggerated confrontational interview style that is now commonplace, remarked to LaVey after failing to break his calm demeanor, "I'd like to tell you where to go, but you'd probably enjoy it."

‡Affectionately known as the "rainbow sheets" due to the variety of colors of paper used to organize them into different topics; they continued to be recirculated within the Church of Satan through the mid-1970s. A selection of these are cataloged and transcribed in Aquino's *The Church of Satan*.

Priesthood. In a January 1972 letter to Michael Aquino, LaVey wrote:

> Seminarial preparations and qualification are rigorous for those attempting to enter the priesthood of any other established religion, so why should they not be equally rigid in the Church of Satan? Why should it be easier to become a Priest of Satan than it is to become a Catholic priest, a Jewish rabbi, or a Methodist minister, when a Priest of Satan actually requires a great deal more wisdom, considering his terrestrial commitment?
>
> [. . .]
>
> The Priesthood of the Church of Satan requires far more perfection of its candidates than do the priesthoods of other religions, for the Priest or Priestess of Satan is the foundation of modern Satanism.[2]

Even if the reader finds these arguments unconvincing, there **still** would remain the same value in his work as a source for magical practice that is present in the work of H. P. Lovecraft. In this view of LaVey's pre-1975 writings, the most important aspect is the evocative imagery that flows from his intensely imaginative and inventive modern take on the darker aspects of the occult.

Either way, we must acknowledge the work of Anton LaVey as a prominent, potent, legitimate source for the magical practices discussed in this book.

The Ritual Itself

As discussed, the claim that *Die Elektrischen Vorspiele* is an actual black magic rite from interwar Germany is likely just a bit of good magical storytelling. This does very little to undermine its potency, however, as the magical mechanics (and faux back story that would do Pauwels and Bergier, and Trevor Ravenscroft, proud) are expertly realized. Indeed, the rite reveals a potent formula unmatched among LaVey's magical writings, and can be adapted into a wide variety of individual and group forms that are every bit as effective as the original.

With the theoretical basis for angular magic now more precisely established, a few more comments concerning the structure and technology of this particular rite are in order.

An earlier form of the Nine Angles served as the seal for the Order of the Trapezoid as conceived within the Church of Satan. There is a subtle nod to this construct in the instructions for the decor of the chamber for performing *Die Elektrischen Vorspiele,* where LaVey specifies that a trapezoid—made of material that can be charged and illuminated—is to hang above the pentagon and match its proportions.

Thus, the rite utilizes the same principles of angles related through the Golden Ratio that are given magical significance via LaVey's Law of the Trapezoid. For this reason among others, *Die Elektrischen Vorspiele* remains the central and most potent rite of the Order of the Trapezoid even today. It is the essence of the Order expressed in ritual form.

Other aspects of the rite worth noting include the sights and sounds resulting from the strobe light and audio requirements within the chamber. Furthering the connection to the evocative "mad lab" representations on the big screen (*Metropolis, Frankenstein,* etc.), the use of the strobe light aids in the feeling that the participants are themselves in an old film—one of the keys to an effective magical ritual is the sensation of complete immersion in the frame of reference from which the ritual operates. Put simply, the more effectively the participants perceive the frame of reference as real and convincing by all the senses, the more likely it is to facilitate the intended transformative effect.

The suggestions for sound within the chamber leave the same impression; the alternating very high and very low pure sounds establish the "alien" feel of the chamber, divorced from the everyday world and creating an environment where unfamiliar standards of sight and sound shock the participants into new modes of thought.

Even given all these requirements for how the chamber is to be outfitted, no particular one is strictly required for effective performance of the rite even though the sum of various effects **is** vital. According to LaVey, "the instructions given here will serve as a useful key to those who can extract the most viable principles and apply them to their own ends."[3] As in all magical workings, the most effective components are those that further the rite's intent according to the aesthetics and preferences of those performing it.

This approach is in keeping with the neo-traditional focus that is present throughout the paradigm of angular magic. Traditional forms may have more rigidity, but even then, in order to be a living system (and thereby suited to the Left-Hand Path), they must be adaptable to the needs and aesthetics of the participants. Otherwise, they are only useful toward predetermined ends and thus are being employed as a Right-Hand Path practice regardless of what aesthetic or methods form their basis.

The Opening

The ritual is to begin with the same general structure given in *The Satanic Bible,* with the specific use of the Sixth Enochian Key. The commentary on this Key in *The Satanic Bible* suggests that LaVey's version of this Key "establishes the structure and form of that which has become the Order of the Trapezoid and Church of Satan."[4] LaVey's rendering of this Key deepens the connection between the ritual and the Order of the Trapezoid, stating that "the spirits of the fourth angle are Nine, mighty in the trapezoid, whom the first hath formed."[5]

Following the opening, the rite provides something to stimulate most of the traditional senses in a unique synthesis of infernal geometry, environment- and consciousness-altering electronics, and a rubric directed as much at the pre-rational "reptilian" brain as any logical thought process. The unusual and clearly non-natural sounds near the extremes of human perception force the participants to be fully "present" in the chamber—they are a manifestation of the Law of the Trapezoid rendered through sound. The electrostatic generators add a significant amount of absolutely real and serious danger to the proceedings, while at the same time their ionization of the air is mood-altering (and introduces the distinct smell of ozone that is normally only encountered if you are too close for comfort to a lightning strike). The neon tubing and strobe lighting create an immersive experience that further disconnects the awareness of celebrant and participants from the everyday world.

It is not uncommon during a performance of *Die Elektrischen Vorspiele* for all to feel a bit anxious at this potent assault on the senses. This is precisely the feeling that the chamber is designed to create, but augmented with a touch of anticipation. The magician knows not to fear or shun this feeling, but rather to apply it to bringing about the changes the rite is designed to effect.

Once the celebrant enters the mirrored pentagon within the chamber, all concentrate their desires for themselves and the World of Horrors onto the celebrant. Whatever they are feeling, the celebrant is feeling tenfold, as he (or she) becomes the focus of attention. For among the secrets of successful performance of *Die Elektrischen Vorspiele* is the overstimulation and ultimately exhaustion of the celebrant. The parallels between this stimulation and its resultant discharge and that of the orgasm cannot be overstated. This is not a sexual rite per se—there is no nude altar, nor any direct contact between the participants and the celebrant—but the effect on the celebrant in particular partakes of the same primal raising and discharging of sexual energy. This was the crux of the work of Wilhelm Reich, and of the very principles explored in his studies such as *The Function of the Orgasm* and *The Mass Psychology of Fascism*.

Ironically, given the largely fantasy-based history in the introduction to *Die Elektrischen Vorspiele,* there is a very specific parallel between one of the central magical techniques of the rite and a particular ritual chamber used within the Third Reich. Given that knowledge of this was very scant in the English-speaking world prior to the mid-1970s, it is very unlikely that LaVey was actually aware of this connection. However, despite the historical shortcomings in lieu of telling a good magical tale, LaVey had remarkably astute intuition about what was actually being employed by the National Socialists in their use of spectacle, wonder, and their longing for the deep past as part of the transformation of their culture.

The Absolute Elsewhere

The Wewelsburg is a late Renaissance-style castle located in Germany, southwest of Paderborn. Its unusual triangular form is partially dictated by the landscape in which it was built, and there has been some form of fortification on this strategic site at least as far back as the Roman invasion in the year 9 of the Common Era. The current castle was built in the early seventeenth century for the Prince-Bishops of Paderborn, on top of a stronghold dating from the twelfth century.[6]

By the early 1930s, it was known that Heinrich Himmler, head of the SS,* was searching for his "Grail Castle," and the Wewelsburg was recommended to him by the *Landrat* (chief administrator) of the nearby town of Büren. This recommendation met with the approval of Karl Maria Wiligut (aka "Weisthor"), the Austrian mystic and Himmler's personal advisor.[7] It seems fair to say that the Wewelsburg evoked in Himmler a gateway to a long forgotten past, and inspired in him the longing to use it as a focal point for his vision of an elite knighthood dedicated to fulfilling themselves through the glorification of Germany.

The castle is infamous for two particular chambers, both in the north tower. The Obergruppenführersaal is a large, windowed hall with a marble floor that contains the symbol in green marble now typically identified with the Black Sun. The twelve *sowilo* (h) runes suggest a solar significance, perhaps even a reference to the appearance of an eclipse (of which there were two visible in that region of Germany during the period of the design and construction of the Obergruppenführersaal).

Reproduction of the Black Sun in the Obergruppenführersaal

*The SS (i.e., the *Schutzstaffel* or "Protection Squadron") were intended to be the elite among the "master race" and thus steeped in its highest ideals, reinforced with powerful rites and ceremonies. A very serious enthusiast of Germanic paganism and its ancient roots, Himmler oversaw virtually all of the interests of the Third Reich that were actually related to paganism and occultism (though in reality there was far less of this in Nazi Germany than has often been suggested). This interest included the *Ahnenerbe*—the organization tasked with Germanic ancestral research, later converted into a think tank for Himmler's occult and pseudoscience ideas—and his relationship with Wiligut.

The crypt, or *Walhalla*, chamber at the Wewelsburg

The even more infamous chamber, below ground level in the north tower, is the *Gruft* (German for "crypt") or Hall of the Fallen.* It is not actually a crypt, which is clear from its appearance and layout; its design is in actuality that of a focusing chamber, where any sound emanating from within the chamber, and any light shining through the four high windows, are focused on the central pit. It is this property that would have made the *Gruft* ideal for a performance of *Die Elektrischen Vorspiele*.

---

*The author visited the Wewelsburg in spring 2015 and was able to spend time alone in both chambers; while there, inconspicuous ritual work was undertaken to connect with the stream of ominous magic and tragic contradiction that flows throughout.

The *Gruft,* also known as the Walhalla chamber, was the site in October 1982 where Michael Aquino performed what has since become known as the Wewelsburg Working. The reasons necessitating the Working itself are internal to the Temple of Set. However, one of its outward results was the reconstitution of the Order of the Trapezoid as a functional entity, charged with guarding the hidden source of the Black Flame of consciousness so that it may not be misused on such a scale again (and can be rekindled in whatever outward form is necessary to facilitate its spread at that time). Aquino's account of the Wewelsburg Working has been a major factor in spreading awareness of the actual facts of the castle's role in the Nazi occultism neo-mythology.*

Examination of the Litany in Die Elektrischen Vorspiele

The litany in *Die Elektrischen Vorspiele* is one of the most important sources for understanding LaVey's magical thinking. This is the case despite sections of it being paraphrased from the work of Maurice Doreal†; many parts of it are entirely original to LaVey however, and, more importantly, the overall synthesis of the borrowed and original parts into a coherent whole is vital to the effectiveness of the rite. Let's take a closer look at some of the key sections and phrases with an eye toward an analysis of their magical intent.

At the point in the rite where the spoken text begins, the chamber has been charged via the various sensory enhancement devices. Immediately following the invocation, the celebrant then traces the angles with his upraised sword, which opens the gate to the future that Is-To-Be. Structurally, LaVey uses this in a manner akin to "casting the circle" in a more traditional type of ceremonial magic. The celebrant

---

*There is an entire chapter in Aquino's *The Temple of Set* that discusses the background and aftermath of the Working in much detail. Additional scholarly sources acknowledging Aquino's influence on the Nazi occultism mythos include: Nicholas Goodrick-Clarke, *Black Sun;* Daniela Siepe's essay "Esoterische Sichtweisen auf die Wewelsburg: Rezeption in 'satanischen' Kreisen"; Eva Kingsepp's essay "The Power of the Black Sun."
†To be fair, LaVey did hint at this in the introduction (although without a full attribution and with enough ambiguity in the reference to make it difficult to track down the true source).

has created the universe in miniature via the invocations, the summoning of the elements, and the tracing of the Nine Angles. Thus, he properly demarcates the ritual space to effect the task at hand.

The initial appeal in the invocation is to the Opener of the Way, thus creating the channel by which the Is-To-Be is brought into line with the desires cast by the participants and celebrant. The characterization of *Die Elektrischen Vorspiele* as the Rite of the Is-To-Be renders it as a performative utterance in its entirety.

The Opener of the Way suggests the jackal-headed Egyptian god Anubis, who acted as a guide for the dead. While this association as "opener" is valid, the title "Opener of the Way" would more correctly refer to the related god Wepwawet. It is possible LaVey used the better-known Anubis in order to enhance the connections of this rite with death,* or simply shared the confusion that many sources do between the jackal-headed Anubis and the similarly portrayed wolf-headed Wepwawet). Interestingly, Wepwawet was also sometimes said to be the son of Set.

In either case, the opening of the way is an important component of the magical mechanism of the rite. Note, however, that Anubis is not being merely asked to open the way, but also to participate in the rite—this is an application of the **law of similarity** from the semiotic theory of magic, with Anubis participating with the others present as equals.

The associations with the mythos of Lovecraft are there at the very beginning of the invocation as well. The celebrant entreats Anubis to "blast . . . forth through the gates of the shining Trapezohedron."[8] Recall that in the Mythos, Yog-Sothoth is the Outer God who symbolizes the **gate**. Death is certainly a gateway to a different type of Being (or nonbeing, depending on what your metaphysical tendencies suggest about the state following death). The irony of suggesting Anubis (or Wepwawet) as a keeper of this particular gate is that a different avatar of Yog-Sothoth—'Umr at-Tawil—has a name that means "the most

---

*Embedded in the interpretation of the rite as a buildup and release of sexual energy on the part of the male celebrant combined with the imagery of Anubis, there could be found an implied reference to the French expression *la petite mort* (literally "the little death," used as a common euphemism for the orgasm).

ancient and prolonged of life." Gates rarely open in only one direction.

The opening paragraph also contains the first performative utterance found in the rite: "The fire of Hell doth provide and the thoughts from within doth prevail."[9] Recall that the nature of a performative utterance is that it creates action (or a change in state) merely by being spoken; another way of looking at this is that performative utterances speak of things that may not yet be true **as if they were already true or had occurred**. Thus, they reconfigure the expectations and realities of those who utter or hear them.

> I decree that the glamour be lifted, revealing the face of the Serpent. By the sounds ye shall see the face of the Serpent, so learn well the word that only a man can pronounce. Thus, I lift the veil from the Serpent and cast him forth among men.[10]

This section is lightly paraphrased by LaVey from Doreal's original text. Recall that Doreal, along with Robert E. Howard (in *The Shadow Kingdom* [1929]), was among the first to write about and popularize the "reptilian aliens masquerading as humans" neo-mythology. The serpent men from Valusia, who figure prominently in Howard's story, appeared later in Lovecraft's "The Haunter of the Dark" as one of the keepers of the Shining Trapezohedron during its long history.

This "decree" can be taken to reinforce the importance of participants in the rite revealing their true selves, rather than hiding behind a metaphorical mask. The "word that only a man can pronounce"[11] is used to distinguish the true humans (possessing the necessary vocal apparatus) from Doreal's serpentine aliens and is perhaps even a veiled reference to the fabled "Lost Word" of Freemasonry.

Keep in mind, too, that the stated purpose of *Die Elektrischen Vorspiele* is "to alter an existing social climate and establish far-reaching change."[12] The more precisely you understand the true nature of the intended target of the magical ritual, the more likely it is that the change will be effective. This aspect of the invocation brings the social climate that is being affected into clear focus and reminds the participants and celebrant not to shun but rather to walk within it as an active force. This is implied by the law of similarity; after all, there is far more opportunity for changing the social structures you participate in than structures observed merely as an outsider.

> [The Hounds] move only through angles, though free are they not of the curved dimensions. Strange and terrible are the Hounds of the Barrier, follow they consciousness to the limits of space. Unseen they walk among thee, in places where the Rites have been said.[13]

This section, also paraphrased from Doreal, is notable for two things: an addition to the text by LaVey, and a line from Doreal he did **not** retain in his paraphrase. The line added by LaVey was the last one; this addition connects the different performances of *Die Elektrischen Vorspiele* in time and space, implying that the rite leaves a "marker" that permits the Hounds to pass through the gate into our curved space when they perceive the "souls of the righteous."[14]

Magically, the Hounds embody the Law of the Trapezoid: they protect those who perceive the secrets of the Angles, but prey on those who know nought but curved space. These gates left behind by performances of the rite provide a means for these emissaries of the Angles to maintain a connection with the World of Horrors.

The line LaVey **didn't** retain is "Only the circle will give ye protection, save from the claws of the DWELLER IN ANGLES."[15] The use of a protective circle was anathema in LaVey's system of magic, the reasoning being that the Satanist was in league with the Powers of Darkness and thus required no protection from them. Furthermore, it would be a bit of an aesthetic clash to be tracing circles in a rite that was purely angular in nature (thus LaVey has the celebrant trace out the angles at the point in the rite where a circle might traditionally be drawn; these angles are not for protection but to further delineate the space within the chamber where the celebrant performs his magical sending).

While drawing heavily from this source, LaVey carefully constructed the pieces that were borrowed to integrate them with his own original ideas. The potency behind LaVey's work is always more about the synthesis than the sources.

> Hiding in the abyss beyond time I found them, and they, scenting me afar off, raised themselves and gave the great bell cry that can be heard from cycle to cycle. Dwelt I then, in lairs remote from man, on the gray shores of time, beyond the world's rim, and ever with me they moved, in angles not known to man.[16]

The celebrant is relating a form of creation myth in this section, establishing the cosmogony wherein the rite functions. The original source of this is a paraphrase of a critical section of the plot of the short story "The Hounds of Tindalos;" it is cast here in more poetic terms and used for building up the neo-mythology that the rite—and the Order of the Trapezoid—continues to draw upon and enhance.

Magically, this is a key component of establishing the **frame of reference** within which the rite operates. Frames of reference are as real as they need to be within the context of a ritual, and the celebrant reinforces this by the extent to which he immerses himself in the role and conveys conviction behind his words and actions.

> O learn the Law, my brothers of the night-the Great Law and the Lesser Law. The Great Law brings the balance and doth persist without mercy. The Lesser Law abideth as the key, and the shining Trapezoid is the door![17]

In *Die Elektrischen Vorspiele* LaVey writes of both a "Greater" and "Lesser" law, but did not elaborate on this in any other written source. Based on work that has continued within the Order of the Trapezoid, combined with the hints given by LaVey, a likely explanation of the meaning of these two facets of the Law is the following.

Over the years LaVey wrote about various aspects of the Law of the Trapezoid, but never gave a succinct definition of it. Recall that, based on his own understanding and various conversations with LaVey on the nature and uses of the Law, Michael Aquino summarized it as:

> All obtuse angles are magically harmful to those unaware of this
> property. The same angles are beneficial, stimulating, and energizing
> to those who are magically sensitive to them.[18]

With this twofold description of the Law, combined with the other hints in the conception of the Law as applied within *Die Elektrischen Vorspiele,* we can create a more accurate picture of the properties and uses of the "Greater" and "Lesser" Law.

The Greater Law "brings the balance and doth persist without mercy."[19] The effect of the Law of the Trapezoid on those unaware and unprepared is to evoke a subtle form of the fight-or-flight instinct. The various symbols that imply danger in Mortensen's Command to Look formula operate on this same principle, and of course Mortensen's work was a vital source for LaVey's own conception of the Law of the Trapezoid.

The Lesser Law "abideth as the key, and the shining Trapezoid is the door."[20] The effect of the Law of the Trapezoid on those aware of and consciously using its principles is beneficial, stimulating, and energizing. The "key" is this awareness and knowing the roots of the Law such that they enhance its action. Whereas the noninitiate instinctively wishes to flee at the sight of these angular environments and symbols, these same environments and symbols act as potent attractors and become tools for effecting change within the angular magician. This Lesser Law is a powerful tool for leaving "seeds" of the inspirations that led the magician to himself, so that others with similar background and interests could then be attracted by the mysteries they hold.

> O my brothers, study well the stone with planes unrecognized by
> those without, for within those glaring facets the Hounds await that
> set the world aflame![21]

The "stone" is the Shining Trapezohedron, which in Lovecraft's "The Haunter of the Dark" provided a means for opening a gate so that the Haunter (i.e., Nyarlathotep) could enter this world. The Hounds lurk similarly awaiting entry into this plane of existence when the proper angular gate has been opened.

> On the grim, gray shore, the monolith prevails, and clutched within the four-fold talons of the ring which Fafnir guards, that shape remains to bring forth that which gives us increase and smites those who would oppose us.[22]

The monolith, instigator of profound change in consciousness and awareness in Stanley Kubrick and Arthur C. Clarke's *2001: A Space Odyssey,* functions here as a focal point for the vision of transformation cast by the celebrant.* It is also a warning: much as the Hounds are guardians of the dawn of consciousness but who will pursue and destroy those unworthy of it, the monolith is created out of destruction of the forms that existed before. From the perspective of a viewer looking up at the monolith, it of course appears as a trapezoid.

> Listen O man of clouded brain and heed ye my warning: move ye not in angles, but curved dimensions. . .[23]

Those who are unable to grasp the significance of strange angles are variously referred to as having "mildewed," "small," and "clouded" minds and brains in *Die Elektrischen Vorspiele.* This is a magical warning that the Hounds will destroy those who encounter them but are unaware of the Law of the Trapezoid; they are too dangerous to invoke or behold unless their angular nature is understood.

> Drift if ye will, into the dimensions of your outer consciousness, and be trapped forever. Ye know not the substance of your creation. I

---

*The dimensions of the monolith are in the very specific ratio of 1:4:9, as the first three square numbers. The novelization of the story also implies that the sequence, and thus the monolith itself, does not stop at only three dimensions.

welcome ye in the name of Set, all ye who delight in great evil and sustain thyselves in miseries unfounded.[24]

As mentioned before, the references to Set have more in common with that figure in the works of Robert E. Howard than to Egyptian mythology. In Howard's books, Set was an evil figure and the enemy of the great hero Conan the Cimmerian; LaVey is casting the god here as a form of Satan, one drawn from the particular literary influences that formed the basis for the ritual. This portrayal again comes with a warning: if the participants are not prepared for the transformative effects of the Law of the Trapezoid on consciousness, it will destroy them.

And we speak with the tongues of serpents, and the baying of the Hounds, and the great bell sound that cracks the barrier-and great are we who rule, and small are ye who suffer.[25]

The "tongues of serpents" continue the references to Howard's version of Set (who also shares attributes of the Egyptian god of delusion in the form of a serpent, Apep), while this imagery combined with that of the Hounds employs the **law of similarity**. The celebrant claims kinship with Set and the Hounds and can also fulfill their role while drawing on their power to enhance his own rulership of himself by wielding angular consciousness.

The day of the cross and the trinity is done. A great wheel with angles in dimensions unrecognized, save for the children of Set, fills the void and becomes as the sun in the Firmament of Wrath![26]

This poetic finale completes the frame of reference of the celebrant and participants as the secret rulers of the society they wish to create. It is post-Christian ("the day of the cross and the trinity is done"), and only the children of Set (those partaking of consciousness who are fully aware of its source and implications) can see this new social order for what it truly is while continuing to guide it toward the fulfillment of the vision cast by the celebrant. They become the sun—nourishing source of light and life—in the Firmament of Wrath (a reference found in several of the original versions of the Enochian Keys referring to the realm which those enlightened by knowledge of the Keys will rule, here being used in a sense similar to that of the World of Horrors).

The Proclamation

After the celebrant has cast his vision, his assistant turns off the strobe and higher-pitched sounds (the electrostatic generators were already turned off just prior to the casting). At this point in the rite, the calm following the storm prevails, as the celebrant and participants are recovering from the overstimulation of the senses that created the proper ritual environment for this type of work. The only sound is a variety of lower frequency sounds mimicking thunder (as the calamitous storm fades off into the distance).

As the celebrant faces east, witness to the dawn of the new future he has cast with his own magical seed, he delivers a proclamation that the participants respond to along with the sign of the horns* (thus they acknowledge him directly for the first time within the rite).

The proclamation is a set of five performative utterances, each consisting of four words—the appearance of nine in this fashion seals the end of one cycle of coming into being and the beginning of a new one according to the vision cast by the celebrant. The utterances claim five desires and speak of them confidently as though they have already come to pass: **Power, Wealth, Wisdom, Recognition,** and **Followers.**[27] The first three are fairly traditional Satanic desires—Faust sought the same things, yet received them at great cost. **Recognition** and **Followers,** however, show a greater maturity beyond just that needed to dominate their fellow men. They represent two qualities that are vital to the fulfillment of the vision that has been cast, arising from "walking unseen among" the very facets of society the participants are intending to change.

---

*See appendix A (page 255) for a description of the sign of the horns.

The proclamation concludes with the declaration of the Twilight of the Gods—*Ragnarök*—further connecting the rite's successful performance with the end of one cycle of existence and the beginning of one anew. *Ragnarök* was not simply a Nordic take on the relatively unimaginative Apocalypse of Christian myth, but a necessary component in the continuous renewal of a progressively refined world. The imagery of dawn breaking in the east strengthens this association, while the reference to "the morning of magic"[28] is probably meant to be a subtle hint about Pauwels's and Bergier's *The Morning of the Magicians.* Loki of course was more responsible than any other single figure in Norse mythology for instigating the necessary event of *Ragnarök;* far from being a simple evil figure, he played a vital role as the catalyst to bring about this necessary and profound change in the state of the world. This is appropriate given his role as a trickster god and likely a hypostasis of Óðinn as the god of consciousness who shares this gift that others may become fully conscious as well.

THE CEREMONY OF THE NINE ANGLES

While *Die Elektrischen Vorspiele* is highly potent in its own right as a work that includes angular magic among many other magical technologies, *The Ceremony of the Nine Angles* must be regarded as the first published account of specifically angular magic in the sense that it is explored in this book.

Like the *Vorspiele, The Ceremony of the Nine Angles* has very specific (albeit much simpler) requirements for the chamber in which it is to be performed. As Michael Aquino notes in "Lovecraftian Ritual" (appendix A), the idealized location is the "King's Chamber" within the Great Pyramid, which contains channels that are oriented toward the stars.

Visually, a pyramid is the dominant mass *par excellence,* being both massive and impossible to move or topple. Its angular shape is imposing, suggesting danger à la Mortensen's theory of the Command to Look. In terms of the Nine Angles, a pyramid is a figure with five vertices (angles converging to a single point) merged into (and concealing) a four-sided figure beneath. It embodies the union of the Five (the self-contained, self-evolving subjective universe) and the Four (the conscious perception of the implicit ordering of the objective universe).

The only light source permitted to enter the chamber for the *Ceremony* should be starlight or moonlight. The masks/headpieces designed to conceal the faces of the participants evoke the visual distortions in Lovecraft's stories that are said to accompany encounters with the Outer Gods. Nyarlathotep is sometimes known as the Faceless One (and referred to as such in *The Ceremony of the Nine Angles*), and thus the participants are also declaring their allegiance with him by likewise being faceless.

Structurally, the *Ceremony* is an explicitly Satanic and Lovecraftian version of the "Sabbatic Goat Rite" from the sources on witchcraft that would have been known to Lovecraft: through the proper setting, words, and actions a Teacher from the otherworld is summoned in the form of a goat, who then reveals secrets that transform the perspective and knowledge of the participants. The hints given in Lovecraft's oblique descriptions of "unnameable rites" are brought to fruition.

The speech and gestures are used as a call-and-response. This has the effect of harmonizing the intent of both celebrant and participants, enabling all to partake of the resulting understanding by unifying their frame of reference. In terms of the law of similarity from the semiotic theory of magic, the participants rise to the level of understanding of the celebrant; then together they declare their kinship with the Outer Gods as they are called forth. All can communicate as equals because they have **become** equals, at least within the context of the rite.

The Nine Angles are a cosmogony: a formula for how the universe came into being, which in a microcosmic sense also provides a model for the self-transformation of an individual within that universe.

In Lovecraft's cosmology, Azathoth occupies a position similar to a creator god; the other Outer Gods are descended from this entity, and its description of being the "monstrous nuclear chaos beyond angled space" places it as the embodiment of the unmanifest void (or the source from which other matter and being may spring). This chaos is not to be seen as random, or wholly unordered; Lovecraft (a connoisseur of obscure words and obsolete meanings of common ones) seems to mean it in its archaic sense of "primordial matter."

Yog-Sothoth, "coterminous with all time and space," is the basic ordering principle that follows onto the primordial chaos of Azathoth. This ordering does not supplant the chaos of Azathoth; it is merely the beginning of the unmanifest void to organize itself into some semblance of coherence.

The opening gestures to Azathoth and Yog-Sothoth—the first two Angles—are performative utterances; by the structure and phrasing of the words, the two are honored by the words being spoken correctly, and with the right context and conviction. These Angles are prior to all the others and must exist before any of the others have any context or meaning; by acknowledging this, the celebrant and participants retain this understanding and capability within themselves.

The World of Horrors

To discuss the World of Horrors in context, let us examine two of the initial references to it in *The Ceremony of the Nine Angles;* this is necessary in order to determine how to relate to the concept in a way that works from understanding and not from the default state of fear.

> Azathoth . . . Thy merriment sustains our fears, and we rejoice in the World of Horrors in thy name.[29]

The World of Horrors is the place where we experience our fears and thus have the opportunity to overcome them. Fear is one of the most primal of emotions, generally operating at a level far below that of rational thought. Azathoth—as the chaotic source from which ordered existence is created—provides the raw material for the thought, matter, and emotion that feed the World of Horrors.

The gesture used with Azathoth is the sign of the horns, made with the left hand upraised.

Yog-Sothoth, master of dimensions, through thy will are we set upon the World of Horrors. Faceless one, guide us through the night of thy creation, that we may behold the Bond of the Angles and the promise of thy will.[30]

Yog-Sothoth—the gate—provides the means of perceiving the world as it truly is. The gate doesn't always lead to a different place in space-time, but it does provide the key to gaining deeper perspective through opening the way to perceptual changes within the subjective universe. As the participants declare their kinship with Nyarlathotep by being faceless themselves within the *Ceremony*, they each assume the role of becoming their **own** guides through this gate to the inner Self.

The sign of the horns is also a gesture of greeting for Yog-Sothoth; however, this time it is done with the **right** hand upraised.

The Yuggothic phrase rendered as "World of Horrors" is *El-aka gryenn'h*. In his 1977 article in *Nyctalops* magazine (reprinted here as appendix A), Aquino writes:

El-aka gryenn'h: "World of Horrors." "El" from the primitive name for the Judaic/Christian god, "gryenn'h" from "grin," originally a facial expression of fear (bared teeth) rather than merriment. Consider the "death grin" explored in *Sardonicus, The Man Who Laughs,* and so on.[31]

Aquino's fondness for the works of John Fowles (especially the philosophical *Aristos* (1964) and the fictional *The Magus* [1965, revised 1977]) is evident from his memoirs *The Church of Satan* and *The Temple of Set*. At the conclusion to *FindFar* (2017), Aquino quotes a passage from John Fowles's *The Magus* that also reveals much of the concept of the World of Horrors:

It came to me that he meant something different by "smile" than I did; that the irony, the humorlessness, the ruthlessness I had always noticed in his smiling was a quality he deliberately inserted; that for him the smile was something essentially cruel, because freedom is cruel, because the freedom that makes us at least partly responsible for what we are is cruel. So that the smile was not so much an attitude to be taken to life as the nature of the cruelty of life, a cruelty we cannot even choose to avoid, since it is human existence. He meant something far stranger by "Learn to smile" than the banal "Grin and bear it." If anything, it meant "Learn to be cruel, learn to be dry, learn to survive."[32]

This passage probably derives from Fowles's interest in the foundational philosophers behind the Existentialism movement, especially Martin Heidegger, whose concept of *geworfenheit* (German: "being thrown") sets the background against which we must find and enhance ourselves. The circumstances, culture, and language into which we are born are outside our control, yet act as significant mediators in how we learn to understand and enhance the inner and outer worlds.

Preparing the Way for the Bond

The celebrant raises his arms above his head at a "sharp" angle, forming a *V*. After the first two Angles, both obtuse, the Third is the first acute angle—as are all of the remaining ones. This is the first Angle that provides a means of action, aided by its much sharper disposition than those who have come before; this is also the last time the celebrant addresses the participants directly until after the Goat of a Thousand Young appears, as he, aided by the participants, is engaged in the complex invocations that open the gate between the dimensions through the proper operation of the Nine Angles.

The Daemons are, the Daemons were, and the Daemons shall be again. They came, and we are here; they sleep, and we watch for them. They shall sleep, and we shall die, but we shall return through them. We are their dreams, and they shall awaken. Hail to the ancient dreams.[33]

This passage is one of the key aspects of the semiotic nature of the Angles, as it encapsulates the full frame of reference within which the Angles function as an expression of Lovecraft's conception of "gods."

"The Daemons" refers to the Outer Gods that are being summoned via the Angles, and this passage describes them as a whole; their trans-temporal nature is explained, along with the mechanism by which they retreat into seeming inactivity, only to continue to work toward the creation that has been set in motion by their emanation from the Ultimate Chaos of Azathoth. They do this via their dreams, which other receptive conscious beings can also experience.

Humanity has been in contact with them via their dreams for ages untold. This has led to mythology and cosmology shared among otherwise greatly disconnected cultures, manifested in both hopes and fears.*

While retaining the same gesture of arms upraised at a sharp Angle, the celebrant now turns to face the altar.

Hail to thee, black prince from the Barrier whose charge we bear. Hail to thee and to thy fathers, within whose cycle thou laugh and scream in terror and in merriment, in fear and in ecstasy, in loneliness and in anger, upon the whim of thy will.[34]

The invocation of Nyarlathotep as the messenger—as Thoth, and Hermes—begins. He is the black prince—the Black Man of the witches, encountered in "The Dreams in the Witch-House"—"whose charge we bear."[35] That is, our capacity for understanding him, and the other Outer Gods of whom he is the messenger, is itself a gift and obligation we have received from this Faceless God. We honor this gift through its use, repaying its obligation by providing a means for the Messenger— and those of whom he is the envoy—to manifest within this world and to learn more of the gift's nature via our experiences. Through actions

---

*Arthur C. Clarke brilliantly described the same mechanism in *Childhood's End* (1953), as humanity has been dreaming since time immemorial in anticipation of the alien race— appearing remarkably similar to traditional representations of Satan—which arrives to guide humanity toward its next crucial evolutionary leap.

such as this, we are **become** Nyarlathotep, and thus enact an essential aspect of the semiotic theory of magic via the expression of the law of similarity. This enables us to communicate with Nyarlathotep—and by extension the other Outer Gods—effectively as equals and thus able to truly Understand each other.

> In thy name let us behold the father. Let the Old One who reigneth upon the World of Horrors come and speak with us, for we would again strengthen the Bond that liveth within the angles of the Path of the Left.[36]

Yog-Sothoth may be the gate, but it is Nyarlathotep alone who has the ability to cross into our plane of existence via that gate without being summoned. As messenger of the Outer Gods, Nyarlathotep provides a connection to them that is available on this side of the gate (which may indeed be safer than transgressing the gate in the other direction). The "father" in this passage is Shub-Niggurath—Nyarlathotep acts as the summoner of the Goat of a Thousand Young.

The celebrant now stands before the altar, with clenched fists and arms crossed (left over right) upon his chest. This sign is the same as the rune *gebo* (X)—the gift whose Mystery demands exchange between equals—further affirming the participants' kinship with the Outer Gods via the Understanding granted to them, which requires reciprocation.

> Hail, Shub-Niggurath, father of the World of Horrors. Hail, father of the hornless ones. Hail, ram of the Sun and deathless one, who sleepest not while we honor thy name and thy Bond.[37]

With the celebrant having successfully invoked Nyarlathotep as the messenger, the gateway is now open allowing for the invocation of Shub-Niggurath as the Goat of a Thousand Young. This is the culmination of *The Ceremony of the Nine Angles* as the purely Lovecraftian manifestation of that which is hinted at in the legendary Sabbatic goat rites of witchcraft.

> I am that I am. Through the angles I speak with the hornless ones, and I pledge anew the Bond of the Daemons, through whose will this world is come to be. Let us speak the Bond of the Nine Angles.[38]

Shub-Niggurath explains its true nature, along with the declaration of intent to "pledge anew the Bond." The Bond created by the acceptance and reciprocation of the Gift is strengthened. Furthermore, the rite affirms that the Angles are the most effective way to communicate with and comprehend the Outer Gods.

> Hail, father and lord of the angles, master of the World of Horrors. We speak the Bond of the Nine Angles to the honor of the flutes of the laughing one, the master of dimensions, the herald of the barrier, and the Goat of a Thousand Young.[39]

The celebrant and other participants affirm their allegiance and their will to communicate through the four of the Angles of the trapezoid. The cosmogony—which then allows for full consciousness of those incarnate within the objective universe—is now complete. True creation—self-guided, with regard only for its own principles—can thus take place; the stead of Awakening is made whole.

The Bond of the Nine Angles

All who are present—including Shub-Niggurath, correctly and successfully summoned to manifestation—recount the Bond of the Nine Angles, reenacting and affirming their allegiance borne of the Gift.

> From the First Angle is the infinite, wherein the laughing one doth cry and the flutes wail unto the ending of time.[40]

The chaos of Azathoth—the First Angle—can be easily misinterpreted as referring to randomness or destructiveness, when in actuality it refers to the emergent properties of complex, dynamic systems that are highly sensitive to their initial conditions. Potential arises, bear-

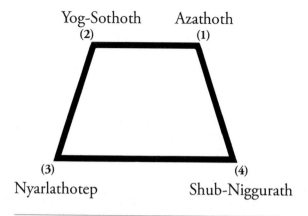

Yog-Sothoth   Azathoth
(2)   (1)

(3)   (4)
Nyarlathotep   Shub-Niggurath

The First Four Angles and the Outer Gods

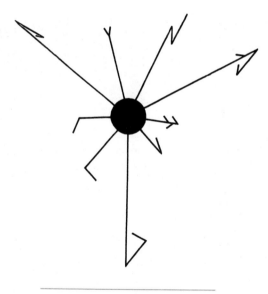

The seal of the First Angle

ing the mark of the initial conditions, which influence the Angles'
unfolding. Azathoth has no visible manifestation, but is known by its
effects on those who encounter it; the paradoxes inherent within it
("the laughing one who doth cry"), and the distant sounds that suggest
its presence implicitly but always just out of reach, provide a means of

knowing Azathoth not directly but only by its reflections and patterns left behind in what comes after.

From the Second Angle is the master who doth order the planes and the angles, and who hath conceived the World of Horrors in its terror and glory.[41]

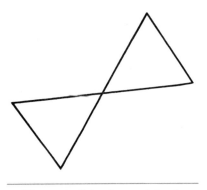

The seal of the Second Angle

The primal, spontaneous ordering of Yog-Sothoth is what initially allows the World of Horrors to exist. The nonthinking nature of the World of Horrors, crudely ordered at best, and driven solely by regular and non-conscious principles, is a blank slate on which more refined psyches can imprint the objects of their deeply held desires for their own transformation. It can seem as though the unconscious and sleeping beings who form the vast majority of the inhabitants of this realm are a force that cannot be overcome and who constantly thwart the right, the thought-based, and the good. The drive for the magician to force the areas of the World of Horrors under her control into forms of her own choosing must be strong, and not easily swayed by mundane setbacks; they are merely new opportunities for refining what must be done and for learning where to apply the proper pressure to bring about lasting change.

From the Third Angle is the messenger, who hath created the power to behold the master of the World of Horrors, who giveth to thee substance of being and the knowledge of the Nine Angles.[42]

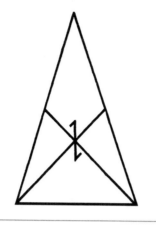

The seal of the Third Angle

In the Seal of Rûna, the Third Angle—represented by Nyarlathotep—is one of the two places where the subjective universe interfaces with the objective universe. Nyarlathotep creates a space wherein Being can take shape (by providing a means of connecting the subjective and objective universes so that they can affect each other according to the will and desires of the psyche). The "power to behold" arises from perceiving a gate that opens the way to partaking of both realms. That which to lesser minds provides an escape from the World of Horrors—whether through fantasy, denial, or submission—enables those who know the Angles to master the subjective and objective universes and become sovereign beings within both.

From the Fourth Angle is the ram of the Sun, who brought thy selves to be, who endureth upon the World of Horrors and proclaimeth

The seal of the Fourth Angle

the time that was, the time that is, and the time that shall be; and whose name is the brilliance of the Nine Angles.[43]

Shub-Niggurath—the Fourth Angle, and second principle through which the subjective universe directly interfaces with the objective universe—provides access to the illusion of time (itself solely a function of the objective universe, at least in the linear and cyclical sense). Shub-Niggurath "endureth" upon the World of Horrors by adding permanence and enabling ourselves "to be"; without this, there is no context for one moment to the next and no means of distinguishing what has come from what is yet to be in the World of Horrors. The task of the self-evolving psyche may be to remain in perpetual motion toward progressively refined ends, but without the mostly asleep inhabitants of the World of Horrors—who unconsciously strive toward predictability and stasis—the individual would struggle to find the way of liberation through antinomianism.

It should be noted here that in *The Ceremony of the Nine Angles,* the four Lovecraftian entities are considered to be facets of Satan as understood within the Church of Satan from 1966 to 1975. They are each individual beings, but Satan is a composite of their properties and behaviors (much as Satan represents many features of gods supplanted and repressed by Christianity). Whether they are considered to be separate beings, or progressive emanations of a single and more complex being, is immaterial to the discussion at hand and the effectiveness of the *Ceremony.*

Through the Bond of the Nine Angles, the Outer Gods are summoned, yet the Bond is not complete at this point; the comparatively crude manifestations of the first four Angles—the trapezoid—are progressively refined through the cumulative effects they bring upon the psyche. More complexity arises within the fully conscious subjective universe than is possible within the objective universe alone; the psyche is not bound by physical limitations, easily able to conceive ideas and objects transcending anything that can arise within a purely mechanistic realm.

The Four and the Five

From the Fifth Angle are the hornless ones, who raise the temple of the five trihedrons unto the Daemons of creation, whose seal is at once four and five and nine.[44]

The seal of the Fifth Angle

The Fifth and Eighth Angles share a resonance both with each other and also with the First and Second Angles with which they share a common vertex (see page 180). These resonances are the property of consciousness that allows it to examine and mindfully evolve itself; unlimited complexity arises from the progressively more intricate interplay between the mind and its creations. The connections bind the Five (the pentagram) to the Four (the trapezoid) in a way that allows each to partake of the essence of the other but does not impose any limitations on their possibilities. That is, they are interconnected, but not fully interdependent.

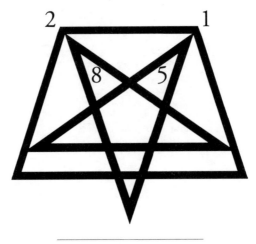

The Resonant Angles

The Hornless Ones are humanity, whose minds are modeled after the traditional representations of devils and demons as horned, independent beings acting in their own interest rather than bound by the limits and ideals of the World of Horrors. The temple is the structure of the pentagram, the symbol within which all the possibilities of consciousness reside; note that the central pentagon within a pentagram forms the chamber where the celebrant in *Die Elektrischen Vorspiele* casts his vision into the Is-To-Be.

The choice of "trihedron" instead of "angle" is a curious one. A *trihedron* is a conjunction of three planes that meet in a single point (one easy-to-visualize example of this figure is a four-faced pyramid, which lies on one side with three sides pointing upward to culminate in a single point). LaVey's fascination with the symbolism of the pyramid as the embodiment of the Command to Look is well known, and this usage appears to be an homage to that obsession by Aquino. More will be said about the trihedron in the context of the Eighth Angle.

The Daemons of Creation are the principles behind the Four, which created the foundation of awakening from which the psyche becomes conscious of itself; the Nine Angles—the combination of the Four and the Five—symbolize this connection.

From the Sixth Angle is the sleep of the Daemons in symmetry, which doth vanquish the five but shall not prevail against the four and the nine.[45]

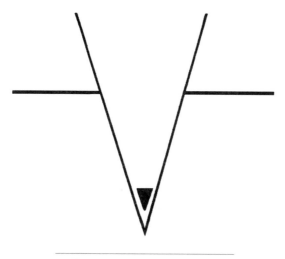

The seal of the Sixth Angle

The Sixth Angle is the angle of Incubation—that of the hidden lying in wait—where thought and magic are deposited to work of their own accord according to how they were set in motion by the First Angle. There conscious awareness of what is to be brought into Being waits until such time as it can be drawn again from the hidden realm to the forefront of conscious effort. In order to permit the emerging works of your creation to continue to form while the mind is focused elsewhere, be not afraid of silence, nor of contemplation, nor of incubation, nor of rest, nor of sleep, nor of death.

Sigil magic, about which we will have more to say in chapter 8, works within the Sixth Angle. The symbol of desire is deposited there, much like a curse tablet hurled into the abyss, where outside the attention of the conscious mind it will continue to work to bring about what it was created to do.

The Hungarian American physicist Eugene Wigner (1902–1995) received a share of the 1963 Nobel Prize in Physics for his work on

symmetry in atomic nuclei; the simplified version of the principle known as Wigner's Classification states that the symmetries inherent in the laws of physics determine the properties of subatomic particles. These symmetries—unchanging and predictable—thus form the underlying natural order within the objective universe, an order which is only perceivable by non-natural psyches (i.e., subjective universes) that are **not** beholden to these laws. The "sleep of the Daemons in symmetry" is both the state that results from denying—or obliterating—consciousness (in which case it may become permanently destroyed), or the deliberate setting aside of conscious awareness regarding a particular aspect of existence that is left to unfold of its own accord.

From the Seventh Angle is the ruin of symmetry and the awakening of the Daemons, for the four and the nine shall prevail against the six.[46]

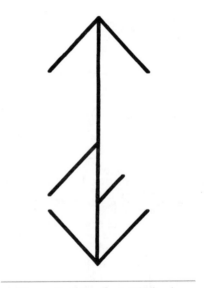

The seal of the Seventh Angle

The "ruin of symmetry" has released that which was incubating in the Sixth Angle, providing an angled path by which it can reemerge to active focus reflecting its evolution undergone in the hidden realm.

The seeds necessary to re-create—or reawaken—consciousness are embedded in both the Four and the Nine. They each prevail against the Sixth, because while the visible manifestation of awareness—the Fifth Angle—may be abandoned or deliberately set aside for a time, it can be re-created at will from these seeds by drawing upon them whenever needed.

From the Eighth Angle are the Masters of the Realm, who raise the temple of the eight trihedrons unto the Daemons of creation, whose seal is at once four and five and nine.[47]

The seal of the Eighth Angle

Note the near-identical description to the Fifth Angle, which nonetheless differs in a few key aspects. The Masters of the Realm were the IV° members of the early Church of Satan, those who held a deep understanding of the philosophy and theology of the Church, and who had proven themselves as master magicians who manifested the highest ideals of Satanism in all aspects of their lives.

According to the formulation of the degree of Magister Templi by Aleister Crowley, the Magister is one whose "work is to comprehend the existing Universe in accordance with His own Mind."* Thus the Masters

---

*Sources for Crowley's conception of the degree can be found in part 13 of *The Vision and the Voice,* and discussions of the degrees of the A∴ A∴ in *Magick (Book 4).*

of the Realm, by virtue of their profound Understanding of both the objective universe and their own subjective universe, are able to leverage that Understanding to re-create and reconfigure at will both their subjective universe and the portions of the objective universe under their influence.

Within the context of the Nine Angles, this ability arises from the Eighth Angle—where the truths wrought of transformation are revealed, and creation (the Fifth Angle) is thereby raised another octave. This pattern of re-creation according to the individual's own conscious awareness is accessible to some extent to all who possess the knowledge of the Angles. Here consciousness is refined to a more complete manifestation and has gained the ability to remake itself in the patterns of its own choosing.

The symbolism of the trihedron—the three-sided pyramid—in the context of the Eighth Angle suggests Crowley's concept of the "City of the Pyramids" wherein the Masters of the Realm dwell.

> From the Ninth Angle is the flame of the beginning and ending of dimensions, which blazeth in brilliance and darkness unto the glory of desire.[48]

Geometrically as well as conceptually, the Ninth Angle is the fulcrum for the entire structure.

The Ninth Angle, as the downward vertex of the pentagram, is the only point of the pentagram that lies outside the trapezoid. Symbolically, this suggests that it provides the external vantage point for both comprehending and generating the entire structure; continuing to trace

The seal of the Ninth Angle

the unicursal figure past the Ninth Angle leads back to the First and thus the cycle begins anew with additional awareness, experience, and momentum.

There is a deep resonance between the Ninth and the Fourth, indicated by the description of "brilliance" that accompanies both. The Ninth is, after all, the last of the five Angles that comprise the pentagram, and thus both the Ninth and the Fourth are the Angles that culminate their respective figures. They are both the ends of cycles and the point from which new cycles begin.

As "the beginning and ending of dimensions,"[49] the pentagram culminates in the Ninth Angle, and is conceptually as well as geometrically a gateway: tracing the interior vertices of a hypercube—the simplest four-dimensional figure—results in a pentagram. This idea is further discussed in Patty Hardy's text "Keystone" (appendix D).

The flame "which blazeth in brilliance and darkness"[50] is the Black Flame of the early Church of Satan and the Temple of Set. The name originates in *The Diabolicon,* an early contribution to the lore of the Church by Michael Aquino, in which he restated various themes from Milton's *Paradise Lost* from an explicitly Satanic point of view. The context and significance of this work are discussed in Aquino's *The Church of Satan.*

The imagery of the Black Flame emanating from the Ninth Angle was used as part of the early seal of the Order of the Trapezoid,

The seal of the Order of the Trapezoid, 1982–present

continuing into the more refined version in use since the reconsecration of the Order in 1982. The origin of the phrase "Infernal Geometry" is thus made more clear.

The Obligations of the Bond

Having reaffirmed the bond, the importance of the Ninth Angle is again emphasized, as it both represents the entire system and acts as the fulcrum point upon which the Nine Angles balance or fall. The oath is reinforced, with the sealing phrase "unto the beginning and the ending of dimensions," which also serves as the culmination (and dismissal) of Shub-Niggurath's participation in the rite as *pars pro toto* of the Outer Gods.

The celebrant now turns to address the participants again.

The hounds are loose upon the barrier, and we shall not pass; but the time shall come when the hounds will bow before us, and apes shall speak with the tongues of the hornless ones. The way is Yog-Sothoth, and the key is Nyarlathotep. Hail, Yog-Sothoth. Hail, Nyarlathotep.[51]

As published in *The Satanic Rituals,* the first phrase of this paragraph was written as "[t]he **gaunts** are loose upon the world." This was changed by Anton LaVey, presumably so as not to have *The Ceremony of the Nine Angles* conflict with *Die Elektrischen Vorspiele.* Also, as Aquino notes in the *Nyctalops* article (appendix A), the Yuggothic term for the Hounds (*Ty'h nzal's*) was meant to evoke the origin of the concept in Frank Belknap Long's story. Subsequent usage of the *Ceremony* and its related concepts in the Order of the Trapezoid employ Aquino's original phrase for the sake of authenticity and correctness.

This paragraph turns the sense of time upside down. Indeed, the Hounds **do** bow before those who know the secrets of the Angles, and relatives of the great apes **have** mastered the tongues of the hornless ones. As a cosmogony, the Angles have emphasized that to use this Gift of self-directed self-awareness to its full potential, the secret lies in reenacting the transmission of the Gift. Consciousness is imbued with the seeds of its own awareness.

Chapter 8 will include suggestions for adapting *The Ceremony of the Nine Angles* as an individual rather than group rite.

THE CALL TO CTHULHU

The Setting

The Call to Cthulhu was written as a "water" ritual to balance the "fire" of *The Ceremony of the Nine Angles*. The realm of the Outer Gods connected with the *Ceremony* is that of the hidden places beyond the stars; Cthulhu however is a **chthonic** deity, associated with the deep places within the earth accessible via the oceans. The ritual must be performed near a significant body of water, as such represents the protective veil that must be pierced in order for Cthulhu to arise from his deathlike slumber. Other than the "Sign of Satan" (i.e., the pentagram), the participants work without robe or other special garments, emphasizing that this is a more primal and less formal rite; the Sign is used not to protect the participants from Cthulhu but rather from **themselves** as they cast their state of mind back to the dimmest beginnings of consciousness.

Structurally, there are some similarities between this rite and *The Ceremony of the Nine Angles*. Both utilize a form of call and response, with the Lovecraftian entity that embodies the rite itself appearing once the law of similarity and frame of reference have been satisfied. The Nine Angles form the basis for *The Call to Cthulhu* as well; this rite takes place at the juncture between the Four—the pre-rational horrors of the human consciousness, remnants of the reptilian brain and our basic mammalian physiology—and the Five—the higher functions of self-aware, self-directed isolate intelligence.

Cthulhu is the High Priest of the Great Old Ones in Lovecraft's pantheon, and thus not an entity of the same type of the Outer Gods employed in the *Ceremony*. As a chthonic being confined to the ocean, Cthulhu is more closely related to figures of earthly mythology than are the Outer Gods (who are generally of less distinctive form and definitely **not** of this Earth). Given the origin of earthly life in the oceans, Cthulhu serves as a conceptual bridge between the strictly biological and the self-aware psychological aspects of humanity. Aquino alludes to this when he notes that "the theme of *The Call to Cthulhu* is that of a 'casting back' through collective, 'racial' memory to the rupture of mankind from the beasts of nature."*

The "honored names" invoked during the rite connect Cthulhu to various deities of the sea, casting them as pale reflections of the **true** entity. Invoking the infernal names following the statement that "great Cthulhu . . . art known to all races of the Deep Ones who walk upon and beneath the Earth"[52] is the key **performative utterance** that facilitates the summoning of the Teacher.

When Cthulhu appears, the call and response differs slightly from that in *The Ceremony of the Nine Angles*. Cthulhu delivers his wisdom in the Yuggothic language, which the participants then echo in English, affirming their increasing understanding of the Gift of self-consciousness for which they then must take responsibility.

The celebrant indirectly invokes Nyarlathotep as the messenger who opened the way to the World of Horrors via the Third Angle. This access was not without danger: it opened the way for the Hounds as well. Consciousness and self-awareness contain the seeds of their own destruction; the monsters of the Id—à la *Forbidden Planet*—cannot be fully avoided but can be held at bay by those who know where they lurk. Early humanity would have been quite the cruel creature until their intelligence and sense of obligation to other forms of life—indeed, their respect for the phenomenon of life itself—developed to the point where they no longer delighted in exploiting the life and natural resources around them. (In many ways, major segments of humanity **still** have not developed past this irresponsible and shortsighted attitude). Cthulhu acknowledges his role in bringing about this intelligence

---

*See appendix A. It may be beneficial to examine LaVey's ritual *Das Tierdrama* in *The Satanic Rituals* as a contrasting viewpoint to the ideas in *The Call to Cthulhu*.

without responsibility: "I walked upon the Earth, and I taught the apes to laugh and to play, to slay and to scream."[53]

But Cthulhu is not the redeemer of any form of intelligent or self-aware life; unlike the savior of biblical legend, Cthulhu died **for himself** and then slept. The Sixth Angle—sleep, or incubation—is said to "boil" the darkness[54] as it causes the Five—conscious awareness—to perish for a time until it returns stronger and more aware of its own unfolding. The sleep is spent with dreams of the master of the planes and the angles (i.e., Yog-Sothoth—the gate—which remains ready to be accessed because it never leaves the mind of the one who successfully traveled through it).

The rite reveals the awakening of Cthulhu as well; he proclaims "the end of the god of death, and of the god of dying"[55] so that those receiving this knowledge may "reject the cause of the death without sleep." These refer to the conception of the Sixth Angle as the repressive effect of the Abrahamic religions and their downfall via the seven-angled star of Babalon (Crowley's conception of one of the most memorable and evocative protagonists in the biblical Book of Revelation.)

A key passage from *The Ceremony of the Nine Angles* is restated. Compare

The Daemons are, the Daemons were, and the Daemons shall be again. They came, and we are here; they sleep, and we watch for them. They shall sleep, and we shall die, but we shall return through them. We are their dreams, and they shall awaken. Hail to the ancient dreams.[56]

with

The Old Ones were, the Old Ones are, and the Old Ones shall be again. I am dead, but I sleep and am therefore not dead. From the depths of the waters I come, and from the depths the Deep Ones also have come.[57]

The Great Old Ones are of course the Daemons, who embody time by transcending it (and thus ultimately existing **outside** of its finite, limiting grasp). While the Old Ones rest outside of the World of Horrors, Cthulhu remains on this side of that gate and endures his deep slumber within this plane of existence. Cthulhu does not merely inspire the ancient dreams, he embodies the ancient dreams through that key element of his manifestation and remanifestation. We may be the dreams of the Daemons, but we arise through the sustenance and exploration of our dreams in the same manner as Cthulhu.

This crucial key to maintaining and evolving the psyche is the central lesson of Cthulhu within the rite:

> Forget neither the Abyss of origin, nor the Old Ones who brought to you the flame of the Abyss, nor the ram of the Sun, nor the Eternal Serpent who raised you upon the Earth and delivered to you the flame from the messenger.[58]

Our biological forms are the product of eons of evolution ultimately originating within the oceans, yet without the "flame of the Abyss" (i.e., the Black Flame of consciousness) we would not possess the same awareness and capacity for mindful evolution as we experience now. Nyarlathotep was not the source, but rather the messenger; similarly, Cthulhu is also not the source, but the one who teaches the Hornless Ones how to utilize this Gift in a way that honors both its source and potential.

7

THE FOUNDATIONS OF WORK
WITH THE NINE ANGLES

As the Nine Angles are a living, still-evolving system of magic, working with them requires not only an understanding of the historical and theoretical background given in the previous chapters, but also a commitment to using the system in new and innovative ways. This chapter and the one following will focus on uses of the Nine Angles in illustrative and operative ways; a thorough grounding in these practices will enable the reader not just to use what has already been created, but also to expand on the underlying neo-tradition. Above all, you must not only read the practices and suggestions in these two chapters, but also truly **enact** and **experience** them—only then will you know whether these ideas and techniques are effective tools for causing change in accordance with your underlying desires.

This chapter describes methods for creating a dedicated space for workings of angular magic. We'll introduce an alternate version of the Bond of the Nine Angles, focusing on a specifically Germanic rendering of the same ideas. The chapter outlines foundational practices that will set the stage for the effective practice of angular magic. This includes a rite to awaken yourself to the angular path—an initiation into the practice of magic of this type. The conclusion of the chapter features suggestions for a daily practice of angular magic, focusing on certain actions and thoughts to be undertaken at certain times; this will deepen your understanding of the foundations of work with the Nine Angles.

CREATING A SPACE FOR ANGULAR WORKINGS

While not always a strict requirement, a suitable chamber for the practice of angular magic enhances the operation at hand and itself becomes part of the magical working. The existing rituals and other influences on the Nine Angles, in combination with the Law of the Trapezoid, suggest some features of an effective chamber. Drawing on *Die Elektrischen Vorspiele* and *The Ceremony of the Nine Angles* in particular, consider the following suggestions for creating an environment dedicated to work with the Angles.

The chamber should be small but not uncomfortably so; this will maximize the effects of the other supporting aspects of the space. The walls and ceiling should not contain any curved surfaces, and the furnishings should be minimal; if the structure of the space includes some angles that deviate from 90°, that is even better in terms of facilitating the appropriate atmosphere.

Limit the outside light admitted into the chamber, although a small amount (ideally from starlight) is preferable to none at all. Use music (when the rite calls for it) that is quiet, alien, and artificial to add to the soundscape's mystery and wonder. Experiment with ultraviolet lighting (do not look directly at the light sources!) and with slowly changing strobe lights (preferably blue or purple). Any decorations on the walls should feature Expressionist or Art Deco styles to capture the right time period for many of the modern influences on the Nine Angles; these designs should also avoid curved forms where possible.

Finally, the top of the altar used for angular magic should be trapezoidal in shape, preferably made from a wood associated with magical traditions such as birch; for more inspiration regarding the altar, see Lovecraft's "The Haunter of the Dark" for the description of the pillar that supports the box containing the Shining Trapezohedron.

As the above suggestions illustrate, the physical and visual components of the chamber are paramount. Through these settings, the magician wields the Law of the Trapezoid and the Command to Look to great effect. The dominant mass—the trapezoidal altar—and the angular designs of the structure and furnishings are key components of the Command to Look in angular workings.

THE BOND OF THE NINE ANGLES

The Bond of the Nine Angles is a key component of angular workings: it describes the individual Angles in a combination of Pythagorean arithmology and Lovecraftian imagery, establishing the frame of reference through which the Angles function in the semiotic theory of magic. It also functions as the foundational piece of lore about the Angles, working with the innate capacity of human minds for processing story and narrative; this capacity plays a key role in forming culture and creating coherence in that culture's understanding of its place within the World of Horrors. Working with the Bond connects you with others studying this system through shared narrative and experience. **One of the forms of the Bond should be memorized**, whether it is the full version in English or Yuggothic, the alternate version of the Bond included in the following ritual, or a personal interpretation created *after* having gained experience and understanding working with the Angles and existing versions of the Bond.

The full Bond is the section of *The Ceremony of the Nine Angles* beginning with "From the First Angle is the infinite . . ." and ending with "From the Ninth Angle is the beginning and ending of dimensions . . ."[1]

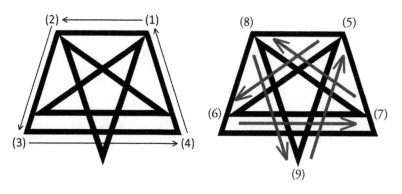

An alternate version—inspired by the style of the *Hávamál* section known as the *Ljóðatal*—is given below. Regardless of the version used, trace each Angle in the air with the left hand following its statement within the Bond, visualizing its trail as a brilliant blue flame that is opening a gateway to the spaces between the stars as you complete the figure.

Stand facing north, arms hanging relaxed at your side, feet forward at a 90° angle to each other with heels touching (forming a *V*) and say:

> *Nine Turns I know, that reveal the unfolding of my thoughts and deeds.*

Raise your left hand in the sign of the horns:*

> *I know a first, the seed holding all that is to be.*

Lower your left hand, and raise your right hand in the sign of the horns:

> *I know what follows, the hallowed dread woven of nothingness.*

Lower your right hand, then raise both arms above your head forming a *V:*

> *I know a third, the bridge spanning the rift between the Self and all the Worlds.*

Cross your arms upon your chest, left over right, fists clenched:

> *I know a fourth, the stead of awakening made whole.*

Lower your arms to your sides for speaking the remaining portions of the Bond. Turn to face the south. Continuing to trace and visualize each of the Angles following its portion of the Bond:

> *And I know a fifth, the knowledge of awareness.*
> *I know a sixth, the riddle of the hidden lying in wait.*
> *I know a seventh, the coming forth of mindfulness taken hold.*
> *I know an eighth, wherein the truths of reshaping are told.*

---

*See appendix A (page 255) for a description of the sign of the horns.

And I know a ninth, the Dark Fire that cleaves Self from the flow of wode.

Having traced the Nine Angles in their entirety, turn to face the east, and reach out before you to conjoin and grasp the Four—the trapezoid, now at your left—and the Five—the pentagram, now at your right—at the places where they meet in the topmost vertices of each figure; that is, the First and Fifth Angles, and the Second and Eighth. As you do so—as the two main parts of the figure are joined to create a gateway to the fulfillment of desire—speak the words:

Helpful to the ones who know the Angles. Of no use to those who see nought beyond the bowed sky.

Lower your arms to your sides.

The gate is now open, and obscurity flees from your mind's eye at once.

A RITUAL AWAKENING TO THE ANGULAR PATH

Having properly outfitted the chamber, we can now begin to do ritual work that draws on techniques and frames of reference particular to the Nine Angles. This awakening—opening the psyche to the possibilities that derive from work with the Angles—hinges on an important principle: Man is asleep but dreams he is awake.

While certainly not the only possible or effective form, the following structure for **angular rites of passage** provides a potent framework for constructing magical workings that utilize the Nine Angles. In contrast to the traditional model of rites of passage—stages of separation, transition/liminality, and reintegration—an *angular* model for rites of passage consists of **four** stages: desire, redefinition, transgression, and realization. This model forms the structure supporting the ritual of awakening to the angular path.

Prior to performing this ritual you will need:

- the book you will use for your magical diary (it must be black, or temporarily covered in black)
- a plain piece of paper on which you have traced—**prior** to the ritual—the five circles needed to construct the pentagram with a compass and straightedge; do **not** yet connect the points that form the pentagon or pentagram itself
- four small, blank pieces of paper on which you will draw the signs for the first four Angles
- a fountain or dip pen with dark blue or purple ink
- four black candles
- a suitably ornate, thronelike chair; if this is not available, drape a comfortable chair in black cloth
- appropriate music (should be sparse and wordless, based on non-natural sounds; selections that suggest the appropriate atmosphere include Tangerine Dream's *Phaedra,* Lustmord's *Dark Matter* or *The Place Where the Dark Stars Hang,* Coil's *Time Machines* or *ANS*)

Arrange the candles and four small pieces of paper on the altar so that they mark the vertices of a trapezoid. Place the paper with the incomplete tracing of the pentagram in the center of the trapezoid.

Note: Prepare all of the above in the chamber ahead of time, and leave the chamber sealed (with any windows covered) for nine hours before the rite is to begin.

The Ritual

1. Enter the chamber; then activate or reveal the source(s) of light. Begin to play the chosen music.
2. Spend a few minutes—but no more than nine—sitting or standing quietly in the chamber with eyes closed, while drawing your awareness away from all concerns that lay *outside* the chamber. Establish your breathing rhythm by slowly inhaling through the nose for a count of four, then exhaling through the mouth for a count of five. Focus your attention inward, bringing all your thoughts toward the task at hand.

3. Stand facing the altar. With arms raised above your head (forming a *V*) state your intent:

ᛝᛉᛟᛝᛟᛈᛝ ᛗᛟᛏᛏᛉᛓᛉᛞᛉᛝᛟ

M'khagn urz'vuy-kin!
[Hear me, Lord of the Angles!]

Through angles mirrored with thoughts, I, [name], draw forth awakening and awareness from the unmanifest void. All that I may bring into being will become known to me. I shall prove myself worthy to receive these Mysteries through the strange angles that take form by my pen, drawing from the wisdom of uncountable centuries as the Form of consciousness transforms itself through its own Laws.

ᛝᛉᛗᛟᛏᛉᛝᛞᛉᛝᛝ ᛝᛝᛉ ᛗᛉᛗᛟᛈᛝᛉᛝ᛬

K'phron-yeh nhi f'ungh'n.
[I manifest and shall speak.]

4. Lower your arms but remain standing before the altar. Draw the sign for the First Angle on the piece of paper next to the candle marking that Angle, with these words:

Within the great center of the cosmos are the hidden seeds of desires that I may yet bring into being. The beginning may be known, but what is to be drawn forth from the great Mystery of Being remains unmanifest until it emerges as the product of my mind.

ᛝᛉᛝ ᛝᛏᛉᛝᛝᛟᛝᛉᛝ ᛝᛉᛝᛝᛟᛝ ᛝᛝᛉᛗᛈᛟᛝ ᛝᛝᛉᛟᛝ
ᛗᛝᛟᛝᛉ ᛈᛝ ᛝᛉᛝᛝ ᛗᛝᛟᛝᛈᛝᛉᛗᛝ᛬

Ki'q Az-Athoth r'jyarh wh'fagh zhasa phr-tga nyena phrag-n'glu.
[Honor to Azathoth, without whose laughter this world should not be.]

5. Draw the sign for the Second Angle on the piece of paper next to the candle marking that Angle, with these words:

The master of dimensions, who doth order the planes and the angles, aligns the cosmos toward its fulfillment by the understanding borne of consciousness. Potential is redefined to open the gates to the possibilities I perceive.

𐎗𐎜𐎀𐎐 𐎌𐎀𐎐𐎗 𐎁𐎜𐎐𐎘𐎗𐎀𐎗𐎐 𐎕𐎘𐎜𐎜𐎀𐎐𐎗 𐎐𐎗𐎕𐎜𐎗𐎐𐎕𐎘𐎀𐎐𐎜𐎗𐎁𐎗𐎀𐎐𐎕
𐎀𐎗𐎀𐎐𐎜 𐎀𐎗𐎕𐎜𐎁𐎜𐎜𐎕𐎘𐎀𐎐𐎜𐎜𐎐.

Ki'q Y'gs-Othoth r'jyarh fer-gryp'h-nza ke'ru phragn'glu.
[Honor to Yog-Sothoth, without whose sign we ourselves should not be.]

6. Draw the sign for the Third Angle (above) on the piece of paper next to the candle corresponding to that Angle, with these words:

The black herald, the one untouched by sleep, transgresses the blind and mechanical ordering of the cosmos, revealing to me the many-angled messages from out of the abysses between the stars. Those who know the Angles thus become fully aware of themselves.

As you stand before the throne, focus your eyes on the space between the candles. When the visual distortion characteristic of encounters with the Outer Gods manifests at the periphery of vision, perceive through the "monstrous sense that is not sight" the approach of the Messenger. Consciousness folds in on itself, and you envision this Messenger not as coming from outside but rather as revealing that your innermost self-awareness seeks to reach out to command the cosmos.

I'a N'yra-I'yht-Otp urz'n naagha.
[Hail, Nyarlathotep, prince of the abyss.]

Sign your name—magical or mundane—in the book in the presence of the Black Man (otherwise known as Nyarlathotep, the Messenger), along with a statement of your intent to study the Angles. Beneath it record the sign of the Ninth Angle (below)— which also represents the Nine Angles as a whole.

W

7. Draw the sign for the Fourth Angle on the piece of the paper at the candle corresponding to that Angle, with these words:

Through the Angles I am become the Old One who reigns upon the World of Horrors, for I have glimpsed the Law, hidden from all but a few, which reveals the truest path between the unmanifest and the fully realized.

ᛌᚱᛝ ᛋᛝᛗᛉᛏᛩᚨᛉᛚ... *(runic/sigil line)*

I'a Sh'b-N'ygr'th, Phragn'ka phragn!
[Hail Shub-Niggurath! I am that I am!]

8. Take your place on the throne—the seat of Azathoth, the ultimate chaos at the center of the cosmos. Speak the words:

> *I proclaim from the monstrous chaos, through which all things arise, that the stead of awakening is made whole. The desire glimpsed through the First Angle shapes the ordering of the Second—thus redefining the path along which I seek the mysteries that lead me to myself. Through the jagged edges of the Third and Fourth Angles I transgress against the limits of perception and possibility, cultivating the real in accord with the unfolding of my will.*

On the paper in the center of the altar, connect the points that trace the pentagon, extending the edges to form the pentagram. As you do this, consider the Mystery that you must draw five **circles**— all with the same radius, signifying the regularity of the objective universe—in order to create the angular pentagram as the symbol of the subjective universe.

9. Declare the final purpose of the rite:

> *The latent promise of the Four now manifests as the Five. Through the Angles I have awakened to the ninefold way of Becoming that shapes the universe through the wielding of consciousness. May the Hounds guard my path and destroy those who do not bring honor to this Gift of Awareness.*

(sigil/runic line)

V'rohz vuy-kn i'inkh-v zy-d'syn.
[From the Ninth Angle is the flame of the beginning and ending of dimensions.]

A DAILY PRACTICE OF THE ANGLES

Each of these practices is a ritual in miniature, deliberately breaking with the sleep that we must constantly fight when moving about the World of Horrors. Perform them wherever you find yourself at the appointed times—seeking inward will provide the necessary angular environment, especially when accompanied by the suggested visualizations as the Nine Angles provide a map to aid the mind's ability to look inward and to transform itself.

By acquiring these practices as a matter of habit, you break from an unthinking, reactive existence and replace it at specific moments with deliberate acts. By constantly drawing attention to the capacity for consciousness to perceive and modify itself, you increase discipline and concentration by keeping a focus on what is to be done now rather than passively drifting from one situation to the next.

Always copy any practices, rituals, or passages that you will memorize into your magical diary. The act of creating this personal grimoire will not only connect you with the magical traditions of the past, but will also document your progress with understanding the Angles and provide a rich set of elements to draw upon in creating your own synthesis of these ideas. Furthermore, practicing the sadly disappearing art of handwriting engages your brain in ways that typing does not, thereby putting more of the ephemeral physical component of yourself at the disposal of your eternal psyche.

Upon Waking

1. After a moment of silence wherein you focus all your awareness on the words to be spoken, say out loud:

   From the seventh comes forth mindfulness evolved.

2. Sit in a comfortable position, in a quiet place, with your eyes closed. Breathe in through your nose for a count of four, then out through your mouth for a count of five; **feel** the rhythm of your breath rather than internally counting out the timing. As you become more

comfortable with performing this meditation, gradually extend the time of its practice to nine uninterrupted minutes.

During the meditation, passively observe your thoughts, noticing the chaotic and unstructured flow that they follow on their own. Notice how once you begin to focus on a specific thought, the seeming randomness is interrupted and you can then more readily direct this flow. Let go of this control, allowing your thoughts to lapse into their random flow; then reassert and perceive this transition from chaos to order happening again and again.

As you gain proficiency with this practice—and become more accustomed to the sensations of meditation in general if you are not already familiar with them—you will find yourself able to still your thoughts entirely. This experience of the Sixth Angle— Death/Sleep/Incubation—then transitioning back into the conscious reawakening of the Seventh Angle—Rebirth/Awakening/ Overcoming—is the key to bringing your deepest desires into being. By learning to perceive those moments when that which has lain dormant suddenly comes back to your awareness with full clarity— those aspects of your destiny that have been set in motion but not yet realized—you will train yourself to think the right thoughts at the right time, thus bringing as much of your existence as possible under the direct control of your will. The Angles provide clues to magical timing, working within rhythms that are a product of consciousness and not beholden to the cycles and demands of the World of Horrors and the objective universe.

3. Perform a version of the Bond of the Nine Angles, thus reaffirming it as a guiding principle within your magical work.

At Noon

At this time when the light shines most brightly, you must work the hardest to summon the darkness. The brilliance of the sun—which is after all a star of the same substance as those visible at night when the sky becomes an entrance not a barrier—echoes the brilliance spoken of with both the Fourth and Ninth Angles. The apparent path of the sun through the sky

provides one of the most easily observable patterns of the basic, unconscious ordering of the objective universe; it is a manifestation of the same
foundation for awakening the Angles realize as they unfold.

In the initial invocations of the Outer Gods in *The Ceremony of the
Nine Angles,* a statement about what has come—and what is yet to be—
appears after the references to the entities representing the first two Angles.
This statement forms the basis of the practice that takes place at noon.*

Find a quiet place, preferably where the sun would shine down upon
you, and face south. Stand in the same stance as that in the morning practice, visualizing the trapezoid in blue flame as you trace its angles in the
air with your left hand. Then speak the words (in English or Yuggothic):

*Z'j-m'h kh'rn Z'j-m'h kh'r Z'j-m'h kh'rmnu. Kh'rn w'nh nyg hsyh
fha'gnu er'ngi drg-nza knu ky cry-str'h n'knu. Ou-o nje'y fha'gnu
qurs-ti ngai-kang whro-kng'h rgh-i szhno zyu-dhron'k po'j nu Cth'n.
I'a ry'gzenghro.*

*[The Daemons are, the Daemons were, and the Daemons shall be
again. They came, and we are here; they sleep, and we watch for
them. They shall sleep, and we shall die, but we shall return through
them. We are their dreams, and they shall awaken. Hail to the ancient
dreams. I'a ry'gzenghro!]*

---

*A brief note on accuracy in the timing of this practice: this is not an astronomical or
astrological operation, and thus it is not necessary to obsess about the timing of the precise moment of "noon" in your current location and time of year. The primary purpose
of this aspect of the daily practice is to make a deliberate choice to withdraw into conscious reflection at a symbolic moment. The meaning you ascribe to this particular experience is far more critical than that you ascribe to the specific timing.

To the persistent image of the trapezoid, add (envisaged in red flame) the pentagram—the five Angles denoting the full potential of awakened consciousness. This reenacts and reaffirms the essential transition from the beginnings of consciousness that arise from the basic ordering of life, to the full self-awareness that the path through the pentagram illustrates.

Early to medieval Christian monastics were especially fearful of the *Daemonium Meridianum*—the "demon at noon." In the King James Bible, the mention of this phenomenon in Psalms 91:6 refers to "the destruction that wasteth at noonday." This personification of the Greek term *acedia* (negligence) attributes a supernatural origin to the common feeling of weariness during the hottest part of the day, which leads to forsaking your duties; this also takes on a deeper meaning as the feeling expands into a general weariness of the world and loss of purpose. It is this lack of focus and purpose that the noon portion of the daily practice addresses at the height of immersion in the daily, regular cycles of the World of Horrors—overcoming it through deliberate wakefulness.

Before Retiring for the Night

The final component of the daily practice should be done soon before sleep, if possible in the chamber devoted to the practice of angular magic, and after you have satisfied all major activities and commitments for the day. This is the time when dreams seed themselves in the unconscious mind and when reflection on the events of the dayside of existence turns toward the nightside where deep change takes place.

1. The same basic parameters for the morning meditation apply here as well, with the same pattern of breathing. The purpose and goals of this session are different, however. The exercises and practices should not last too long, with half an hour as the suggested upper limit to ensure the proper focus and concentration.

2. Gaze upon an image of the Nine Angles to fix it in your mind; you will know it has been properly internalized when it remains easy to

visualize once you close your eyes.* As you gain greater proficiency with this visualization, add more advanced variations such as: tracing the Angles in your mind's eye instead of just seeing them as a static image; envisioning the Four and the Five as separate figures that come together to form the whole; seeing the Angles as multiple three-dimensional figures that merely appear as the familiar two-dimensional representation due to perspective; adding another pentagram into the pentagon at the center of the original pentagram; and so on.

Solid visualization skills will prove to be quite valuable with magical work in general, but especially with a system that is based on intricate geometry. As you do so, the spatial relationships become further ingrained in the psyche, and your lived experience enhances the effects of the metaphor.

3. As an optional but recommended exercise, this is an appropriate time to practice writing with the R'lyehian alphabet (see appendix F). This adds to the symbol-heavy evening exercises, which are also designed to induce perceptual changes—and perhaps dreams— that result from contemplating geometric ideas (see appendix D, "Keystone"). Familiarity with the R'lyehian alphabet will add to the symbols available for use in sigils, visualization, and constructing effective magical rituals and environments—**magic is, at its**

---

*A highly recommended book for sharpening your visualization skills is *Seeing With the Mind's Eye: The History, Techniques and Uses of Visualization* by Mike and Nancy Samuels (Random House, 1975).

core, an act of communication with that which is to be transformed, and adding to the symbols available for communication enriches its possibilities.

4. Angular divination should be a regular component of the evening practice as well; however, it should generally only happen at most every **third** night. The discussion of divination and sigil magic in chapter 8 will make the reasoning behind this limitation more clear. In brief, **angular divination** is a technique of illustrative magic by which the Angles suggest to your psyche ways in which it might reconfigure itself—see the discussion of the Norns in chapter 5. The Angles are not providing the answer but are functioning as a mirror through which you can gain clarity.

5. Concluding the evening practice, the night-taking phrase—to be verbalized as consciousness begins to fade into sleep, while also visualizing the seal of the Sixth Angle (below)—is: "Within the Sixth Angle flow the dreams that shape the Is-To-Be."

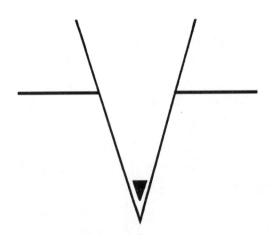

Daily Practices without Set Times

The daily practices for enhancing your understanding of angular magic and its applications do not end with these three exercises that take place at specific times. There are other techniques that you should train yourself to engage in whenever the opportunities present themselves. Among the other benefits of this training, a general

The Seal of Rûna, with Third and
Fourth Angles indicated

mindfulness will begin to be ready at hand and you will gain greater
control over the phenomena that you encounter while exploring existence within the World of Horrors.

As you are walking about throughout the day, take notice of any
time you cross an intersection where the streets or paths do not come
together at a right angle.* At such moments, draw your full awareness
to focus on the Third and Fourth Angles—Understanding and Being.
Recall that these are the two Angles that touch the ring of nature in
the Seal of Rûna, emphasizing the interface between the objective and
subjective universes. Another way to view these two Angles—and their
function in the mindful evolution of sentient beings—is to conceptualize
them as the principles of Significance and Life; the interplay between
these two provides a great key for determining where the focus needs to
be to utilize the Nine Angles as a tool for self-transformation.

Another method of applying this same technique—akin to the
teachings of Gurdjieff and Ouspensky regarding the need for continual self-awakening, or becoming fully aware of yourself as a thinking
being that is making deliberate actions—is to become aware of the
angles within the structure of any room that you enter. This hidden

---

*Stefan Grabiński alludes to a fear of angled intersections—manifesting the Greater Law
of the Trapezoid—in his story "The Glance" (1922): "He didn't know why, but suddenly
it seemed that the angle of the intersection was too sharp for his nerves. Quite simply,
an overwhelming anxiety arose within him that there—'beyond the bend,' 'around the
corner'—one could meet with 'a surprise'" (Stefan Grabiński, *The Dark Domain*, 137–38).

reminder revealed to your psyche creates an opportunity for interrupting the automatic (and thus below the level of conscious intention) way we move about throughout the day. Calling forth awareness at such moments—and attaching that awareness to a symbol system that suggests new ways of exploring their meaning—trains yourself to keep wakefulness close at hand.

This chapter focused on establishing a basic practice working with the Angles through the creation of sound foundations and effective habits that will enhance any type of magical work you engage in. Once you have had success working with them, they will become the stones from which you build the many-faceted temple that is **your** practice of angular magic.

8

ILLUSTRATIVE AND OPERATIVE WORK WITH THE NINE ANGLES

The rituals and other magical practices in this chapter—combined with the Awakening Rite and the daily practices covered in the previous chapter—form the basis for creating your understanding of the Nine Angles. They are not the last word on the Angles, but serve to encourage the reader to explore the system in a deeply personal way to further develop this living system. Above all, you must **experience** these ideas, not merely study them, in order to make them into a viable component of your lived experience rather than just an intellectual curiosity. Work within the Order of the Trapezoid and the Temple of Set continues to develop and enhance the understanding that creates this uniquely Left-Hand Path system, and public resources that either body may publish should continue to inform your own work with the Angles as well.

Examine and experiment with the magical work given in this chapter to the extent that it calls to you. This chapter does not present the material in any particular order, and each section stands alone, although virtually all the rituals and practices have relationships to the others that can reveal new understanding of the Nine Angles that transcends the sum of its components.

The practices in this chapter are more advanced than those in chapter 7; it is highly recommended that you first gain proficiency and experience with the ideas in that chapter prior to undertaking extensive work with this one.

In this chapter, we'll work with angular time in a ritual context. Traditional practices with geometric figures gain a new dimension with the *Star Trapezohedron*. The practice of *angular divination* is introduced, along with examples and suggestions for its effective use. The well-known techniques of sigil magic take on a distinctively angular point of view, and the significance of the Sixth Angle—*Sleep,* or *Incubation*—features in a ritual that provides a means for developing mastery of the use that Angle. Finally, the importance of dreams in the fiction of H. P. Lovecraft reappears as a set of ritual practices designed to facilitate such dreams for your own operative and reflective purposes.

WORKING WITH ANGULAR TIME

Background and Overview
The Bond of the Nine Angles reveals that "from the Fourth Angle is the ram of the Sun, who brought thy selves to be, who endureth upon the World of Horrors and proclaimeth the time that was, the time that is, and the time that shall be; and whose name is the brilliance of the Nine Angles."

Thus in addition to the Fourth Angle's role as completing the foundation from which consciousness can become fully aware of itself, working with this Angle is essential in magical operations that comprehend and manipulate **time.**

First, let's review a few key concepts.

Curved time is that which we experience as physical inhabitants of the orderly cosmos. Conscious beings perceive it as **linear** or **cyclical.** Linear time suggests moving in one direction only, limited and shaped by the curves of the "spherical" cosmos. **Cyclical** time is that of the progressions of the seasons or the stars, or the "eternal return" embedded in mythological models of religious and social structure.

0. Perfection
1. Being
2. Birth
3. Chaos
4. Creation
5. Order
6. Re-creation
7. Death
8. Understanding
9. Perfection

Curved time

0. Perfection
1. Chaos
2. Order
3. Understanding
4. Being
5. Creation
6. Sleep/Death
7. Awakening/Birth
8. Re-creation
9. Perfection

Angular time

The concept of **angular time**—introduced by Frank Belknap Long in the story "The Hounds of Tindalos" (1929)—reflects the subjective experience of the non-natural, self-aware psyche. In angular time, much like the human thought process, ideas and awareness unfold in ways that obey different rules than the predictable processes of nature. A flash of insight may circumvent a much longer process of logical analysis; a moment of inspiration may create an entirely new worldview or a previously undreamt-of work of art. Angular time is the essence of **lateral thinking** (discussed in the section in this chapter on angular divination).

One of the most profound explorations of angular time within the Order of the Trapezoid and the Temple of Set was the "Shub-Niggurath Working,"* which concluded during the Temple of Set's annual International Conclave in 1992 and opened the **following** year during the International Conclave in 1993. The solo rite presented here takes inspiration from that seminal Working.

The ritual expands on the concept of **angular time** to differentiate your personal timeline—the manner in which your self-awareness unfolds and you gain a greater conception of your own Being and how to enhance it—from the linear timeframe that constrains existence in conventional space-time. To understand further the conceptual background of this ritual, and to suggest other imagery and dreams that may enhance the experience, read Lovecraft's *The Silver Key* prior to performing each half.

Ritual—Part One

Part one of this ritual occurs **first** in *circular* time, but **last** in *angular* time. The two parts should be performed exactly one year apart, both to accentuate the relationship between circular and angular time, but also to provide ample time for further self-transformation in the interim. **If your life, interests, and understanding remain the same over such a period of time, then this ritual will only serve to continue to bind you to that stasis.**

Prior to commencing the ritual, prepare as follows.

During twilight, gather a small amount of dirt from a place that is special, sacred, or otherwise mysterious to you. Place the dirt in an open container on the altar in the chamber devoted to angular magic, and also procure a second small sealable jar that will hold a portion of the dirt following the first part of the working. Seal the chamber for at least nine hours prior to the rite.

Choose music based around deep, sustained drones.† In contrast to

---

*Conceived and constructed by a former Grand Master of the Order known here as Rudra, and until now only written about in sources internal to the Temple of Set.

†Appropriate suggestions include *Zeit* by Tangerine Dream, *Dark Matter* by Lustmord, or *V01d* by Hlidolf.

the usual practice of using the music as mysterious sounds in the background, for this rite the volume of the musical background should be loud enough to fill the chamber.

1. Invoke the Ninth Angle as the Black Flame of self-aware, self-directed consciousness:

[ritual script glyphs]

V'rohz vuy-kn i'inkh-v zy-d'syn ur'bre-el hy'j whreng'n nakhreng'h yh'whreng'n kyenn'h.

[From the Ninth Angle is the Flame of the beginning and ending of dimensions, which blazeth in brilliance and darkness unto the glory of desire.][1]

Through Angles mirrored with thoughts, I draw forth awakening and awareness from the unmanifest void. The dark fire of Isolation and Inspiration illuminates my way, even as I bear the ultimately responsibility for remaining true to the path that the Angles reveal to me in their unfolding.

Hail, Shub-Niggurath, ram of the Sun, who proclaimeth the time that was, the time that is, and the time that shall be, and whose name is the brilliance of the Nine Angles.

2. Speak the Bond of the Nine Angles.

Stand facing north, arms hanging relaxed at your side, feet forward at a 90° angle to each other with heels touching (forming a *V*) and say:

Nine Turns I know, that reveal the unfolding of my thoughts and deeds.

Raise your left hand in the sign of the horns:

I know a first, the seed holding all that is to be.

Lower your left hand, and raise your right hand in the sign of the horns:

I know what follows, the hallowed dread woven of nothingness.

Lower your right hand; then raise both arms above your head forming a *V:*

I know a third, the bridge spanning the rift between the Self and all the Worlds.

Cross your arms upon your chest, left over right, fists clenched:

I know a fourth, the stead of awakening made whole.

Lower your arms to your sides for speaking the remaining portions of the Bond. Turn to face the south. Continuing to trace and visualize each of the Angles following its portion of the Bond:

And I know a fifth, the knowledge of awareness.
I know a sixth, the riddle of the hidden lying in wait.
I know a seventh, the coming forth of mindfulness taken hold.
I know an eighth, wherein the truths of reshaping are told.
And I know a ninth, the Dark Fire that cleaves Self from the flow of wode.

Having traced the Nine Angles in their entirety, turn to face the east, and reach out before you to conjoin and grasp the Four—the trapezoid, now at your left—and the Five—the pentagram, now at your right—at the places where they meet in the topmost vertices of each figure; that is, the First and Fifth Angles, and the Second and Eighth. As you do so—as the two main parts of the figure are joined to create a gateway to the fulfillment of desire—speak the words:

Helpful to the ones who know the Angles. Of no use to those who see nought beyond the bowed sky.

Lower your arms to your sides.
The gate is now open.

3. Turn to face the altar. Through the timeless medium of angular space, communicate with your ascendant Self—the manifestation of your awareness and self-knowledge a year ahead from the present in mundane time. Seek to understand the message signifying some facet of this "future" being, sent back from the time when it has manifested. This becomes a seed for the magic you will create between now and when that aspect of your being comes to fruition. Visualize this seed disappearing into the dirt on the altar, where it will find nourishment and growth, ultimately flowering in the manner you have chosen so that your ascendant Self can then perceive it for it truly is. Record in your magical diary the symbol or message that you receive.

4. Seal some of the dirt in the small jar while keeping the rest in its place on the altar until nine days have passed.

5. Do not close the ritual, and do not speak of it to anyone.

6. At least nine days later, and again at twilight, scatter the portion of the dirt that has remained on the altar at its original location with these words while visualizing the message or symbol you received as the seed:

> *The Daemons are, the Daemons were, the Daemons shall be again.*
> *I have become the gardener who creates the fertile fields in which*
> *my magic will grow. From this single seed, I will nourish my being*
> *that it may flower into wonders beyond my expectations and dreams.*
> *In a year as counted among the curved space of the cosmos, I will*
> *celebrate the harvest that reveals the success of my cultivation.*

Ritual—Part Two

The second part represents the **latter** operation as reckoned in the timespan of three dimensions and five senses, but serves as the **beginning** of the ritual itself since this action in the chamber sends the message back to the magician one year *previously*.

Reference your magical diary for the origin of the dirt, the symbol or message you received, and the music used during the first part of the ritual, so that the same components are used in part two. Gather more dirt from the location at twilight. Also, place the jar containing the small portion of dirt from the first portion of the rite on the altar.

7. Invoke the Ninth Angle as the Black Flame of self-aware, self-directed consciousness.

V'rohz vuy-kn i'inkh-v zy-d'syn ur'bre-el hy'j whreng'n nakhreng'h yh'whreng'n kyenn'h.

[From the Ninth Angle is the Flame of the beginning and ending of dimensions, which blazeth in brilliance and darkness unto the glory of desire.]²

Through Angles mirrored with thoughts, I draw forth awakening and awareness from the unmanifest void. The dark fire of Isolation and Inspiration illuminates my way, even as I bear the ultimately responsibility for remaining true to the path which the Angles reveal to me in their unfolding.

Hail, Shub-Niggurath, ram of the Sun, who proclaimeth the time that was, the time that is, and the time that shall be; and whose name is the brilliance of the Nine Angles.

8. Speak the Bond of the Nine Angles (see pages 213–214 of Ritual—Part One for the text and gestures).
9. Turn to face the altar. Through the timeless medium of angular space, send **back** to your previous conception of yourself a message about what must manifest to enable you to become what you are *now*. Communicate with the manifestation of your awareness and self-knowledge as it existed a year behind the present in mundane time. This will become a seed for the magic you will create between then and now to bring that aspect of your being to fruition. Visualize this

seed disappearing into the dirt on the altar, where it will be nourished and grow, ultimately flowering in the manner you have chosen so that you will perceive it for it may become.

10. Mix the dirt from the jar with the fresh dirt gathered from your garden.

11. Do not close the ritual, as it has only now begun, and do not speak of it to anyone. During the next period of twilight, scatter **all** of the dirt back at its original location with these words while visualizing the message you have sent to your previous conception of your being:

> *The seed has sprouted, and now I transcend the boundaries of time as known in the orderly cosmos by overlaying it with my own true timeline realized through the Angles.*

THE STAR TRAPEZOHEDRON

Uniting the Four (the trapezoid) and the Five (the pentagram) draws forth from out of the abysses between the stars the causal principles behind the Outer Gods—consciousness confronts the precursors that led to its emergence, and thus comes to have greater awareness of itself and its possibilities.

Perform this ritual beneath the stars, or within a closed chamber completely devoid of curved surfaces and lit solely by starlight or moonlight. The magical working reveals Starry Wisdom and its close relationship to the Hermetic maxim of "As Above, So Below"—expressed within a purely Left-Hand Path context drawing on the astronomical implications of the Nine Angles and their relationship to the Mythos.

The Ritual

1. Let the magician face the Seven Stars, tracing a trapezoid in the air
   with his left hand, visualizing it in a brilliant blue flame while mak-
   ing the gestures indicated.
   - He makes the sign of the horns with the left hand, then traces
     the top line of the trapezoid sharply from right to left at the
     level of the eyes
   - He makes the sign of the horns with the right hand, then traces
     the left line of the trapezoid downward and to the left
   - He raises both arms above his head, forming a *V*, then traces
     the bottom line of the trapezoid sharply from left to right at the
     level of the solar plexus
   - He crosses both arms upon his chest, left over right, with fists
     clenched, then completes the trapezoid by tracing the right line
     upward to the left

   If he knows them, and will dare speak them, and will keep silent
   about them to those unversed in these Mysteries, he may accompany the gestures revealing the ominous trapezoid with the relevant
   portions of the Bond of the Nine Angles.

2. Then let him advance to the north, and with his left hand trace an
   inverse pentagram envisioned in red flame, and say:

   *I rise from the earth to the Seven Stars that I may order my own
   Becoming.*

3. Then let him advance to the west, trace again the infernal pentagram, and say:

   The coruscations of the daemon-light reveal the path to myself.

4. Then let him advance to the south, trace again the infernal pentagram, and say:

   *Beneath the shadow of the burning dome, cycles emerge anew. This
   is the end of eternity and the beginning of infinity.*

5. Then left him advance to the east, trace again the infernal pentagram, and say:

By the breast of the lion, I create sovereignty in the inner and outer worlds"

6. As the First and Fifth, and Second and Eighth, Angles are conjoined, a gate opens to reveal the path of the Remanifesting psyche.

7. Let him then trace the *Yn'khe Rohz,* burning brilliantly in its conjoined purple flame.

8. And then he shall say:

Z'j-m'h kh'rn Z'j-m'h kh'r Z'j-m'h kh'rmnu. V'k'naa v'ty'h nhi cvy, nhi v'quy'h nhi nyr K'ghr-kha n'fhtagn-gha. Krell v'fnaghn'k' krell d'yn'khe cyvaalic h'y-cvy-rohz.
[The Daemons are, the Daemons were, and the Daemons shall be again. By the gate of One and Five, and of Two and Eight, I reject the curse of the death without sleep. The key is known to me, that key whose seal is at once four and five and nine.]

9. Let him repeat the signs of the trapezoid, but not those of the infernal pentagram, that the stead of awakening may thus remain whole.

Commentary on the Star Trapezohedron

The Nine Angles are the two-dimensional representation of a multidimensional portal beyond the stars that is known as the Shining Trapezohedron.

The trapezoid indicates the foundation for Awakening—the arrangement of the cosmos that had to be in place before conscious self-awareness could take root. The four points of the trapezoid—and their associated keywords and Lovecraftian entities—are not the objective universe itself, but rather the pre-rational *reflection* of these sources as they unfold. Those remaining pre-rational aspects of ourselves—the "reptilian" brain, or the non-conscious parts of our self-awareness that we retain as members of the animal kingdom—must still be accounted for even when creating and realizing complex thoughts.

The pentagram symbolizes the self-aware and self-evolving psyche. It is self-aware because it can perceive and reflect on its own existence; it is self-evolving because it can use this self-awareness to modify itself and its tendencies. The five points of the pentagram—and their associated keywords—capture the essence of what it means to have this self-awareness and to wield it; they tell the story of how the mind evolves of its own will.

The Four and the Five "attach" to each other at the conjunction of the First/Fifth and Second/Eighth Angles. The First and Second—chaos and potential from which order begins to spontaneously arise through its repeated interactions—sets up the World of Horrors as limiting the possibilities of the unmanifest void; they are reborn in their full potential in the Fifth and Eighth Angles. This connection and resulting resonance between similar facets of being at different places in the recurring octave of their unfolding creates a **gate** with those Angles as its boundaries; this gate draws energy and influence from the objective universe (the ring in the Seal of Rûna) through the Third and Fourth Angles (the only ones to touch the ring directly), and these become fodder for the subjective universe to further refine itself.

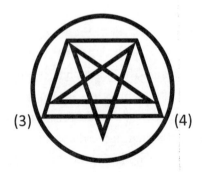

The Seven Stars are a circumpolar asterism known to the ancient Egyptians as the Thigh of the Bull, in most of continental Europe as the Great Wagon or Great Bear, in the United Kingdom as the Plough or Charles's Wain, and in the United States as the Big Dipper.

Algol—the "demon-star"—is a binary star in the constellation Perseus in the western sky, so nicknamed because it ominously "blinks" as the brighter star of the pair is obscured by the smaller, dimmer star.

Sirius—to the south in the constellation Canus Major—is the brightest star in the night sky. It has been important since ancient times, notably to the Egyptians who tracked the timing of the annual flooding of the Nile by its disappearance and reappearance. This period also coincided with the beginning of the Egyptian year according to its calendars, the most well known of which was a stellar calendar named "The Book of the End of Eternity and the Beginning of Infinity." The ancient Greeks knew that the appearance of Sirius heralded the onset of the hottest part of summer and referred to the star as "burning" or "flaming."

Regulus—known as "breast of the lion" in the Babylonian star catalog called the *MUL.APIN*—is the brightest star in the eastern constellation of Leo (the lion). The lion's regal nature denotes royal power in both the inner and outer worlds of the magician; he becomes the king ultimately responsible for knowing himself and creating the world within his influence as that most conducive to his own purposes and desires.

All of these (including the bright star Dubhe in the Seven Stars) are members of the collection known as the Behenian Fixed Stars, a catalog of fifteen stars considered especially effective for magical operations in medieval astrology in Europe and the Arabic world.

ANGULAR DIVINATION

Background

Angular divination is a set of practices for furthering your own understanding of the Nine Angles and exploring their possibilities as a tool for illustrative magic. The magical and philosophical basis of angular divination differs from other traditional forms of divination and functions within an explicitly Left-Hand Path context.

The Left-Hand Path approach to divination involves suggesting to your psyche new ways in which it might reconfigure itself. The information thus received and made meaningful is not the revealing of a static fate; rather, it is the discovery of a new tool that may suggest a way to reshape your *Wyrd*—the sum total of your past experiences that give rise to your possibilities for further action and reflection. The Angles represent glimpses of possibilities within a dynamic, unfolding future in which you seek your most effective path. The Angles are thus a tool for shaping what may be, not for fitting into a predetermined fate.

Understanding the frame of reference's use of **time** is vital to any divination system—the way of affecting the future depends on how you conceive its relationship to the past and present. With the Nine Angles, the Fourth is the key to the magical understanding and uses of time:

> From the Fourth Angle is the ram of the Sun, who brought thy selves to be, who endureth upon the World of Horrors and proclaimeth the time that was, the time that is, and the time that shall be and whose name is the brilliance of the Nine Angles.[3]

> The Daemons are, the Daemons were, and the Daemons shall be again. They came, and we are here; they sleep, and we watch for them. They shall sleep, and we shall die, but we shall return through them. We are their dreams, and they shall awaken. Hail to the ancient dreams.[4]

There is also an implied connection with the Ninth Angle—Perfection, the roots of desire through the Black Flame of consciousness itself—as per the Bond both the Fourth and Ninth burn with the same "brilliance" and influence the self-awareness necessary for perceiving and manipulating time. Recall:

> From the Ninth Angle is the beginning and ending of dimensions, which blazeth in brilliance and darkness unto the ending of time.

The Angles do not exclusively belong to a specific cultural matrix, and this not only frees them from existing mythic structures but also enables their practitioners to adapt them to whatever additional symbolism they may find beneficial or evocative. The Angles also do not rely on their supposed antiquity for their power or allure (even in light of the Pythagorean connections that Aquino writes of in his "Commentary on the Seal of the Nine Angles" [see appendix B]). This postmodern universality sets the Angles apart from divinatory systems with deep roots to the past that form a major portion of their allure, such as the tarot and the I Ching.

Naagh-R'unai

For work with angular divination, you should create a set of nine trapezoidal tiles, each carved or painted with one of the nine numbers from the set of R'lyehian symbols (see appendix F). Suggested materials for the tiles (called *Naagh-R'unai* or *Runes of the Abyss*) are hardened clay or wood; the background of the titles should be black with the numbers in a brilliant blue. The tiles should have a base and height of about 1 to 1.5 inches (approx. 2.5 to 3.75 centimeters).

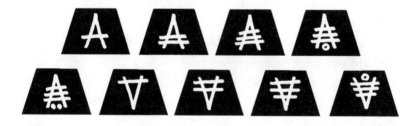

The numbers 1 to 9 in the R'lyehian Alphabet

Framing the Question

The effective use of any divination system requires the formulation of an appropriate question. Such a question is an application of the semiotic theory of magic in that the phenomenon you are affecting—the information being sought through the act of divination within the frame of reference of a particular system—transitions from recipient to communicator. The **operator**—the magician asking the question—in turn becomes the **recipient**.

Recall the map of the semiotics of magic from chapter 5:

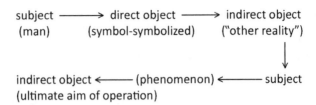

In terms of this map applied to angular divination, the operator encodes what she wishes to know in the form of an appropriate question and communicates it to the Angles. Then, the operator receives a response in the form of the drawn tile(s), which she must decode by ascribing meaning to it in the context of the Angles. The operator perceives the possibilities of her question through its effective formulation, and the decoding of the answer results in a change within her subjective universe to accommodate the newly revealed possibilities. The effectiveness of this encoding/decoding primarily derives from the operator's understanding of the Nine Angles; through other exercises designed to increase that understanding, the effectiveness of angular divination increases as well.

The most effective questions that benefit from angular divination are those related to perceiving *where in the angular cycle a given course of action presently exists* (type **A**), and those related to *revealing which parts of the cycle may need more attention in order to move it forward toward realization* (type **B**). You must then evaluate the "angular answers" to such questions in the same way as any other potential signal arising from the friction between your individual psyche (i.e., the subjective universe, which is desiring the change) and the objective universe (which above all values uniformity and predictability).

Casting and Interpreting Angular Divination
There are two methods of casting that have proven themselves especially useful. Both use the same simple frame ritual:

1. Begin with a small period of silence to clear the mind and prepare for sending and receiving.

2. Speak out loud:

𐤀𐤍𐤉𐤅𐤋𐤊 𐤋𐤏𐤕𐤊𐤋𐤀𐤏𐤀𐤉𐤊

M'khagn urz'vuy-kin
[Hear me, Lord of the Angles]

3. State the question.
4. Without lust for result, mix up the angular tiles and draw either *one* or *three* (keep the tiles themselves and container hidden from view unless in use).
5. **Before** looking at the tiles, state out loud:

𐤇𐤀𐤊𐤋𐤏𐤏𐤅𐤏𐤉𐤀𐤕𐤊 𐤅𐤊𐤉𐤊 𐤍𐤀𐤊𐤅𐤏𐤀𐤊

K'phron-yeh nhi f'ungh'n
[I manifest and shall speak]

6. Look at the tile(s) drawn, and speak the line from the Bond of the Nine Angles (the original version in *The Ceremony of the Nine Angles*) associated with each number on the tile(s).

The difference between the two methods is in whether one tile or three are drawn. While each operator will need to experiment for themselves to determine the method that works best in different situations, in general the one-tile version is more effective for type **A** questions, whereas the three-tile variation is more effective for queries of type **B**.

When drawing one tile, you must consider the angles before *and* after (in angular, not circular, order) that of the one drawn in evaluating the response. **None of the Angles exist in isolation**, and consecutive ones (in both directions) always participate in a mysterious relationship that you must explore as part of internalizing the meaning and significance of any particular Angle. While learning to use angular divination effectively, you should use the one-tile arrangement exclusively as this provides a simpler set of possibilities to interpret. This doesn't mean the possibilities are less profound, meaningful, or applicable; it just means that you are training your understanding of the Angles with less complicated exercises until you are more comfortable and conversant with applying the ideas. In the one-tile drawing, there are eighteen possibilities to consider—one of nine tiles is drawn, you examine each of these nine in two contexts (the before/after Angles in angular time, and in the different ordering of circular time).

For the three-tile arrangement, place the first one drawn as the bottom point of an inverted triangle, with the next two tiles placed above. Take the first tile to be the current *balance angle,* or fulcrum, on which the situation addressed by the question balances; the other two are the *decreasing* and *increasing* influences on the question, respectively. This is the more complicated arrangement to read, not only because of the increase in number of tiles but also because you must consider alternative angular relationships in order to create a coherent interpretation. It is especially fortuitous when the three-tile casting reveals three Angles in their natural order; consider thoroughly the directions and insights such a casting suggests. With the three-tile casting, there are 504 possible arrangements (or permutations).

An example three-tile arrangement

So how does one interpret the results of an angular casting?

Angular divination is a form of **lateral thinking***—problem-solving through creative and indirect approaches that avoid step-by-step logic and obvious reasoning. Lateral thinking is about the *movement*

---

*See De Bono, Edward. *Serious Creativity: Using the Power of Lateral Thinking to Create New Ideas* (Harperbusiness, 1992).

value of ideas; it does not itself cause a breakthrough in problem-solving or creativity, but instead is a tool for escaping unproductive patterns, which *then* leads to accessing the needed inspiration.

Bear in mind the definition of divination given previously, that it is a means of suggesting to the psyche ways in which it might reconfigure itself. The particular angle(s) drawn imply a means of winnowing down the uncertainty of the question. A *potential* answer is thus extracted from the Unknown, where you can evaluate it in terms of how effectively it spurs new thoughts in the resolution of the question. In this sense, its use is analogous to Schmidt and Eno's Oblique Strategies cards* that function to spur breakthroughs for creative blockages; in other words, the Angles are not providing the answer per se but are functioning as a mirror through which you can gain greater clarity.

The Oblique Strategies cards help their user to overcome creative blockages by encouraging her to take a fresh look at the creative problem from different perspectives. This is a form of divination that instead of claiming "this is the answer to all your uncertainties," rather suggests "look at the problem this way and explore whether it triggers the change in perspective that you need." The particular cards drawn suggest new ways to approach the problem and interrupt stagnant patterns of thought. Angular divination, while drawing inspiration from the Oblique Strategies cards, differs from them in that the Angles are specific markers in the way a creative process unfolds that you can read for insight; they are also a more structured approach than the Zen-inspired Oblique Strategies. (Or perhaps you could say that the cards work primarily in terms of the First Angle, since they focus on the unleashing of potentialities).

---

*The music producer Brian Eno (b. 1948) and artist Peter Schmidt (1931–1980) created the Oblique Strategies cards in the 1970s as a tool for enhancing and "unsticking" the creative process. The set of cards includes aphorisms and open-ended suggestions such as "Honour thy error as a hidden intention," "Work at a different speed," and "Not building a wall; making a brick." The artist draws a card from the deck at random and follows the suggestion without judgment or reservation. The true test of the cards' effectiveness is in whether the results are aesthetically pleasing and artistically satisfying; the creators still hold the ultimate responsibility for the legitimacy of their creations.

Example Casting of One Tile

Let's look at a couple of real examples of questions and readings of the Angles—utilized during the writing of this book—so that the principles and practices behind angular divination become more clear.

First, here is a reminder of the Angles and their orderings in both **angled** and **curved** time, along with the original set of keywords that encapsulates the meaning and significance of each Angle according to its place in the cycle:

0. Perfection
1. Chaos
2. Order
3. Understanding
4. Being
5. Creation
6. Sleep/Death
7. Awakening/Birth
8. Re-creation
9. Perfection

The Angles unfolding in angled time

0. Perfection
1. Being
2. Birth
3. Chaos
4. Creation
5. Order
6. Re-creation
7. Death
8. Understanding
9. Perfection

The Angles unfolding in curved time

In response to the question, "Where should I apply my effort to focus on finishing the writing of this book?" you then draw the Second Angle ("Order") from the *Naagh-R'unai*.

Read out loud the portion of the Bond that describes the Angle:

From the Second Angle is the master who doth order the planes and the angles, and who hath conceived the World of Horrors in its terror and glory.[5]

The initial observation you note, to begin to put this Angle into perspective, is that in **angular** time—the non-natural sense of time, and cause and effect, perceived by sentient beings—the Second Angle follows the First ("Chaos") and precedes the Third ("Understanding"). Secondly, in **circular** time—the observable way that events unfold in accord with the laws of the cosmos and normal perception—the Second Angle is between the Fifth ("Creation") and the Eighth ("Re-creation").

Drawing the Second Angle might suggest that the process of writing the book is still "stuck" in the stage where it is beginning to have some semblance of order and organization in your mind, but it is not yet particularly well formed in terms of what you have written down or outlined. Having begun to move past the First Angle (Chaos—unrealized potential), look ahead to what the Third Angle must entail: you can characterize it as *Understanding*—the beginning of true apprehension of the significance that the topic behind the book must convey. As the Third Angle is one of the two that intersect with the circle of the objective universe in the Seal of Rûna, moving the process of creation to this stage is crucial for capturing your thoughts and understanding of the subject of the book and giving them real existence within the objective universe.

An alternate perspective arises from viewing the place of the Second Angle in the continuum of *circular* time, situated between the Fifth ("Creation") and Eighth ("Re-creation"). The orderings in circular time tend not to be as valuable to examine, because they are typically more "obvious" due to their generally matching the default patterns and orderings within the world; in other words, the examination in *angular time* is typically more revealing as it suggests a truly alternate perspective. Here, the particular ordering drawn from the Angles suggests that the writing of the book is currently in a form of limbo between the basic, but not fully formed, initial creation and the more refined re-creation that arises from having written enough of the book that its creation has begun to change its author as well. Having changed his understanding and perspective during the process, the author would then be able to bring the fully formed and refined book into creation.

You may decide this suggestion and interpretation are completely off-base for your question. The point of angular divination is not to provide an unmistakable answer but rather suggest unexpected **possibilities** to consider. **Whether or not such a possibility works out or leads to the desired results, uncertainty has been constrained and you are closer to clarity.**

Example Casting of Three Tiles

Questions concerning what should be done to move a process along, or finding ways to explore what may be needed to overcome a creative blockage, work better with the more complicated drawing of three tiles. Let's explore an example from the creation of this book.

The question when I was struggling to determine what topics to cover in a particular section was: "How should I seek inspiration for completing the chapters about the history of the Nine Angles?" The *Naagh-R'unai* that I then drew were the Sixth (as the pivot), Ninth, and Third Angles.

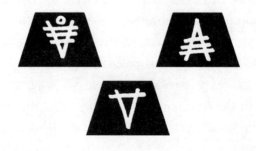

Starting with the decreasing Angle (top left), the relevant portions of the Bond are:

From the Ninth Angle is the flame of the beginning and ending of dimensions, which blazeth in brilliance and darkness unto the glory of desire.[6]

From the Sixth Angle is the sleep of the Daemons in symmetry, which doth vanquish the five but shall not prevail against the four and the nine.[7]

From the Third Angle is the messenger, who hath created the power to behold the master of the World of Horrors, who giveth to thee substance of being and the knowledge of the Nine Angles.[8]

Recall that the first tile drawn in the three-tile arrangement is the "pivot" Angle, or the one that is currently of central importance. The second is the diminishing influence, and the third is the increasing influence; these two provide context and form the impetus for examining the question from the point of view of how its subject may be evolving over time.

In this particular case, taking these Angles under advisement, I arrived at the following reading of the signs the *Naagh-R'unai* suggested to me for consideration. The descending Ninth Angle—the beginning and end of the cycle of the Angles—is the "seed" for any creative endeavor. The Ninth is both source and destination for reflecting consciousness in on itself—along with the desires that arise from it—in order to evolve as a product of its own inspiration. As a symbol of the Black Flame of Isolate Intelligence—the self-aware, self-evolving consciousness—it will burn most brightly at the beginning of a project such as this; then it remains available to return to as needed.

With the Sixth Angle as the pivot or balance Angle, the meaning is fairly clear that this may be a time for processing and assimilating knowledge and understanding, rather than actively creating (writing in this case). This reflection made me realize that I had been doing so much research into various antecedents and previous explorations of the Nine Angles that I needed to stop for a while to integrate all this new information into a deeper understanding. In other words, I had greatly increased my knowledge but not my understanding, and thus was not ready to write about what I had learned yet. Drawing the Third as the ascending Angle only reinforced this interpretation, since Understanding (keyword for the Third Angle) was precisely what I needed to increase before I was prepared to continue.

Final Remarks on Angular Divination

Angular divination is a tool that magical work with the Angles has only hinted at until recently. It is one product of the second major revival of work begun with the nine-year exploration of the Angles within the Order of the Trapezoid as a means of rediscovering and greatly expanding our understanding of one of our core technologies. The explanations and examples given in this book provide a means for others to work with this aspect of the still-evolving magical system of the Nine Angles; as with all other facets of the Angles, it is only through innovation conducted with a deep understanding of the history of this neo-tradition that you can come to truly Understand the Angles and their possibilities.

SIGILS

Theory and Background

Sigils—signs encoding magical intent—reveal much about their effectiveness when we examine them in the context of the semiotic theory of magic.* While the most well-known method for sigil construction is the *word method*—reducing and redrawing the letters in the statement of intent until nothing is left but a single abstract symbol capturing

---

*The history of sigil magic, including the theory and practice behind their construction, is covered thoroughly in Frater U.˙.D.˙.'s *Practical Sigil Magic: Creating Personal Symbols for Success* (Llewellyn, 1990).

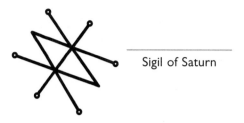

Sigil of Saturn

the "essence" of the statement—any symbol that conveys the necessary message to the subconscious can have the intended effect.

The mechanism behind sigil magic is the anchoring of desire—what you wish to change or create—to an abstract symbol, then binding that symbol to the subconscious mind.

As the Nine Angles are a system that is **visual**—even more so than it is verbal—this leads to some quite effective applications using the techniques of sigil magic. In terms of the Nine Angles, sigils work primarily within the Sixth Angle. The Sixth Angle is that of Incubation, begun by depositing thought and magic there to work of their own accord (according to how they were set in motion by the First Angle) until such time as they emerge from the hidden realm to the forefront of conscious effort. The Sixth Angle describes the way that ideas remain dormant until the conditions are right for their reemergence.*

When creating sigils based on the Nine Angles, portions of the figure itself provide rich symbolism for signifying the meaning and function of the different Angles. For example, the seal for the Sixth Angle (page 234) suggests the state of potential embedded in rest, and also recalls the "symmetry" spoken of regarding that Angle in the Bond.

---

*A prime example of this incubation-revitalization cycle is the seeming disappearance of the runes for hundreds of years, before interest in them arose again in the last place (Sweden) where they were previously used. One of the reasons this reemergence occurred there had to do with the rune stones present throughout the country; these signposts kept their memory alive even though interest in studying or practicing the runes had mostly lain dormant for centuries. Sweden, along with all of Scandinavia, was the last region of western Europe to be Christianized, and thus the true traditions had not been hidden or suppressed there for as long as was the case in other areas. The Sixth Angle can also work on far shorter time scales, of course.

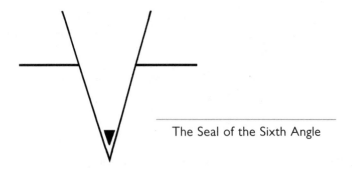

The Seal of the Sixth Angle

Generally, sigils should focus on simplicity in order to make them easier to visualize as well as to implant them more directly into the subconscious.

The Mechanics of Sigil Magic

The practice of sigil magic occurs in three stages:

1. **Formulating** the *statement of intent*;
2. **Sigilizing**—creating a symbol—within the chosen *frame of reference*; and
3. **Implanting** the symbol—and the meaning you have imbued it with—into the subconscious mind.

The *statement of intent* is akin to a **performative utterance**. The intended outcome is spoken of as if it had already become true; the magician—if she sincerely pursues the Left-Hand Path—is, by virtue of her mastery over her own existence, empowered with the proper authority to perform an effective utterance.

The *frame of reference* is the combination of theoretical framework and aesthetic (or style) that the magician utilizes in creating a suitably evocative sigil. In the case of the Nine Angles, sigils created within that frame of reference work from the magical theory underlying the Angles themselves, as well as follow the aesthetic of incorporating oblique angles into the sigils while avoiding curves (other than as minor design elements of flourishes).

The third stage—*implanting*—is what activates the sigil, setting it into motion so that it may act as a beacon for the desire. Contrary to oft-repeated instructions—typically associated with techniques inspired by the British artist and occultist Austin Osman Spare (1886–1956)—you do not need to forget a sigil in order for it to be effective. You **do**, however, need to create enough distance from its meaning and intent so that you avoid viewing the sigil only in terms of your expected outcomes, which can then blind you to other possibilities that may arise. Think of this technique as training yourself to be observant of unexpected situations—beyond just those evident to the rational mind—that may lead to the fulfillment of the underlying desire. In this way, sigils work as an inducement to lateral thinking (see the section in this chapter on *angular divination*).

Sigils **do** need to be properly implanted into the subconscious as part of creating this necessary "space" between action and the ability of the sigil to continue to work below the level of conscious thought. Effective techniques range from dramatic to subtle and symbolic and may vary depending on both your own needs regarding a specific sigil and the methods that you respond to best. Some common suggestions included burning or burying the image, staring at it in low light until retinal fatigue sets in then removing the sigil from sight, placing it under your pillow while sleeping, or concentrating on it intently while masturbating and then destroying the sigil at the moment of climax. Regardless of the technique, the intent is to implant the image in the subconscious in a very visceral way by bypassing the rational mind (thus avoiding judgment about the intended result).

Suggestions for Practice

The *word method* is one classic type of sigil magic. It works well within the semiotic theory of magic because it creates a very effective bridge between words—themselves a type of symbol—and abstract images that encode the meaning of the words.

The basic technique of the word method is to write out the statement of intent, then cross out repeated letters. For example, the phrase

MY WILL IS TO SEEK MYSTERY IN THE MUNDANE

becomes, after striking all repeated letters,

M Y W I L S T O E K R N H U D A

From this point, there are two general choices: combine and simplify the remaining letters into a suitable image, or create a *new* word from what remains. In the case of the new word, you will still be implanting this in the third stage of activating the sigil, but through repeated vocalizing of the word rather than concentrating on an image (whether the vocalization should be chanted, whispered, screamed, or otherwise depends on your intent and experience of what method works best for you).

Continuing with our example, a new word/phrase arising from the original statement of intent could be *WILSTOM KRYENHUDA*.

With the symbolic version, one possible permutation is as follows, with the original sigil on the left containing all of the elements of the statement of intent, and the simplified version on the right with minor flourishes:

MY WILL IS TO SEEK MYSTERY IN THE MUNDANE
MY WILL IS TO SEEK MYSTERY IN THE MUNDANE
M Y W I L S T O E K R N H U D A

There are many possible specifically **angular** approaches to sigil construction. The following are merely a few starting suggestions, and the reader is highly encouraged to experiment. The sigil thus *also*

encodes any statement of intent that arises from the divination. In this way, you will turn the insights from the **illustrative** magic of Left-Hand Path divination into an **operative** act that causes change within and beyond yourself. This helps to create the conceptual bridge between the insights gained and the operative acts they then inspire. Thus, the illustrative magical act of divination informs operative magic; thinking about change is only a starting point, with the true test being the results of actions that follow from that insight.

You can construct a sigil from the signs associated with each Angle. This is a useful technique when you must further contemplate the meaning suggested by a particular angular casting. While by no means the only possible set of such basic symbols, the following table shows a set of suggested—and known to be potent—sigil components representing each of the Angles:

THE SIGNS OF THE ANGLES

A 1
⟋ 2
Δ 3
⊔ 4
⟨ 5
∀ 6
⟊ 7
⟀ 8
W 9

Continuing with our example angular casting, one possible combination of the sigil components is the following. The three component signs (using our example angular divination that drew the Third, Sixth,

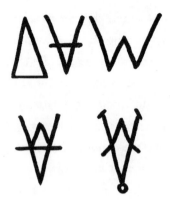

and Ninth Angle) are on top, with the bottom left as the initial sigil combining these signs, and the bottom right showing a simplified and more abstract representation of the same sigil.

The Nine Angles as Sigil

The symbol of the Nine Angles itself can be considered a sigil embodying the underlying concepts at the core of the magical system. Two suggestions for the underlying phrase that becomes the abstract symbol, hinted at within the Bond of the Nine Angles, are

Z'j-m'h gry-h'y
[daemons of creation]

and

zhar-v zy-d'syn
[the beginning and ending of dimensions]

Both of these capture something essential about the concepts that form the Nine Angles as an illustrative and operative system of magic. They also hint at the primary actor (the "daemons of creation," or the hornless ones seeking enlightenment to these mysteries), and the function of the Angles as a gateway to other modes of thought and perception (being both the "beginning and ending of dimensions").

DEAD BUT DREAMING

This ritual reveals the depth of the Sixth Angle, the angle of incubation, where thought and magic are deposited to work of their own accord—following how they were set in motion by the First Angle—until such time as they can be drawn again from the hidden realm to the forefront of conscious effort.

The rite should take place at night in a secluded location, beneath the stars. Clothing should be all black, and you should wear no magical or "occult" jewelry. The only lighting at the beginning should be a single source of flame, and you will need a small piece of paper and a writing implement.

1. Stand with arms outstretched and parallel to the ground, saying:

   The Daemons were, the Daemons are, the Daemons shall be again.
   The Daemons were, the Daemons are, the Daemons shall be again.
   The Daemons were, the Daemons are, the Daemons shall be again.

2. With your left hand clenched in a fist, thumb between the first and second fingers, trace a line envisioned in blue flame sharply from right to left at the level of the solar plexus.

3. Tracing the unicursal hexagram with the left hand, starting from the topmost point and moving down and to the left, speak these

phrases revealing the keywords for the Sixth Angle in conjunction with each segment:

Of silence, I am not afraid
Of contemplation, I am not afraid
Of incubation, I am not afraid
Of rest, I am not afraid
Of sleep, I am not afraid
Of death, I am not afraid

Then to the center of the hexagram, direct these words:

All things evolve according to how they were set in motion with the
First Angle, and this holds the seeds to their emergence from the
Sixth Angle to return to my mindful awareness.

4. As your last words fade away, your breath dispersing into the air around you—transformed by the processes that sustain this temporary vehicle for your Essence—create a sigil on the paper to symbolize that which must be set aside for a time.
5. Burn the sigil with the flame, depositing into the hexagram that magic which needs to incubate further before you can reawaken it to fulfill its Wyrd. As the flame consumes the sigil, envision the hexagram fading into the darkness as it absorbs the ashes.
6. Close the rite with the words:

I know a sixth, the riddle of the hidden lying in wait.

When the stars come right again—you will sense when this is so—return to this place to draw on inspiration from what has continued to develop without lust for result.

AN ANGULAR RITE OF PASSAGE

This rite is useful for confronting yourself with the true source of frustration and hindrance that prevents you from fulfilling a particular intent. If you find yourself constantly facing distraction, or unable to do what must be done, clearing space and providing clarity in this manner may be beneficial.

Passing through the stages of **desire, redefinition, transgression,** and **realization,** you will see with clarity what you must confront—and discard—in order to clear your path. This could lead to something as mundane as beginning to overcome your lack of commitment to taking proper care of your body, or as deeply profound as realizing that you must remove a certain person from your life because they hinder your freedom and self-development. Like the Black Mass as analyzed through the magical theories in the present text, it is an extremely powerful magical technique that increases in potency when used sparingly.

It is best to perform the rite in an open place—for example, a clearing in the woods—on a cloudless night in a location where the stars are visible. You will need a lantern or other source of light that is not too bright and your magical diary for reading the text during the rite and for recording the sigil/symbol described at the end.

If it is not practical to bring your trapezoidal altar with you to the location, then draw (or form with sticks or other straight objects) a trapezoid in the center of the space. This will take the place of the altar and act as the focus of the work with the four Angles that facilitate angular rites of passage.

1. Begin in the shadows on the periphery of the area where the rite will take place. Speak:

   𐎀𐎗𐎊𐎒𐎚𐎒𐎅 𐎒𐎙𐎛𐎔𐎒𐎐𐎊𐎗𐎀𐎊𐎅

   M'khagn urz'vuy-kin
   [Hear me, Lord of the Angles]

2. Perform a version of the Bond of the Nine Angles that you have *memorized*.

3. Speak:

   𐎅𐎗𐎒𐎚𐎒𐎊𐎒𐎅𐎊𐎗𐎊𐎒𐎚𐎒𐎅 𐎅𐎗𐎒𐎊 𐎐𐎗𐎒𐎀𐎅𐎒𐎚𐎀𐎅

K'phron-yeh nhi f'ungh'n
[I manifest and shall speak]

4. Emerge from the shadows, walking into the area where the rite will take place. Then, pace about the central trapezoid—taking straight paths with sharp turns rather than walking in a circle.

5. When you have returned to the beginning of your path, stop and visualize what it is you intend to facilitate with this rite, while saying:

    My desire rises from within, as I come forth to illuminate it in the light of the Black Flame.

6. Pace about the central trapezoid three times, again taking sharply angled paths. When you have returned to the beginning, trace in the air before you the lower three lines of a trapezoid with your left hand, envisioning it as blue flame that lingers in the air before you.

I have moved from the shadows into the light, and now glimpse the possibilities for redefining the boundaries of what may be.

7. Close your eyes and direct your thoughts to the freedom that is now within your group. Turn to your left, and as you open your eyes quickly slice your outstretched left hand through the air at a downward angle—as though ripping a new fissure in reality itself. Then speak the words:

    The patterns of Becoming are taking shape through transgression . . . boundaries become fluid and I disregard them at will. As I home in on the limit that binds, it evaporates into the air as do my

words, and fades into nothingness where it may no longer hinder my
self-directed destiny.

8. When you have fixed this newly realized inevitability in your mind as a certainty that will come to pass, gaze upward at the stars. The night sky becomes an entrance not a barrier, and you record in your diary the pattern of the stars visible directly above. Connect them with lines that become a sigil signifying this newfound understanding of what you must do; afterward, handle the sigil with one of the suggestions in that section of this chapter.

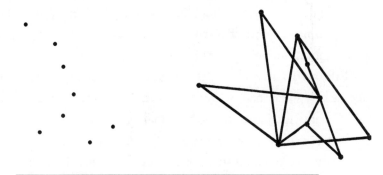

An example arrangement of stars and possible sigil

9. Conclude the rite with the words:

The patterns I have created are reflected in the movements of the self-
sustaining fires above, windows into the eternity that I willfully partake
of knowing that it is a product of my own creation and realization.

Speak of the rite to no one, and wait to include the contemplation of its possible results in your meditation until nine days following its conclusion.

STRANGE ANGLES AND DREAMS OF THE FANTASTIC

One of the experiences that often arises from success with understanding and effectively using the Nine Angles is the appearance of dreams featuring strange angles and related imagery. The following rite may assist with deliberately enticing such dreams to occur. Dreams were, after all, one of Lovecraft's most important inspirations, and experiences with the dream world (such as those of Randolph Carter, who effectively **was** Lovecraft manifesting in his own fiction) form the basis for some of his most evocative stories.

Alone in a quiet place—if possible, in the same chamber where you explore magical work with the Nine Angles—read one of the two stories that feature strange angles as a central plot device ("The Haunter of the Dark" or "The Dreams in the Witch-House"), **or** one of the foundational "dream cycle" stories ("Nyarlathotep," "Polaris," or "The Silver Key"). Immerse yourself in their imagery and plots, vividly picturing their locations and characters in your mind's eye.

Take a walk in a place that suggests the same aesthetic or environment as the story that you read. Return with either a small, distinctive object from this place, **or** with a small image that you drew in your diary that expresses the experience in abstract form.* The object or image functions as a talisman or anchor that you will place under your pillow for aiding in the facilitation of strangely angled dreams.

Immediately before retiring for the night, construct a pentagram on a new piece of paper; then connect the points to form the pentagon—extending them to form the pentagram—with red ink. As you gaze upon the completed pentagram, commit it to the tablets of memory while speaking the words:

> *My dreams open a gateway into the abysses between the stars.*
> *I shall see deeply into dimensions that remain hidden from those*
> *who see nought but curved space, and return to awareness of the*
> *World of Horrors with new understanding of my mastery over the*
> *trajectory of my own existence. I'a ry'gzenghro!*

---

*Learning to create spontaneous magical "doodles" in response to an evocative experience or environment is a skill worth cultivating. You will learn to express your own internal symbol system—akin to the Spare's "alphabet of desire"—and can use this to "fix" the experience in a medium that can be used as part of magical rituals such as this.

Variation A. If your desire is simply for dreams of the strange, drift into the abyss of sleep with the above words echoing in your mind while envisioning the circles and angles of the constructed pentagram.

Variation B. If you wish for dreams of imagination and inventiveness, where new ideas will be revealed to you that should then form the basis for a new creation in the medium of your choice, add the words:

> *Untold wonders shall be revealed to me! Within the realms of creation I will seek new ways to work my will upon the universe. New vistas of thought and beauty show me the way toward my own inner flame as expressed through my craft.*

Variation C. Or, if you seek dreams of destruction, wherein you remove power from your enemies by envisioning their dissolution, exclaim this addition to the spell (substituting a specific name if truly warranted):

> *I set my enemies in the place of destruction, where the gryphons tear their flesh apart from their bones and sinews. I spit upon their ashes, and trample upon their name. I erase their image from the book of life, and decree that henceforth none shall recognize their existence or remember their evil deeds.*

Variation D. Alternately, if your dreams will serve you through extending compassion to another person or animal, deeply feel these supplemental words as you send them into your subconscious:

> *I shall lift the burden from [name], and he/she will seek with me the wonders of the dreamlands that provide peace and comfort. Together we shall sail up the river Oukranos past the gilded spires of Thran, to forgotten places with ivory columns beneath the tranquil moon.*

Variation E. Finally, if you desire your dreams to deepen your lust for another and draw them nearer to you, seduce the unmanifest with these additional words:

[name] shall appear closer to me through the secret pathways revealed in my dreams! In the name of the great god Pan as I drift into the void of night, I pierce the mind of the one I desire who shall then respond with lewd abandon.

And I have exposed to the curious reader things which are told to few. Farewell, and guard your tongue.[9]

ATHANASIUS KIRCHER (1602–1680)

"AFTERWEIRD"

BY STEPHEN E. FLOWERS, PH.D.

What you have read, and I hope studied in the same way Wilbur Whateley poured over his moldering manuscripts, is a remarkable and unique text of eldritch lore. It is not the *Necronomicon,* but it may well contain the theoretical basis for that mythic volume.

In his seminal tale "The Call to Cthulhu," H. P. Lovecraft wrote: "The most merciful thing in the world, I think, is the inability of the human mind to correlate all its contents."

I am afraid in this regard Toby shows the reader no mercy in this tome, as he is providing a set of obscene geometrical keys to do exactly that: correlate the contents of the mind, but not on the terms of someone or something else, but on the mind's own terms. *Infernal Geometry and the Left-Hand Path* has provided a geometrical tool for this "correlation of contents" in such a way that a gateway to personal power can be opened.

One of the main reasons I joined the Temple of Set was to uncover the secrets of the Nine Angles. The ideas implied in *The Ceremony of the Nine Angles* written by Michael A. Aquino for inclusion in Anton LaVey's book *The Satanic Rituals* (Avon, 1972) fascinated me as a sign of the great ancient traditions whose "signature" was a ninefold sign: the Ennead of the Egyptian *neteru,* the *Valknútr* of the ancient Odinic North, the Enneagram of the Central Asian Sarmoug Brotherhood all seemed to me to be linked—but *how?* This book tells that story in very practical terms, terms that are *useful* to the reader.

The operative secrets revealed in this book could not have been revealed at this time by anyone else but Toby Chappell. As present Grand Master of the Temple of Set's Order of the Trapezoid, he has the unique authority and imprimatur to do this work. So this was not an exposé of secrets that the Order did not want to let get out. It is a lesson to a world ready to benefit from it.

Another important thing you will have experienced in the study of this book is an insight into how all great traditions are formed, and how even the great traditions of the eldritch past were formed at the dawn of time. Pseudo-traditions that spring from the fertile imaginations of single individuals rarely stand the test of time. They may appeal to a contemporary audience for a while, but eventually they fade, or are transformed by subsequent generations into shapes and monstrosities that their founder would hardly recognize. In the genesis of the material you find in this book, there is a span of about one century—from Lovecraft to LaVey, to Aquino, to Flowers, to Webb, to Hardy, and so on, to a whole range of thinkers and students. This is the blooming of that Yankee Rose. Each contributor to the root idea added something, which only that individual was capable of adding. It was an unfolding of a seed concept from beyond.

This book has many of its foundations in Left-Hand Path traditions. There are legitimate dangers linked to the actual Left-Hand Path. Here I do not speak of those dangers imagined by the superstitious, but of the actual dangers posed by stepping outside of superstition and simple faith in unseen and unexperienced things. These dangers can be avoided by a disciplined approach and a firm foundation in personal Initiation. For a general history and analysis of various Left-Hand Path schools, see my book *Lords of the Left-Hand Path* (Inner Traditions, 2012).

I will leave the reader with this final personal reflection. In the pages of this book we have an explanation of the oft-seen Seal of Rûna; in its circle and nine lines is the summation of an entire philosophy. The Seal is the bridge between all worlds and the aperture between the paths of human development. Take care of it, and it will take care of you.

I'A RY'GZENGRHO

STEPHEN E. FLOWERS, PH.D., studied Germanic and Celtic philology and religious history at the University of Texas at Austin and at the University of Göttingen, West Germany. He received his Ph.D. in 1984 in Germanic Languages and Medieval Studies with a dissertation entitled *Runes and Magic.* He is the author of numerous books, including *Original Magic, Icelandic Magic, Rune Might* (under his magical name Edred Thorsson), *The Fraternitas Saturni: History, Doctrine, and Rituals of the Magical Order of the Brotherhood of Saturn,* and *Lords of the Left-Hand Path: Forbidden Practices and Spiritual Heresies.* He is a Grandmaster of the Order of the Trapezoid, Emeritus.

THE APPENDICES

INTRODUCTION TO THE APPENDICES

It is impossible to cover the entirety of the history, development, and uses of the Nine Angles in a single volume. The six appendices that follow share both some of the foundational works as well as additional resources that will reveal more of the rich history of ideas that meet their unique synthesis in the Nine Angles as presented in this book. All appendix material reprinted here appears with the kind permission of the respective authors.

"Lovecraftian Ritual" (appendix A) was written by Michael Aquino in response to an article about Lovecraft and Satanism in *Nyctalops* #10. "Lovecraftian Ritual" reveals much about the circumstances that led to the creation of the two Lovecraftian rites in *The Satanic Rituals*. The article discusses Lovecraft's attitude toward the occult and how his work can nonetheless serve as an effective inspiration for **actual** occult explorations in the hands of a knowledgeable practitioner. This article is also the only previously publicly available analysis of some of the linguistic mysteries behind the Yuggothic language created for these rituals.

In the late 1980s, at the height of the Satanic Panic in the United States, Stephen Flowers began to dust off some long-dormant aspects of Satanic practice as covered in *The Satanic Bible* and *The Satanic Rituals*. Many of these analyses were published in *Runes,* the private journal of the Order of the Trapezoid within the Temple of Set.

From his conversations with Aquino concerning the origin and significance of the Nine Angles, Flowers wrote a few additional articles exploring this system. Inspired by this renewed interest, Aquino wrote his "Commentary on the Seal of the Nine Angles" (appendix B) as an explanation of the deep Pythagorean influence on the Nine Angles in his original conception, cast through the aesthetics of Lovecraft and magical technology of Satanism.

The first published writing of Flowers on the Nine Angles, "The Nine Angles of the Seal" (appendix C) focused on tracing the Angles and orienting them in time and space. Here he casts the Angles for the first time as the seed of a complete magical system, acting as a tool for understanding how the products of the subjective universe come into Being and how they relate to the mundane and linear processes at work within the objective universe. He later followed this article with the more detailed and speculative *"V'Ynk-he Rohz*: The Cycle of Nine"* (1992), which introduced the concept of **keywords** for the Angles, and focused on the relationship of the Angles to the inner and outer rings of the Seal of Rûna.

Developments in the Nine Angles were contributed by many within the Order of the Trapezoid. One of the more provocative contributions is "Keystone" by Patty Hardy (appendix D), who was later to serve both as Grand Master of the Order of the Trapezoid (1998–2001) and then High Priestess of the Temple of Set (2004–2013). "Keystone" focuses on the mathematical relationships encoded in the Nine Angles and Seal of Rûna, and the effects that the study of mathematical resonances have on the human psyche.

In a microcosmic sense, a mythic cosmogony (or model that describes the origin of the universe, whether scientific, mythical, or a blend of both) expresses the way that thoughts, ideas, and actions come into being. The richly detailed creation of the world described in the *Eddas* encodes many of the ideas that form the basis of the Northern Germanic Tradition. The "Angular Alchemy" section of Stephen Flowers's "The Alchemy of Yggdrasill" (appendix E) analyzes the origin of Óðinn—and the possibility for other living things to become fully self-aware and conscious—in terms of the Nine Angles, showing other manifestations of these core principles within but not bound to a particular cultural matrix.

---

*First presented to the Temple of Set at its 1992 International Conclave in Danvers, Massachusetts (exactly three hundred years following the Salem Witch Trials, when the town was then known as Salem Village). The article is presently only available in the archives of the Order of the Trapezoid.

The use of a magical language created specifically for Lovecraftian and angular magic was a vital component of the effectiveness of *The Ceremony of the Nine Angles* and *The Call to Cthulhu*. Chapter 6 and appendix B discuss the original creation of the Yuggothic language and the considerations that went into its development.

What was missing from this alien language, only approximately pronounceable by human tongues, was an alphabet that conveyed the same sense of mystery and utilized the Law of the Trapezoid as a design principle to facilitate the necessary effects on the human psyche. While we are used to expressing a wide variety of languages (with varying degrees of effectiveness) with the Latin alphabet, in the deeper past languages often used an alphabet that was specific to that language and more precisely matched the phonemes (individual sounds) used in that language.

Twenty years after the original publication of the Lovecraftian rites in *The Satanic Rituals,* a member of the Order of the Trapezoid named Sir Tmythos (Timothy McGranahan) created and published an alphabet specifically designed for use with the Yuggothic language. This alphabet, dubbed the R'lyehian alphabet, is given in appendix F showing both the handwritten and printed versions.

LOVECRAFTIAN RITUAL

BY MICHAEL A. AQUINO, PH.D.

It was in one of those small, musty bookshops lining Hollywood Boulevard that I came across a copy of *Nyctalops* #10, sandwiched roughly into a shelf between an 1895 edition of *The King in Yellow* and a rather decrepit-looking book labeled *Qanoon-e-Islam*. Leafing through *Nyctalops,* I was pleasantly surprised to encounter Rob Hollis Miller's provocative and perceptive article "Lovecraft and Satanism." Therein I found myself quoted twice—once from my introduction to Anton Szandor LaVey's *The Satanic Bible,* and again via excerpts from the H. P. Lovecraft essay and rituals which I wrote for LaVey's *The Satanic Rituals.* Miller's analysis of both the essay and the rituals was admirable, so much so that I decided to offer *Nyctalops* an exclusive exposé on the actual story behind that material.

During 1971–72, while Anton LaVey was writing/assembling the other essays and rituals for *The Satanic Rituals,* he invited me to contribute a Lovecraftian section to be included in that book. I accepted, but I soon found that I had undertaken no small task. Lovecraft's stories abound in references to his monstrous gods, but of actual "nameless rites and unspeakable orgies" there are few detailed descriptions. Such

Originally published in *Nyctalops* #13 [May 1977] and included in the appendices of Aquino's *The Church of Satan.*

" *fiction*"

rituals as are described at length—as in "The Horror at Red Hook," "The Festival," and "Imprisoned with the Pharaohs"—are reported by horrified, ignorant onlookers.

Then, too, there were conceptual problems that would have to be addressed. What was the Lovecraftian cosmological system, and how did the notion of "gods" fit into it? Why should such "gods" be worshipped by human beings at all—particularly if they were malignant? Was HPL expressing contempt for humanity by illustrating its morbid desires for self-obliteration, or was he creating a more subtle and complex philosophy?

good question.

From Lovecraft's own letters and non-fiction essays, it is evident that he drew a sharp line between mythology and reality. In a 1935 letter to Emil Petaja, for example, he disavowed his belief in any form of the supernatural and argued that the universe is simply a product of random force/matter mutations. Why, I wondered, would so adamant a materialist devote so much effort to the creation of a new body of literary mythology? Obviously not for money, nor did HPL vaunt his stories for their artistic merit. The general explanation given out by the "Lovecraft Circle"—that he wrote for personal amusement and with at least some commercial ambition—is unconvincing (at least to me). There is an atmosphere of sincerity in his stories that transcends mere yarn-spinning. In fact, it is this very quality of authorial conviction which so markedly separates HPL from his disciples and imitators, whose stories, clever as they may be, are instantly identifiable as "just" stories. (Exceptions are authors such as Colin Wilson who use the technique of the Lovecraftian novel to illustrate and explore their own philosophical hypotheses.)

This quality of conviction in Lovecraft's "fiction" cannot be overemphasized. It is the secret of that author's phenomenal popularity with both readers and would-be imitators. It also explains why most of those same imitators have failed to gain equal popularity. A similar quality of authorial conviction distinguishes Tolkien's *Lord of the Rings* from its many imitations, it may be added.

Another unique characteristic of Lovecraft's stories is their extraordinary detail and precision from a scientific and scenic standpoint. Linguistic dialects, historic data, geographic vistas, and abstract theories are refined so sharply as to reduce plots to secondary importance. (Only in *The Case of Charles Dexter Ward,* I think, did HPL machine the plot itself to comparable degree; the use of timed release of information, flashbacks, and plot groundwork in that novel is brilliant. Compare it to *The Dream-Quest of Unknown Kadath,* in which the sequence of the various episodes is relatively unimportant, the stress being on the visual imagery itself.)

The paradox of Lovecraft's personal materialism and vivid writing was profoundly disturbing to me. And it smacked of inconsistency as well: If HPL were so firmly convinced that the universe and its contents are merely mechanical, how could he account for his mental visualization of entities, objects, and processes outside that mechanical order? (Consider especially the philosophical sequences in "The Silver Key" and "Through the Gates of the Silver Key.") Are not such concepts so alien to the integral symmetry of natural law as to truthfully be identified as violations of them?

Perhaps the answer is that Lovecraft indeed spoke his true mind in his stories—but not relative to the objective, natural world which our senses impress upon us. Rather his focus is inward—toward the power of the human mind to conceive and create non-natural phenomena and to imbue those phenomena with subjective existence. The subjective idealism theories of J. G. Fichte, the objective idealism "sequel" of Hegel, and the more recent phenomenology of Husserl (cited by Colin Wilson, whose own *The Outsider* swings a mean existentialist club) are pertinent references. Such an interpretation would account for the gripping realism of the Lovecraft stories, while not contradicting their author's contention that they were not to be taken as portraits of objective reality.

I decided to put my theory to the test by constructing a Lovecraftian ritual that would stimulate the non-natural, creative/visualizing abilities of the human mind. I began to rough out the text for *The Ceremony of the Nine Angles.* And immediately I was aware that something else was wrong.

If the ceremony were theoretically designed by humans for humans to illustrate veneration of a Lovecraftian god, then the English language (or any other human tongue) would not be inappropriate. But the basic assumption of the Lovecraft mythology was that such gods—or, one might say, "god-entities of the subconscious mind"—were mental creations prior to the development of logical reasoning processes per se: the spontaneous product of primeval, non-ordered high intelligence. (An excellent illustration of this was the uncannily Lovecraftian monster created by the Id of Dr. Morbius in the 1956 film *Forbidden Planet*.)

The single most essential feature of any civilization is its language. Once a system of communication has been established, all else follows; it is simply a matter of time. To approach that special quality of authenticity found in Lovecraft's own work, therefore, *The Ceremony of the Nine Angles* would have to be composed in non-human language, illustrate non-human concepts, avoid objective patterns of logic, and be bewilderingly enigmatic in its overall purpose. At the same time there would be no point in reducing the text to complete nonsense, else the "normal" reader would find it valueless as a practical tool of ceremonial magic.

So I set out to create a Lovecraftian language. The pattern, of course, is to be found in HPL's famous incantation from "The Call of Cthulhu": *"Ph'nglui mglw'nafh Cthulhu R'lyeh wgah'nagl fhtagn."* The expansion of this pattern into a linguistic base for a complete ritual text is not as difficult as one might suspect: it is essentially a question of creating artificial words to match English words or phrases, which can be accomplished by some fairly random accordion-playing on a typewriter keyboard. Then a non-human quality to the vocal and mental/vocal rendition of the words is created by the juxtaposition of vowels, consonants, dashes, and apostrophes in such a way as to impair—but not entirely prevent—human utterance.

Linguistic consistency was achieved by the manufacture of artificial declensions and conjugations for certain key nouns and verbs, as well as by consistent use of repeated words and phrases throughout the text. Especial care was taken with regard to the appearance and sound of

specific terms of unusual importance, and I was enough of a prankster
to lace the text with obscure references, hidden meanings, and outright
satires. A very few of these have been guessed, but a complete decoding
has never been printed. Even Anton LaVey is unaware of this "ritual
behind the ritual." *Nyctalops* readers, then, may be the first to really
understand this particular duet of "nameless rites."

(Parenthetically I may add that the controversial English magician
Aleister Crowley used a similar language-creation technique for some
of his own incantations, based upon the Enochian or Angelic language
appearing in the diaries of John Dee. Crowley's task was somewhat
easier than mine, since the 19 Enochian Keys already provided him
with a substantial vocabulary and some grammatical technique. He
had merely to catalogue the words, create a few new ones as desired,
and build his new incantations from this "dictionary." To see how the
original Enochian underwent periodic revision, see [in this order] Meric
Casaubon's *A True and Faithful Relation of What Passed for Many Years
Between Dr. John Dee and Some Spirits,* Israel Regardie's *The Golden
Dawn,* Aleister Crowley's *Equinox,* and Anton LaVey's *Satanic Bible.*)

The English translation to *The Ceremony of the Nine Angles* is
designed to be read prior to the conduct of the ceremony itself, so that
participants will be aware of the concepts actually enunciated in the
Yuggothic tongue during the ceremony proper. Such knowledge, combined with the emotional, nonhuman effects of the spoken Yuggothic,
brings the ritual to its full effect. The setting and visual preparation of
the participants per the instructions are equally important. What many
armchair magicians do not understand is that, not unlike Shakespeare's
plays, magical rituals are both unimpressive and impotent on paper.
They must be performed in the flesh. Critics, novelists, and "students"
rarely display the courage, energy, or intelligence necessary to achieve
success with a magical ritual. And so they hunch over their typewriters,
glare at *The Magus, The Sacred Magic of Abra-Melin,* or *The Litany of
Ra,* and denounce it as superstitious nonsense. Therein they demon-
strate their own sophistry—and guarantee that their writings will never
evoke the power of conviction so easily achieved by H. P. Lovecraft.

Houdini

The Ceremony of the Nine Angles took about two months to research, write, and revise. Some sequences looked satisfactory on paper, yet failed in practice. The completed ceremony was sent to Anton LaVey in San Francisco, and a short time later he asked me to balance the "fire" impact of the text with a "water" ritual invoking Cthulhu. Since the Yuggothic language was now ready at hand, it was but a week's work to provide *The Call to Cthulhu*.

Before embarking upon a decoding of the two ritual texts, I should like to respond to four provocative points raised by Mr. Miller in his *Nyctalops* article:

The comment in my Lovecraft introduction in *The Satanic Rituals* about "Lovecraft being aware of rites not quite 'nameless' . . . often identical to actual ceremonial procedure . . . around the turn of the last century" was added to my text by Anton LaVey prior to the book's publication. As far as I am concerned, it is an ungrounded statement. From HPL's letters and conversations we know of the impact that his "dream-ritual" experiences exerted on his fictional themes, but nowhere is there evidence that his stories were influenced by contemporary magical societies. In fact he was openly contemptuous of both the magical literature available in his day (see his letter to Willis Conover of 7/29/36) and individuals who avowed themselves practicing magicians (letter to Emil Petaja of 3/6/35). Had he taken the trouble to look beyond the books of Rohmer, Waite, and Levi to Crowley's *Equinox,* Casaubon's *A True and Faithful Relation of What Passed for Many Years Between Dr. John Dee and Some Spirits,* or Budge's compilations of Egyptian magical texts, he might well have modified his literary view. And had he actually investigated the practices of the A∴ A∴, the Green Pang & 14K Triads of China, or the Thule Gesellschaft of pre-Nazi Germany, his scorn for practicing magicians also might have abated. I think we can assume that Lovecraft's prejudice in these areas derives from his contact with Harry Houdini, whose disgust with the fraudulent seances and stage-magic of the day was scarcely a secret. In the case of the man who once gave thanks for the mind's inability to correlate all its contents, it is perhaps equally merciful that a brain of his calibre was not exposed to the exhilarating stimuli of actual Black Magic. Else HPL might have left mankind a legacy far more estranged from "normalcy" than his works of fiction.

Mr. Miller questions my statement that "servility is definitely lacking in a Lovecraftian ceremony" (as opposed to the climate of conventional religious observances). He argued that "most of the followers of those (HPL) gods were degenerate and ignorant." In point of fact, the disciples of the Old Ones may be separated into two categories—the "intellectuals" (e.g., Curwen, Ward, Carter, Blake, Akeley, Peasley, "I") and the "subhumans" (the ignorant *Untermenschen* useful only for slavery or food). If this brings to mind the Nazis' similar classification of humanity, it is neither accidental nor surprising; see chapter #6 of de Camp's HPL biography for a candid exposé of HPL's racial beliefs. The most revealing story along this line is probably "The Horror at Red Hook." To make Lovecraft acceptable to his egalitarian public, August Derleth did what he could to play down his idol's elitism, but Lovecraft's letters suggest that he took this opinion with him to his grave. "Cursed are they who voice inconvenient truths, for they shall be given hemlock to drink . . . or simply be 'reinterpreted' by others."

It is a little easier to deal with Mr. Miller's question concerning the old Satanic concept of "Indulgence." Within the Church of Satan, "indulgence" was not equated with excess per se. The point was not to get sick by eating like a hog or to become delirious from a week's worth of orgiastic sex. Rather it was to attain some concrete understanding of actual extremes in order to make a reasoned approach to an Aristotelian Mean.

As for "where the beginning came from," that question was not addressed in either *The Satanic Bible* or *The Satanic Rituals,* but it was dealt with in an article entitled "Genesis II" that I wrote for the Church of Satan newsletter *The Cloven Hoof* in 1972. For an answer to the problem of how "something may be created out of nothing . . . and why" may I suggest Hannes Alfvén's *Worlds-Antiworlds: Antimatter in Cosmology* (W.H. Freeman & Co., 1966). As to the creation of intelligence against this tableau, that has been addressed in texts not available outside the Temple of Set. . . . Now to ye decipher'g of ye Abominations from ye Outer Spheres:

THE CEREMONY OF THE NINE ANGLES

The "nine angles" are the 5 points of the pentagram and the 4 edge-angles of the Φ-trapezoid (defined by the pentagon within the pentagram). The pentagram and the Φ-trapezoid may thus be considered both complementary and mutually definitive. Theoretical setting for the ceremony is the "King's Chamber" of the Great Pyramid of Giza, a structure whose true function has not been conclusively explained to date. The King's Chamber possesses inconspicuous, astronomically oriented light channels from the exterior of the Pyramid. This environment may be approximated in a ritual chamber through the mirroring of starlight from appropriate constellations. Where this is not possible, ionization of the atmosphere via electronic apparatus or indirect ultraviolet light may be employed. Distortion of recognizable human features may be accomplished by makeup, masks, or face-coverings of nylon mesh. The individual and group impact of such distortion must be experienced to be appreciated.

The Sign of the Horns is an identifying signal among Satanists, given by clenching the fist above the body, with the index and little fingers extended, to symbolize the horns of the Goat of Mendes—patron of the ancient Egyptian cult-center of Ba-neb-Tett, later corrupted into *Baphomet,* the Satanic goat.

The following terms are defined in the order in which they appear in the text.

Ki'q: "honor"

Az-Athoth: "Az" from the traditional "Aztlan" mother country of the Aztecs/Plato's Atlantis; hence "Az-Athoth" becomes "Thoth (Egyptian god of magic and wisdom) of Atlantis."

El-aka gryenn'h: "World of Horrors." "El" from the primitive name for the Judaic/Christian god, "gryenn'h" from "grin"—originally a facial expression of fear (bared teeth) rather than merriment. Consider the "death grin" explored in *Sardonicus, The Man Who Laughs,* and so on.

Phragn: Linguistic root for concepts of being/existing, adapted from the Latin *fragmentum*, something that is broken or incomplete.

Fhagn: Root for concepts of night and dreaming, taken directly from the HPL incantation.

Zyb'nos: "Bond," from the Latin *bini*.

Vuy-kin'eh: "V" prefix denotes possessive case in Yuggothic, "Kin" (angle) from the Greek root for "kinetic" (contained) energy.

Z'j-m'h: A non-human rendering of "demon" from the Greek *daimon* ("divine spirit" or "tutelary divinity"), later corrupted into a Hellish term by superstitious Christians. A not-inappropriate honorific for the Old Ones . . .

Quz: Root for concepts of death, from the Latin *quolquis* (who).

Kh'reng: Root for blackness or darkness.

Ty'h nzal's: "Hounds" (from Frank Belknap Long's "The Hounds of Tindalos"). LaVey altered my original English translation to "night gaunts," apparently not seeing the phonetic tie and evidently thinking that "hounds" would seem less impressive (or might clash with another text in *The Satanic Rituals*).

Zhri: "Cry," taken from *zhro* of the Descending Node incantation in *The Case of Charles Dexter Ward*.

Naagh: Root for "Abyss," adapted from J.R.R. Tolkien's Nazgul and *Nâz-* prefix. (Translation at one point altered to "grotto" by LaVey.)

F'ung: Root for "speak/speech," being a new translation of the title *Fungi from Yuggoth*.

Urenz: "Prince" from the hieroglyphic *ur* ("great man" or "prince"). Note the modifier "black" from the consonants of **kh'reng** ("darkness").

Aem'nh: "Father(s)," from the name of the Egyptian ram-god Amon.

W'ragn: To laugh, scream, or sing (more or less equivalent from a Great Old One standpoint!); from "rage."

W'hrengo: "Terror/delight" and "fear/ecstasy." The notion of the blending of diametric opposites is crucial to this ritual. See passages concerning the Dweller from Abraham Merritt's *Moon Pool* (G.P. Putnam and Sons, 1919)—based in Ponape, the Micronesian model for HPL's R'lyeh.

Kyno: "Will," treated as a variation of kinetic energy.

Hu-ehn: "Name" from "hue" (color) from "The Color Out of Space."

Y'goth-e: From "Yuggoth," here identified with the Left-Hand Path of Black Magic.

Kyl'd zhem'n: "Those without horns," from the Satanic term for mankind: the goat without horns.

Phragn'ka phragn: "I am that I am." The first words of Amon/Shub-Niggurath upon evocation and thus a hint as to who **really** addressed Moses from the burning bush . . .

Syn: From "sin," here used for both "time" and "dimension" as an integral continuum.

The First Angle identifies infinity and the concept of Azathoth.

The Second Angle identifies Yog-Sothoth.

Zaan: "Plane," a tribute to HPL's magical violinist.

The Third Angle identifies Nyarlathotep. With three angles a triangle becomes possible. Consider the dream-origins of Nyarlathotep, the poem and prose-fragment concerning him, and the triangular emblem and symbolism of Ra and the Heliopolis cult of Egypt. The Ra-triangle later became the symbol of the Hermetic Order of the Golden Dawn and its derivative Orders during the Æon of Horus prior to the Age of Satan.

Zhem'nfi: "Ram of the Sun" (Amon-Ra). The light of the Sun is the "brilliance of the Nine Angles."

A building constructed with five trihedrons is a pyramid, referring in this case to the original use of the Great Pyramid and other non-mortuary pyramidal structures.

The Seal is again the pentagram, intrinsically defining the Φ-trapezoid.

The "sleep of the Dæmons in symmetry" refers to the destruction of the Egyptian initiatory tradition by Judaism/Christianity. It vanquished the "five" (the visible tradition), but not the "four" (the secret tradition = the Order of the Trapezoid and the Shining Trapezohedron) or the "nine" (the Council of Nine/Nine Unknown—governors of the Church of Satan and now of the Temple of Set).

The Seventh Angle identifies the downfall of Christianity heralded by the seven-pointed star of Babalon (of Aleister Crowley's Order of the Silver Star (A∴ A∴)).

The Eighth Angle identifies the Masters of the A∴ A∴, the Church of Satan, and now the Temple of Set, who have attained to knowledge of the City of the Pyramids and raise the truncated pyramid—the Great Pyramid restored to an astronomical and communicative function—the Great Trapezohedron.

The Ninth Angle identifies the Black Flame spoken of in *The Diabolicon*. It will be seen that the Yuggothic phrase for the "Seal of Nine" translates phonetically to the previously enigmatic **YANKEE ROSE** at the end of the Satanic Bible. see next page

THE CALL TO CTHULHU

In diametric contrast to *The Ceremony of the Nine Angles,* this ritual emphasizes primitive concepts by ordinarily clothed people in a "wild" location. Hence there are strong lycanthropic undertones. The bonfire, torches, and unorganized assembly of the participants all add to this atmosphere. The identifying medallion (inspired by the star-stones of ancient Mnar) is not to protect them from Cthulhu; it is to protect them from one another. The rationale behind this will become evident from an actual celebration of the ritual. The theme of *The Call to Cthulhu* is that of a "casting back" through collective, "racial" memory to the rupture of mankind from the beasts of nature.

✳ **The Eternal Serpent**: translation of the hieroglyphic Set-heh ("Eternal Set") in the serpent-personification of that entity. See also James Thomson's *A Voice from the Nile*. (Thomson also authored *The City of Dreadful Night,* quoted elsewhere in *The Satanic Rituals*.)

Cylth: "Deep Ones," a racial name derived from "Cthulhu."

Water Demons **The names of Cthulhu** are those of water-dæmons and serpent-monsters from a variety of mythological traditions. They are followed by HPL's famous incantation from "The Call of Cthulhu."

Y'gth: Used here in the "planetary" sense as "Yuggoth"; in view of the unsophistication of the ceremony as opposed to *The Ceremony of the Nine Angles,* this simple reference is appropriate.

K'heh: Again from *heh,* the hieroglyphic term for "eternity."

The Cthulhu-entity was able to attain the Earth-dimensions via the angular environment of the Messenger Nyarlathotep, hence mention of the Third Angle.

Here the **Hounds of Tindalos** are referred to as "jackals," identifying them with Anubis, originally the "son" of the triad Set/Nepthys/Anubis and a guide of the intelligence in non-"living" dimensions.

Here the words for **"death" and "sleep"** have been taken from the HPL incantation. The "laughing one" is Azathoth.

The "god of death" is the Judaic/Christian god who stresses abstinence in life in exchange for reward after death.

The "god of dying" is Asar or Osiris, the original model for YHVH, whose cult in Egypt was based upon the presumed glory and promise of the dying process itself.

Wow

Vampire

"Death without sleep" is the total extinction of the personality, either before or after "physical" death. Death with sleep refers to Cthulhu's own Undead life, not unlike that of the traditional blood-vampire. — *of*

Here **"Old One"** is translated using the term "father" (**aem'nh**).

The awakening of the *cylth* after the reign of the god of death refers to the coming of the Age of Satan in 1966.

The extinction of the angles of the watery Abyss refers to the Childhood's End of mankind. Appeals to primitive, racial memory are no longer necessary, as the capacity for higher intelligence is now dawning among the *cylth*. A concept only roughed out within the Church of Satan, this has now become the Setamorphosis of the Elect of the Temple of Set.

V'yn'khe rohz: "By the Seal of Nine."

Some concluding remarks may be in order. Even from this abbreviated scanning of the two rituals, it will be evident that the translations and explanations often "open more doors than they close." This is bound to be frustrating to those who seek instantly finite answers to all phenomena within their range of perception.

I must answer that persons so inclined are rarely qualified for the practice of Black Magic, and that *The Ceremony of the Nine Angles* and *The Call to Cthulhu* are deliberately designed to be devices for operative magic. The literary aficionado will invariably feel more secure with the passive stories of the "Lovecraft Circle" of fiction authors.

For those *cylth* who become "restless" after this cursory exposure to the two ceremonies and begin to wonder whether they really "work" . . . there's only one way for you to find out. **I'a ry'gzengrho!**

COMMENTARY ON THE SEAL
OF THE NINE ANGLES

By Michael A. Aquino, Ph.D.

Generally speaking, some of these angles were taken from Pythagoras, who talked in terms of the significance of "**numbers**" rather than "**angles**." From my readings on the subject, I am convinced that Plato's discourses upon geometry and the significance of the various "Platonic solids" are essentially taken from Pythagoras's work, just as Pythagoras came up with these notions following his lengthy stay in Egypt as a priesthood initiate. Fascinating how these "trails" just keep going backward until they vanish into the mists of pre-recorded history.

Bear in mind that *The Ceremony of the Nine Angles* was composed within the conceptual and iconographic limits of the Age of Satan. Nor was it intended to be an extensive, exhaustive "last word" on the angles or other included concepts; it was conceived as a noetic vision and Greater Black Magic expression. The following comments pertain to my ideas at that time and deliberately avoid embellishing *The Ceremony of the Nine Angles* with the more sophisticated concepts to which I have since been sensitized through my own work and the many brilliant examinations by other Setians.

First published in the May 1988 issue of *Runes* (the private journal of the Order of the Trapezoid).

268

First Angle: **Unity.** The concept of the Universe as the totality of existence. Note that this does not admit to monotheism (except in the sense of Deism), because there is no room for conceptual distance between a God and a worshipper. The "laughing one" is **Azathoth,** who is "blind" and an "idiot" because in a condition of perfect unity there is naught else to see, not any knowledge of anything else possible. (Understand, of course, that I was taking H. P. Lovecraft's gods rather beyond his storytelling version of them. I don't in the least represent these as Lovecraft's own ideas, although I rather think that he would not have found fault with such elaborations.) In geometry a singularity identifies a locus only; there is no extension in any direction. Even the locus is "both there and not," since it has no dimensions at all. Hence there are an infinite number of loci, for example on a one-inch-long line: an interesting mathemagical paradox.

Second Angle: **Duality.** The profound and necessarily total change of unity into symmetry and polarity (and its symbolic representations: Horus and Set, Yang and Yin, etc.) The "orderer of the planes and angles" is **Yog-Sothoth,** who is, as the shaper of energy and matter, described as the author of Earth in its matter/energy/evolutionary configuration. Note that in pure duality there is no room for judgment between the two; there is only one or the other. In duality geometry creates a single extension (a line).

Third Angle: This is a very critical stage, because the existence of a third element introduces the notion of choice between the two opposites, either absolutely or relatively (Aristotelian system) or of choice to aspire or not to aspire to universal perfections (= Platonic/Pythagorean system). This is **Nyarlathotep,** otherwise **Set,** otherwise **Lucifer/Satan,** otherwise **Prometheus,** otherwise **Thoth,** who has created the power of perspective and the independent psyche of judgment. Here "knowledge" becomes possible. In geometry we now have the triangle, which is the most rigid of figures and also creates a two-dimensional plane. Note that, per *The Book of Coming Forth by Night,* the Horus/Set relationship actually fits into a threefold matrix rather than a twofold one. Set is an independent Intelligence with perspective upon the non-conscious objective universe on one hand and the chaos of the anti-objective universe (HarWer) on the other. The simple Horus/Set duality results from primitive Aristotelian thinking (so kick me, Tharrud Terclis!).

Fourth Angle: The ram of the Sun (**Shub-Niggurath/Amon**) is a manifestation of the "awakened" human psyche as energized by the Messenger. It is thus that "Satan" is known to humanity: a personalized reflection, as it were, of the results of the messenger's working. Satan's other name (**Lucifer**) is that of light and enlightenment, hence the "brilliance" of the Nine Angles. With the number four we have geometrically a three-dimensional displacement in space. Hence existence of matter and energy becomes possible. Hence time becomes possible, as the measurement of change in matter and energy.

Fifth Angle: Humanity as the physical vehicle for the expression of the Satanic psyche as discussed in the Fourth Angle. Concept of the body as a necessary medium for the self-realization of the psyche, at least in its early stage. Translation of this into physical representation of supra-energy/matter Forms such as Set via the creation of images, building to temples, and so on. A temple with five trihedrons is a four-faced pyramid (as Giza), the 4/5/9 seal is the seal of the Order of the Trapezoid: a marvel of integrated, interrelated 4/5/9 values. As noted elsewhere, even the addition of 4 + 5 + 9 = 18, which takes you into the "returning' qualities of 9 as expounded upon in Anton LaVey's "Unknown Known" in *The Satanic Rituals.* In geometry 5 creates the pentagram, hence the Golden Section, hence the concept of perfection. This is why to Pythagoras (and his priestly mentors) 5 was the most sublime of numbers, and why the pentagram was used as the seal of the Pythagorean Brotherhood.

Sixth Angle: If Crowley considered his Tenth Aether to be accursed, then this would be the accursed (or should I say "hexed"!) of the Nine Angles. It is the hexagon and hexagram. The hexagon corrupts the Golden Rectangle; it adds an angle and a line to the pentagram and pentagon, thus destroying them. Six is symmetry obese and unnecessary (two and four are quite adequate for the principle). The seeds of the destruction of the hexagonal forms are carried within them, however,

for they necessarily embrace two trapezoids (the four) and the pentagrams defined by those trapezoids (the five); hence 4 + 5 (the nine).

Seventh Angle: The destruction of the status of monotheism by
the addition of a line/angle to the hex. The legacy of the First Beast of
Revelation and his sevenfold Seal and Star of Babalon (A∴ A∴). The
forces of the Aeon of Horus overcoming those of the Aeon of Osiris.
Yet the only thing that can be said of seven is that it is an effective
destroyer of six. It has no creative properties of its own; it has neither
the strength of symmetry nor the magical powers of its asymmetrical
predecessors (1, 3, 5). Proponents of six-isms instinctively fear seven:
They warn about such things as the seventh son of a seventh son, of
the Seven Towers of Satan in Yezidi legend, of the Seventh Seal, of the
Jewel of the Seven Stars. Seven is thus a harbinger of doom to six: a
shadowing-forth of the Apocalypse to come. Geometrically and numer-
ically, like the Æon of Horus, seven has an "identity crisis." Additions
or multiplications or powers of seven yield all sorts of random values
and relationships.

Eighth Angle: The temple containing the trihedral angles is a
truncated pyramid: the power of the trapezoid perfectly manifest in a
Golden Section-based three-dimensional structure. Thus its architects
are the Masters of the Realm (the all-embracing term for the IV°+ in
the original Church of Satan): the Sorcerers who beam from their towers the Powers of Darkness to rebuild the world corrupted by six and
shattered by the seven, and their seal is the Seal of the Order of the
Trapezoid (seal of the Priesthood of the original Church of Satan).

Ninth Angle: The culmination of this dynamic process: the Black
Flame in its perfection: the "will to power" of Nietzsche in a glory
of desire: the extension of the Enlightened Will and Initiated psyche
throughout all dimensions of space, time, and thought: what in the
Aeon of Set would be Uttered as *Xeper.*

THE NINE ANGLES
OF THE SEAL

BY STEPHEN E. FLOWERS, PH.D.

Many Knights and Dames of the Order have probably been, like myself, fascinated by the powerful working called *The Ceremony of the Nine Angles* created by Grand Master Emeritus Michael Aquino for Anton LaVey's book *The Satanic Rituals*. It was always clear that the "nine angles" referred to nine angles made by the Seal of the Order of the Trapezoid: a trapezoid superimposed over a pentagram, two points aloft.

Originally published in the March 1988 issue of *Runes* (the private journal of the Order of the Trapezoid).

What I wanted to do was identify the numbers of the angles and see what magic could be wrought with this knowledge.

During the Set-VIII Conclave, I had the opportunity to discuss some of the conceptual background to *The Ceremony of the Nine Angles* with the High Priest*. He explained that in his conception the Nine Angles were beyond conventional (3-D) space and that they existed more as qualities rather than loci in space. This is an ontological aspect that must be kept in mind constantly when considering the characteristics and magical usages of the Nine Angles. In fact the Nine Angles cannot be confined to any two- or three-dimensional representation. However, on a symbolic or metaphorical level, useful and revealing insights may be gained by observing such models through the lenses of two- and three-dimensional perspectives.

In the meantime, Sir Michael has sent me a document in which he has outlined in some detail his concepts and interpretations of the nine angles. A version of this document will appear in a future issue of *Runes*—and perhaps straighten out the obscene mess you are about to read. Here I will put the model of the "nine angles" under those lenses of the two- and three-dimensional perspectives.

It seems clear to me that the nine angles were defined by the Pentagram of Set and the Trapezoid juxtaposed in the manner depicted in the Seal of the Order.

The history of this general emblem is outlined in Grand Master Emeritus Aquino's article "Evolution of the Trapezoid Insignia" in *Runes* IV:2 (March XXI), pp. 11–16. But a question always remained in my mind as to the likely location and enumeration (ordering) of the nine angles when considering this figure. A likely answer came to me in two parts. First, it is said of the Ninth Angle:

From the Ninth Angle is the flame of the beginning and ending of dimensions, which blazeth in brilliance and darkness unto the glory of desire.[1]

---

*Referring to Michael Aquino, who was High Priest of the Temple of Set at the time

Therefore, it would seem clear that the Ninth Angle is defined by the nethermost point of the Pentagram from which the Black Flame arises. Even in LaVey's conception the Infernal Flame blazed from this angle. Second, if we employ the principal of leftward (counterclockwise or widdershins) motion in our analysis, all of the angles automatically fall into place. Only one ordering and enumeration is possible when we place the ninth, or last, angle at the apex and in a unilinear fashion we trace our way through the angles in a widdershins direction:

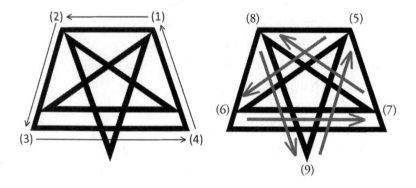

Thus a two-dimensional symbol of the ultra-dimensional reality of the Seal of Nine Angles, the **V'yn'khe Rohz** (as it is in Yuggothic), is actualized.

Practical magical uses of the **V'yn'khe Rohz** are actualized, and range over a wide spectrum of possibilities. The tracing of the angles in this configuration is a powerful mode of opening the Gates to other dimensions. It can spark a higher understanding/Understanding of the process by which phenomena within the World of Horrors, and without it, come into being. In this regard the Seal of the Nine Angles most certainly can be linked to the enneagram as taught by Gurdjieff and his followers, or with the Nine Worlds of Yggdrasill. Another operative use of the "Yankee Rose" is as a paradigmatic channel for visualized images. Visions cast through these angles by the Will of the Trapezoidal Magician shall come into being, just as all other things come into being through these Nine Angles. Whole articles could be devoted to these practical uses, which I hope will follow. I urge you to experiment.

For now let us analyze the descriptions of the Nine Angles given in *The Ceremony of the Nine Angles* and begin to unlock the secrets of this sign. For the sake of clarity in this article I will only present the English versions of the texts, leaving the secrets of Yuggothic for another night.

> From the First Angle is the infinite, wherein the laughing one doth cry and the flutes wail unto the ending of time.[2]

This is the angle of the Infinity of absolute unity—really the point, geometrically speaking. It is the unity beyond time and space, but from which both emerge. In it exist the full spectrum of emotional, spiritual polarity; joy and despair, pain and pleasure are one. In the wailing vibrations of the "obscene flute" endless manifestation is generated.

> From the Second Angle is the master who doth order the planes and the angles, and who hath conceived the World of Horrors in its terror and glory.[3]

Dualistic ordering of the World of Horrors is revealed in the geometrical ordering of the basic building blocks of the cosmos by the master (note the lowercase *m*) who has designed the World of Horrors. The point has become the line. Again an emotional polarity of terror and glory is invoked.

> From the Third Angle is the messenger, who hath created the power to behold the master of the World of Horrors, who giveth to thee substance of being and the knowledge of the Nine Angles.[4]

This is the intermediary principle of the solid triangle—and hence the two-dimensional plane. This allows for a perspective on the dualistic universe and provides geometrical solidity and thus the possibility of objective knowledge of the objective (nine-angled) cosmos.

From the Fourth Angle is the ram of the Sun, who brought thy selves
to be, who endureth upon the World of Horrors and proclaimeth
the time that was, the time that is, and the time that shall be; and
whose name is the brilliance of the Nine Angles.[5]

With the four angles the three-dimensional world becomes possible.
Here the Trapezoid is crystallized, and with it the non-natural Form of
the Self, or psyche, is also crystallized and becomes able to perceive time
and at once seeks to master it.

From the Fifth Angle are the hornless ones, who raise the temple of
the five trihedrons unto the Daemons of creation, whose seal is at
once four and five and nine.[6]

With the Fifth Angle we enter into a new level or dimension. The
Trapezoid is complete, and the Pentagram is now coming into being.
The "hornless ones" are humanity, the physical vehicle that carries the
Gift of Set and thus can become a creative (shaping) force in the World
of Horrors and beyond. In this angle lies the root of the fully developed Seal of the Order which combines the numbers $4 + 5 + 9$, which
equals 18 $(1 + 8 = 9)$ or 2×9—all of which shows the cyclical eternal
return aspect of the number nine. The Fifth Angle is the fulcrum of an
ultra-dimensional lever of great magical power, four angles "above" it
and four angles "below" it.

From the Sixth Angle is the sleep of the Daemons in symmetry,
which doth vanquish the five but shall not prevail against the four
and the nine.[7]

The Sixth Angle is a point of rest, of stasis, which is really stagna-
tion. Symmetry is stasis. This stasis has sufficient power to crush the
simple root form of the vehicle of the Gift of Set which arose in the
Fifth Angle. That is why it is imperative for the "hornless ones" to strive
"upward" to the Ninth and "downward" to the Fourth Angle in order to

Become and to be able to gather the powers and understanding to themselves to be able to overcome the stasis and death of the Sixth Angle.

From the Seventh Angle is the ruin of symmetry and the awakening of the Daemons, for the four and the nine shall prevail against the six.[8]

The Seventh Angle is a tool, a weapon, used by the awakened psyche to smash the symmetry of the Sixth Angle. This act of breaking through the barrier of symmetry and stasis needs help from powers already gained from the Fourth Angle, and also from beyond, from the Black Flame of Set itself. Between these two forces the Seventh Angle is activated, the barrier is broken through and Becoming is accelerated.

From the Eighth Angle are the Masters of the Realm, who raise the temple of the eight trihedrons unto the Daemons of creation, whose seal is at once four and five and nine.[9]

This is the Principle embodied in the Masters of the Temple, who are the Masters of the Realm. A fully manifest principle of magical sovereignty is activated and it is responsible for the building and maintenance of the Temple—the greater vehicle for the working of the Black Flame in the world.

From the Ninth Angle is the flame of the beginning and ending of dimensions, which blazeth in brilliance and darkness unto the glory of desire.[10]

The Ninth Angle is the Black Flame itself, which in truth is the beginning and ending of the unfoldment of the Seal of the Order, as discussed above. In it is the root of light and darkness. In it is the source of the Will which is beyond all good and evil.

These comments only scratch the surface of what this configuration can be made to yield to the Will of the Working Knight or

Dame. As Grand Master of the Order, I urge each of you to construct according to your Wills a simple representation of the Seal of the Nine Angles of sufficient dimension to serve as a focus of concentration in your working chambers. Through Work with this configuration of lines and angles the power of and utility of this elaborate Gate—or set of Gates—will unfold.

KEYSTONE

By Patty A. Hardy, Grand Master Emeritus of the Order of the Trapezoid

This article is the result of Sir Setnakt's provocative remarks in the April issue of *Runes* and the image of the Seal of Rûna found on the back cover of that issue among the cryptic glyphs of the *Naath-R'unai*.

Impelled by Sir Setnakt's reference to the Seal of Rûna and to those "who would try to undo its knot," I began by tracing the Seal on a sheet of paper, computing each angular measure and looking for Golden Ratios. This was easily done:

$\alpha = \pi/5$ radians $= 36°$
$\beta = 2\pi/5$ radians $= 72°$
$\gamma = 3\pi/5$ radians $= 108°$
$\delta = 3\pi/5$ radians $= 108°$
$\epsilon = 2\pi/5$ radians $= 72°$

$AC/CE = CF/EF = \phi$
$CF/CE = CG/CF = \phi$
$AG/AC = CF/AB = \phi$
$AD/DJ = IJ/JK = \phi$

Originally written in 1992.

Gazing at the figure, and seizing on such insights as it might present to me, I sensed further possibilities, and the figure seemed to unfold beyond the flat surface of the page.

Both the Grand Master* and the Grand Master Emeritus† have written commentary on the Seal of Nine. It has been associated with the Order of the Trapezoid since the days of the Church of Satan, and forms a portion of the Seal of Rûna. I consulted these commentaries and studied the Bond of the Nine Angles, in addition to contemplating the Seal of Rûna.

THE SYMBOLIC

When humans are unable to guide their actions by ordinary perceptions they resort to mathematical ideas.

J. Peter Denny, "Cultural Ecology of Mathematics," 178

What is the source of the power of a geometric symbol?

From prehistoric times, the most intelligent among humanity recognized the power of geometric symbolism. The old proverb, "a picture is worth a thousand words," simplifies the situation greatly. For evolutionary reasons the neurological equipment of human beings is biased heavily toward the interpretation of spatial information and of motion in space—think of a monkey leaping through the treetops.

Human speech grew out of the need to communicate both emotional states and information in the most compact form possible. Speech is a potent tool, yet it is poorly suited by itself for certain types of information nor is it the only expression of the human capacity to abstract. The use of pictures keyed to oral explanation and experience to signify processes involving visualization and complex coordination would have been one of the earliest discoveries of humanity, and one ideally suited

---

*Stephen E. Flowers at the time of the original article
†Here referring to Michael A. Aquino

to the transmission of secret knowledge: prediction of future celestial and earthly events, architectural designs and procedures, and all sorts of process-description.

Unlike phonetic writing, which discloses its message to anyone who can recognize the relationship between glyph and sound, the abstract pictograph or glyph guards its content, disclosing it only to one who has access to initiated explanation OR one whose native talents, intuition, and experience are sufficient to recognize the reality which gave birth to the symbol.

Mathematical notation stands somewhere between these two realms, being in theory accessible to all. J. Peter Denny has argued that abstraction of this kind is useless to humans who do not change their environment—what we would call natural humans—and points to the differences in level of articulation of basic geometric and arithmetic concepts between hunting-band societies, trading cultures, and members of industrial societies.

Yet at all times individuals existed who sought to comprehend and command the world through dealings with unseen powers, and who in this regard stood apart from the rest of their culture. It is this elite which formulates its understanding as esoteric diagrams.

Let it be observed that there is nothing mystical about this matter; it is the antithesis of mysticism. However fraught with error the beliefs of a priesthood or guild might have been, the original power of the group lay in the grasp of some extremely practical secret unknown to the masses, concealed in their symbols—this is what Massey dubs "the physical nature of the Gnosis." An uninitiated person perceiving what lay behind the symbolism had to be brought into that cult as one deserving of its prerogatives, or else silenced to protect the secret.

Before proceeding to discussion of the Seal itself I mention two more facets of visual abstraction that may be important.

The first concerns perspective and aspective representation. The Egyptologist Heinrich Schaefer has demonstrated, in comparing Greek and Egyptian representational art, that their treatment of space and content proceeds from fundamentally different assumptions.

Perspective representation entails a set of conscious ideas about space and point-of-view which are neither obvious nor necessary. "Primitive" art the world over, and the drawings of children and most persons unfamiliar with art, are indifferent to perspective. In aspective representation, position and size pertain to meaning rather than visual appearance. While this may take crude forms, such as is found in drawings where the size of a person indicates their importance rather than their height, aspective representation may conceal some information from those unfamiliar with the graphical conventions involved. When interpreting a geometric emblem both systems of representation must be kept in mind.

Finally, neurological factors may be important in perceiving the meaning and intent of geometric and mathematical symbolism. While a general cross-sensory mapping of spatial orientation takes place in the thalamus, an ancient part of the brain, discrimination of angles and construction of perspective from visual cues takes place in the cerebral cortex. There is medical and practical evidence that visualization is subject to hemispheric lateralization, being one of the strengths of the "nonverbal" hemisphere of the brain.

It is possible that prolonged active contemplation of abstract geometric forms causes unusual patterns of brain activity and facilitates changes in consciousness (see H. P. Lovecraft's short story "The Dreams in the Witch-House"). This power to change consciousness through passive contemplation has traditionally been ascribed to the abstract mandalas and *yantras* of Asia, and it is certainly a belief implicit in Western sacred geometry. Neurological signs of such effects could conceivably be detected via EEG testing but to my knowledge this has not yet been attempted.

THE FORM OF THE HIDDEN

The trapezoid superimposed on the non-natural pentagram and resting on the circle of the natural order forms a conceptual bridge between these distinct realms. This suggested a spatial reinterpretation of the figure before me: the circle occupying one plane, the pentagram another,

and the trapezoid forming a path between those planes. The Seal then appeared as a projection onto the page of a pathway between planes.

Having realized this, I questioned my perception of the Seal. For if this were a perspective sketch, what were the true forms involved?

Here it is appropriate to mention some little-known mathematical facts about "occult" insignia.

Writers on the history and philosophy of mathematics state that the Pythagoreans did not extend the concept of dimensionality beyond solid geometry, and that the idea of higher dimensions could not take hold until the rise of analytic geometry in Europe centuries later. I can find no evidence to fault this view. Yet I find it singularly suspicious that the pentagram, the badge of the Pythagorean brotherhood, is not only a key to the Golden Ratio but a two-dimensional projection of the interior vertices of the pentahedroid or hypertetrahedron, the simplest possible four-dimensional figure.

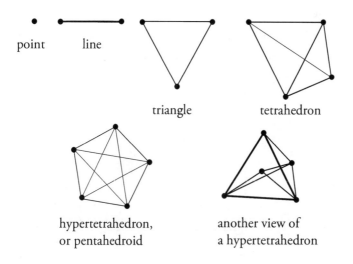

point   line

triangle   tetrahedron

hypertetrahedron,
or pentahedroid

another view of
a hypertetrahedron

Nor is this the only "occult" symbol of hyperdimensional aspect. Denning and Phillips have documented the appearance of the ogdoadic star in Renaissance art and identified it with a hermetic tradition. Whether this be true or no, they have described a modern occult group making use of this symbol. It is easy to compare the ogdoadic star with a two-dimensional perspective view of a tesseract, or hypercube, and see that the ogdoadic star is a tracing of the interior vertices of this figure.

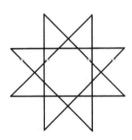 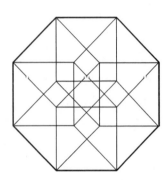

Equally curious, from a mathemagical perspective, is the fact that another conventional perspective representation of the hypercube shows this: six cubes are distorted in ordinary space to appear as truncated pyramids bridging the *ana* and *kata* cubes of the hypercube [shown below at the right]. (*Ana/kata* are the polarities that Rudy Rucker uses to refer to direction along a fourth spatial axis perpendicular to the three of our normal experience, *up/down, right/left,* and *near/far.*)

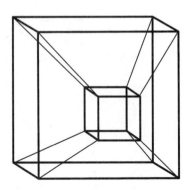

Returning to consideration of the Seal, then—the possibility exists that this form is a representation of a dimensional gate bridging the natural order and the non-natural realm of consciousness. The trapezoid is the keystone of this gate, having the traditional form of the keystone of an arch, being mutually defined by the ring of nature in size and by the non-natural, hyperdimensional pentagram in essential form. The threshold of this portal is formed by the points of contact with the natural order.

As I have remarked, a geometric figure, especially a unicursal figure, may describe a process. Time is frequently treated as the fourth dimension of our experience. To this interpretation of the Seal I now turn.

THE TRACING OF THE NINE ANGLES

During correspondence on this topic, Sir Setnakt drew my attention to the Pythagorean aspect of the Bond of the Nine Angles; the notes of the Grand Master Emeritus on the Seal of Nine treat this Pythagorean symbolism in detail. A brief summary follows.

The Bond of the Nine Angles distinguishes the first four Angles associated with the trapezoid from the subsequent five Angles of the pentagram. The first four Angles are closely identified with Lovecraftian *neteru,* or Forms, establishing the fundamental character of our consciousness: Azathoth's chaos; the dualistic and dimensional ordering defined by Yog-Sothoth; Nyarlathotep's message of consciousness; and the endurance of Shub-Niggurath, who defines temporal perspective. The connection between these concepts and Pythagorean numerical philosophy—the point, the line, the triangle, and the solid tetrahedron—is evident.

These latter powers—self-consciousness and temporal perspective—have triggered an unfolding of various non-natural historical events: the raising of the Pyramids under the rule of initiatory schools and the sleep, "not dead but dreaming," of those schools during the rule of an aggressive and imperial monotheism. With the Aeon of Horus (and with the Theosophical "New Age" introduced at the same time—note that the Yin/Yang logo lacks all angularity, yet poses a subtle challenge to symmetry) these initiatory schools have "awakened" and in our time have brought forth Masters. It is not without interest that it is the third and fourth Angles, those of self-consciousness and temporal perspective, which touch the ring of the natural order in the Seal of Rûna prior to launching these temporal manifestations.

The Seal of Rûna may thus embody a description of the relationship of these *neteru* or Forms in an inner, creative realm, and the temporal unfolding of their potential in the outer realms defined via contact with the natural order. That's a macrocosmic interpretation. Microcosmic interpretations involve application of the *neteru* or associated Pythagorean ideas for structuring the manifestation of concepts in the World of Horrors. Thus the phrase, "casting a vision through the angles."

Here is a simple example. Social change starts with the status quo, a function of mindlessness. Participants are blind to their contribution to a situation, indeed cannot perceive the situation, being embedded in it. This is the "Idiot God" stage. Since it is only possible to discriminate any stimulus by observing a difference, the first step in awareness comes when somebody observes a case where custom isn't observed, yet the sky doesn't fall and the spirits don't smite the heretic.

Once de-identification takes place, it is possible to distinguish necessity from custom, and the newly aware individual can "behold the master of the World of Horrors," tracing out the process by which the custom arose. Finally, the one who makes change—the one who triggers the evolutionary War in Heaven—is the Luciferic spirit who goes hither and yon "raising consciousness" ("the ram of the Sun, who brought thyselves to be") and slicing the timeless perpetuity of the status quo into "the time that was, the time that is, and the time that shall be." At this point, a concept has been launched from inner planes into the World of Horrors, from dream into action.

What of the process of manifestation associated with the five Angles of the pentagram? Wilson and Shea, in *The Illuminatus! Trilogy*, avow that a fivefold treatment of historical process is the guarded secret of the

Illuminati, and put forth a tongue-in-cheek exposition of this theory. I mention this to alert the reader to the possibility that we are engaged in an exercise illustrative of Wilson's Law of Fives, the principle that all events and processes can be related to the number five given enough ingenuity. On the other hand I find it curious that Sun Tzu's analysis of warfare—now hawked in bookstores as a tract applicable to business— begins with strategic assessment of five factors critical to success, and that the product-development cycle used by one large corporation is divided into five phases.

More relevant, perhaps, are mathemagical hints found in patterns of natural growth: phyllotaxis, the shell of the nautilus, the horn of the ram. These are examples of gnomonic expansion, a proportioned growth peculiar to life, resulting in invariance of form. Living beings alone produce forms of pentagonal symmetry. The Hidden includes secrets about the fashion in which the will-to-live has taken tangible form. Do these secrets apply to the trajectory the magician must consider as the vision is cast through the widdershins spin of the Nine Angles?

People speak of an idea having a life of its own, but can we find any formalization of this concept that will serve us in understanding and predicting the spread of ideas? The psychohistory of Hari Seldon is not here yet; it may well be asked if such a thing is possible. Forecasting is more an art than a science, even though new tools and theories are constantly being invented and explored.

Evolutionary biologists have written of "memes"—constellations of ideas and beliefs whose propagation and development seem analogous to that of parasitic and symbiotic life forms—and students of organizational behavior have begun to consider broad-spectrum theories of interaction that span biological systems, computer systems, and market transactions. Whether these strange cross-disciplinary efforts will develop into revolutionary scientific fields of practical application, as cybernetics did, remains to be seen. What we seek is not so much the ability to forecast the future as the ability to identify natural-order constraints and inertial factors that influence the trajectory of change.

THE DOOR

Late in the work on this essay I "stepped back" from the Seal of Rûna and tried to look at it once again with a fresh perspective. I noticed the simple elements: the geometric star, the trapezoid, and the circle. I recalled the image in *2001: A Space Odyssey,* the rising of the sun over the black monolith—which, from the perspective of the viewer, was a trapezoidal form—and a further thought occurred to me. I thought of the Daemons of Creation in the Bond of the Nine Angles, and recalled that the Egyptians used the same word, *s'ba,* for three ideas: star, door, teach.

This is not the place to delve into a treatment of archeo-astronomy. But we who speak of the Powers of Darkness should not forget that H. P. Lovecraft was an amateur astronomer as well as a dreamer, that the ceremony in which the Bond of the Nine Angles is recited was to be illuminated by controlled moonlight or starlight, and that the King's Chamber of the Temple of the Five Trihedrons was lit by channels admitting the light of certain stars. The Grand Master has spoken of the magnetic pull of the ring of Nature that draws the Self through the Nine Angles; the sense of exaltation the Elect feel under the light of the stars is the expression of that hunger for the Unknown as it is evoked by Nature in its immensity.

While this paper takes an intellectual approach, the intellectual pursuit of the supra-rational is met with due response from the Hidden realms of the psyche. When I checked my diary I noticed that the first mention of my study of the Seal was dated precisely eighteen days prior to the Transformation Working of June 18–19: I had fallen asleep after computing the angular measures and experienced dreams about the past and the future.

During the Transformation Working itself I framed the momentum set up by the conscious trajectory of my life—the choices made while awake—as the force behind the launch of a specific idea. My notes on process under "The Tracing of the Nine Angles" were the result of this focus on manifestation of will.

There can be no final conclusion. I have put forth a few of my thoughts and speculations concerning the Seal of Rûna and the secrets concealed in its geometric form. Any widening of the perimeter of the Known must entail a proportional increase in the scope of the Unknown, yet this inquiry expands and enhances the Self rather than diminishing it before the Hidden. Thus the motto of that perpetual Quest as the Magus of Rûna has formulated it: *Reyn til Rúna*.

BIBLIOGRAPHY

Aquino, Michael A. "Commentary on the Seal of the Nine Angles." *Runes* 6, no. 3 (June 1988): 1–4.

———. "Lovecraftian Ritual." *Nyctalops* 13 (May 1977): 3–6.

———. "The Ceremony of the Nine Angles." In *The Satanic Rituals* by Anton LaVey, 181–193. New York: Avon Books, 1972.

Dawkins, Richard. "Memes: The New Replicators." In *The Selfish Gene*, 189–201. 2nd edition. Oxford: Oxford University Press, 1989.

Denny, J. Peter. "Cultural Ecology of Mathematics: Ojibway and Inuit Hunters." In *Native American Mathematics*, edited by Michael P. Closs, 129–180. Austin: University of Texas Press, 1986.

Flowers, Stephen E. "V'Yn'Khe Rohz: The Cycle of Nine." *Runes* 10, no. 5 (September 1992): 1–10.

Goldstein, E. Bruce. *Sensation and Perception*. 3rd edition. Belmont: Wadsworth, 1989.

Hardy, Patty A. "Horizonglass." *Scroll of Set* 15, no. 2 (April XXIV): 1–2.

Malone, Thomas W., and Kevin Crowston. "What Is Coordination Theory and How Can It Help Design Cooperative Work Systems?" In *Proceedings of the Third Conference on Computer-Supported Cooperative Work*. Los Angeles: ACM Press, 1990.

Massey, Gerald. *The Natural Genesis*. London: Williams and Norgate, 1883.

Rucker, Rudy. *The Fourth Dimension: Towards a Geometry of Higher Reality*. Boston: Houghton Mifflin, 1984.

Shaefer, Heinrich. *Principles of Egyptian Art*. Oxford: Clarendon Press, 1974.

Tompkins, Peter. *Secrets of the Great Pyramid*. New York: Harper & Row, 1971.

Tzu, Sun. *The Art of War*. Oxford: Oxford University Press, 1963.

Vinette, Francine. "In Search of Mesoamerican Geometry." In *Native American*

Mathematics, edited by Michael P. Closs, 387–407. Austin: University of Texas Press, 1986.

Whitaker, Roger L. "Neuronal Tracings and the Physiology of Angular Prosthesis." *Runes* 9, no. 3 (August XXVI): 2–7.

Wilson, Robert Anton, and Robert Shea. *The Illuminatus! Trilogy*. New York: Dell Publishing Co., 1975.

THE ALCHEMY OF YGGDRASILL

BY STEPHEN E. FLOWERS, PH.D.

I. ALCHEMY OF THE NORTH

The Northern Tradition understands well the principles of alchemy. Its very cosmology, cosmogony, and eschatology are expressed in formulas any alchemist could understand—if they have learned to ask the right questions. This methodical investigating of the mysteries (reyn til rúna) of how things are created, developed, and transformed is keyed, like so much else of the Hidden Heritage, to the ninefold paradigm. This nine-fold symbol, with significant variations, is also known in traditional Northern studies as the Valknútr—Knot of the Chosen, or Slain, or among the Persian brethren as the Naqsh—whence the Gurdjieffian Enneagram.

Alchemy is a technology of transformation not limited to any one kingdom of existence—it can transform mineral, vegetable, animal, or spiritual "substances." There is no one formula for this technology—even the classical Western alchemists of the Middle Ages and Renaissance used variations in their formulas. We will learn nothing

---

Also available in *Blue Rûna: Edred's Shorter Works Vol. III (1988–1994)* (Rûna-Raven, 2001).

of practical value if we simply impose the classic alchemical formulas upon data foreign to them. Independent data—such as the traditional cosmogonic process of the ancient North—can teach us new formulas if we proceed in a precise way informed by inspiration.

In a practical sense what appears here is a formula for the **generation** (creation) of any desired thing—be it an object, situation, or state of being.

II. NORTHERN COSMOGONY

The ancient Germanic cosmogony is most clearly and continuously outlined in sections of 2–19 of the *Edda,* written by an Icelander named Snorri Sturluson around 1222 CE. Although ostensibly a Christian, he was far more interested in preserving the heritage of his Northern ancestors than he was in any form of Church (or even Classical) Teaching.

The *Edda* tells us that in the beginning there was nothing but *Ginnunga-gap* (magically charged void). This interpretation of *Ginnunga-gap* was offered by the great Germanic philologist, Jan de Vries, in an article published in 1930 in the *Acta Philologica Scandinavica* (vol. 5). At the southern extreme of this void arose Fire (*Muspellsheimr*) and at the northern extreme arose Water (*Niflheimr*). These polar opposites were attracted to each other. As the Fire neared the Water, Space (Air) manifested—through which sparks flew toward *Niflheimr*. But as the Water of *Niflheimr* neared the center it hardened (and expanded) into Ice, which contains solid Salts and extrudes from its essence a Venom—which is struck by sparks of Iron. These sparks activated a Yeast (living substance) in the liquefied Ice. [Note that the Ice contains three substances: Salt (solid), Venom (vapor), and Yeast (liquid).]

Where these elements converge in the mild midst of *Ginnunga-gap,* there arise two beings from the dripping Ice: first Ymir (a proto-humanoid form) and then Auðumbla (the cosmic bovine). Ymir lives on the milk produced from Auðumbla's udders and she lives by licking the Salty Ice. Out of the Ice Auðumbla forms the shape of a second humanoid: Buri. Buri replicated himself asexually and thus Borr came into being.

In the meantime Ymir also produced other humanoid entities: under his left arm there grew a pair of humanoids, but his left foot engendered with his right foot a whole race of frost-giants (Old Norse: hrím*þursar*).

A daughter of the "frost-giant" <u>Böl</u>þorn, named Bestla, mated with Borr. Borr and Bestla had three sons: Óðinn–Vili–Vé. This is really a threefold but singular entity, who is/are the first of the race of Æsir.

Óðinn–Vili–Vé rebelled and killed their maternal ancestor, Ymir, and from the parts of his form they shaped the cosmic order—arranging the earth in the middle and rationally ordering the rest of the cosmos. The stars, sun, and moon are appointed their places, etc.).

The Æsir actually created dwarves to compete the work of physical creation. (This point is clear only in the Elder or Poetic *Edda*.)

Óðinn then undertakes the Ordeal of Yggdrasill—he hangs himself on the World Tree in order to gain Runic Knowledge. On the Tree he apprehends the ultimate Mystery, and returns to enact what he has learned.

Óðinn then undertakes the building of an enclosure of the gods (Æsir)—called *Ásgarðr*. From *Ásgarðr,* Óðinn ventures out (again in his threefold aspect) and discovers the natural bodies of human beings. In the text these are symbolically represented as "trees" named *"Askr"* (Ash) and *"Embla"* (Elm?). Upon these the threefold Gift is bestowed: Consciousness, Life-Breath, and Aesthetic Form.

This brief, and in some places simplified, recounting of the cosmogonic process outlined in Snorri's *Edda* and elsewhere in Germanic mythological texts will serve as a basis for further discussion. A complete study of all the details of the process (which has been undertaken) expands, but does not fundamentally alter, the "alchemical" and Ennegonic Formula.

It is clear that the threefold entity known as Óðinn ("Master of Inspired Consciousness") is the first consciously creative entity in this process. He is the result of a synthesis of the polar extremes of Fire/Air and Water/Ice, and so contains all the potential present in the original magical charge of *Ginnunga-gap*. Óðinn then proceeds to act as the "first alchemist." He takes the base substance (Ymir) and subjects it to an analysis (*solve*); it is broken up and broken down into its component parts and rearranged according to the subjective (semi-conscious) contents of Óðinn's mind and will.

A study of the meaning of the three names of Óðinn–Vili–Vé reveals the Secret here: Óðinn = "Master of Inspired Consciousness," Vili = "Volition," and Vé = "Sacrality" (i.e., the conscious division between sacred and profane—the quality of conscious discrimination). Óðinn is the first individual being with these three qualities: Transcendental Consciousness possessed of Will and able to Discriminate between "this" and "that."

III. ALCHEMICAL PRINCIPLES

In the Germanic cosmogony presented above certain features consistent with those we also know as alchemical clearly emerge. There is a movement from primal unity (a coagulated state) through an analytical process (dissolution) into a transformed, re-coagulated state, each time under the guidance of an increasingly more awakened consciousness. This is carried out through confrontations between polarized qualities most simply explained as concepts of Form (Water–Ice, etc.) and Energy (Fire–Air, etc.). The Germanic cosmogonic mythos provides a doorway to learning of the Secret of how to bring things into being. This doorway can be unlocked by those who learn how to use the ninefold key which opens it.

The primal, or first, unity is *Ginnunga-gap*. In it all things are contained. It is beyond all limitations of time and space; in it are unified in a completely undifferentiated way all polar opposites—*Ginnung* is the absolute unity of Form Mass and Energy. The cosmos emerges from this undifferentiated chaos and returns to it on a cyclical basis.

Before any conscious, or even living beings can come into existence, four pairs of opposing elements must manifest and be activated:

THE GERMANIC COSMOGONICAL ELEMENTS

Form	Energy
Water	Fire
Ice	Air
Iron	Yeast
Salt	Venom

The first two pairs (1–2) manifest the concrete order of the cosmos, while the second two pairs (3–4) constitute the manifestation of living information in the natural cosmic order. Most of the cosmic ordering is made up of substances and processes restricted to the first two pairs. The living information (genetic code) dynamically, but still from our perspective unconsciously, evolves to a point where enough information (from *Ginnung) has been cross-referenced to make a mutation into a semi-conscious being possible. This is the first of the Æsir:* Óðinn–Vili–Vé—the first reunification of the spectrum of all the qualities present in *Ginnung*.

However, this (re-)unified entity is not yet a fully conscious (divine) being. His first impulse is to rebel—to destroy the root from which he sprang and to reorder it in a way more in accordance with his will. This is the first self-aware act of creation. The creation is carried out under the guidance of a conscious and rational plan. Here all the hidden and mysterious laws of nature are laid down. Essential to the process is that the "old order" was deconstructed (Ymir killed and dismembered) and a new order established (from the parts of the old order) according to the subjective will of the creator.

Having established certain laws of nature—that is, archetypal processes—which take on lives of their own, the Æsir create a host of agents of formation (dwarves, or dark-elves) which act as the craftsmen who bring into physical reality the ingeniously fashioned principles of the Æsir. The dwarves are well known in Germanic mythology as the craftsmen of the gods.

They are the technicians who execute the plans of the gods, but why are also freed by their semi-conscious status to create all manner of forms (including mutations and manipulations of mineral substances, as well as vegetable and animal species). In this process the Æsir are absent as they have withdrawn into another dimension to contemplate the next, most momentous alchemical work.

Óðinn emerges from his withdrawal to undergo the Ordeal of Yggdrasill—in which he extends the essence of himself throughout the structure of the world-order which he has fashioned—he contemplates his own Self through the World-Tree which acts as a multidimensional mirror of that Self. The culmination of this act is the apprehension of the ultimate Mystery (*Rúna*) and the gaining of real Runic Knowledge.

This moment of realization that there is something greater than that of which the Aesir were conscious when they first shaped the World is the result of their contemplation of the entirety of the Work. The possibility of something even greater than self-awareness arises— and although the keys to this Mystery are imparted to Óðinn (in the form of the Runes) it is also clear that these are only keys and that an eternal Quest is necessary to actualize them.

All Knowledge gained in this Quest is then used as a program for further development as well as for the creation of further plans for the evolution of the original creation.

The first act Óðinn undertakes with this new Knowledge is the building of *Ásgarðr*—a separate, shielded fortress in which the experiment in divine evolution can be carried out.

But this separate fortress, which transcends the mundane universe, must be grounded. It must have a form or vehicle in the mundane universe for purposes of its own evolution, and it must also have a direct connection with the mundane, or horizontal, universe itself.

In order to effect this link, the threefold Óðinnic entity ventures out from *Ásgarðr* and takes the natural bodies of human beings (really nothing more than ape-like creatures) and endows them with the threefold Gift of Consciousness, Life-Breath, and Aesthetic Form. Perhaps the reason why they are symbolized as trees is that these humanoid creatures were, at that point purely creatures of appetite—

serving a function little more significant than eating and excreting.

But endowed with the divine Gifts, humans (*mannoz*) become Agents of Consciousness in the horizontal plane. What the dwarves were to the creation of the natural cosmos—helpers and allies—human beings are to the continuing creation of the non-natural realms.

IV. ANGULAR ALCHEMY

Angles are complex entities. They are essentially defined by two lines which converge at a given point in space and which can be further defined by the precise quality of the relationship one line has to the other (e.g., the number of degrees between the two lines). There are also many hidden dimensions behind each angle.

Those who have studied the Seal of Rûna will have suspected the nature of the ninefold key to unlocking this alchemical process: an aperture between the original unity of *Ginnungagap* and the realms of manifestation is created by the first Angle (**Chaos**). This chaotic unity is broken by the second Angle (**Order**) which describes the manifestation of the four principle elements (Water/Fire/Ice/Air). The third Angle (**Knowledge**) manifests the patterns of life and establishes the pathways of information.

A second unity is established in the fourth Angle (**Being**) as the life/coded information process engendered in the third Angle is completed in the form of the first beings capable of self-knowledge. The ring of nature and the trapezoid are completed with the forging of the fifth Angle (**Creation**) as the Æsir rebel against the established order, overthrow it and create the cosmos anew in their own images. The sixth angle (**Death/Sleep**) is a moment of stasis for the Æsiric creators as they allow their demiurges, or craftsmen, the dwarves, to finish the physical cosmos according to the principles established by the Aesir in the creation of the dwarves themselves.

In the seventh Angle (**Birth/Awakening**) **the Ordeal of Yggdrasil is completed wherein** Óðinn becomes conscious of something greater than himSelf, and something which laid outside his consciousness when he reshaped the World (in the fifth Angle)—this something is the Mystery (*Rúna*). This initiatory experience Transforms Óðinn into a god among gods. He is conscious as is no other god of his own limitation and even ignorance, he learns to see more and more clearly and to dream yet more inspired visions of what the divine realm could be. This leads him to design and have constructed the Enclosure of/for the Gods, *Ásgarðr,* as an idealized community of conscious entities. This is a place where he plans for them to evolve and develop, and is indicative of the eighth Angle (**Re-creation**). The re-creation is not a carbon copy of the first creation, it is now informed by a Sense of Mystery (*Rúna*) and other information gained in the experience of the seventh angle, *Ásgarðr* is, however, the ultimate staging ground for Becoming throughout the Worlds.

The process first set into motion from a previously unknown, or unarticulated, original point begins to come full circle when the threefold Gift is bestowed upon a natural creature—*Mannaz*. However, this process, the subject—the enactor—of which is the Flame, cannot come full circle until the Gifted Race brings it full circle of their own volition—through initiation. This ultimate realization of the source of consciousness, the Flame, closes the cycle and in so doing shall create a new race of gods.

V. CONCLUSIONS

One of the essential Runic messages of the exploration of this process is the alchemical Necessity of returning to the roots of things in order to transform them. The exhortation *Reyn til Rúna* mandates a return to the essential, original Forms of things, constantly synthesizing them with the subject's present state of Being. This often necessitates the periodic, and perhaps only temporary, rejection of tradition for its own sake. This process creates a moment of pure Wakefulness, and having awoken, the initiate sees, and having seen the initiate acts effectively with knowledge.

In this article we have presented the outlines of a guide to the successful completion of a complex creative process—any complex creative process—whether it is building a house or creating a new universe.

The alchemic theory presented here is not only a key to the creation and transformation of things/phenomena in the "objective universe," but also a structural map to certain aspects of the subjective universe— the self which is the true subject of initiation.

This study is far from a complete discussion of the alchemical Mysteries present in the Ennegonic Formula of Yggdrasil. What you have before you is not an end, but only an eternal beginning, with so much more to discover than what we already know about the process, what lies in Skuld looks to be full of power and wonder.

The R'lyehian Alphabet

Based on the Work of Tmythos
(Tim McGranahan)

In 1992, a Knight of the Order of the Trapezoid named Sir Tmythos (Timothy McGranahan) published for the internal use of the Order a suitably "alien" alphabet for transcribing the Yuggothic language. While a font rendering these glyphs has been previously released publicly via the H. P. Lovecraft Historical Society, this is the first time the alphabet is available—in its complete context—outside the Order.

Three forms are presented for each letter: the written R'lyehian form, the printed R'lyehian form, and the Latin alphabet (with notes as appropriate).

THE R'LYEHIAN ALPHABET

Written	Printed	Latin	Written	Printed	Latin
(glyph)	(glyph)	'	(glyph)	(glyph)	H
(glyph)	(glyph)	Y*	(glyph)	(glyph)	B
(glyph)	(glyph)	N	(glyph)	(glyph)	R
(glyph)	(glyph)	C, K, Q, K†	(glyph)	(glyph)	U¶
(glyph)	(glyph)	S	(glyph)	(glyph)	M
(glyph)	(glyph)	T	(glyph)	(glyph)	A\\
(glyph)	(glyph)	V, W	(glyph)	(glyph)	1
(glyph)	(glyph)	G	(glyph)	(glyph)	2
(glyph)	(glyph)	L	(glyph)	(glyph)	3
(glyph)	(glyph)	I, E, Y‡	(glyph)	(glyph)	4
(glyph)	(glyph)	O	(glyph)	(glyph)	5
(glyph)	(glyph)	P	(glyph)	(glyph)	6
(glyph)	(glyph)	D	(glyph)	(glyph)	7
(glyph)	(glyph)	Z, J§	(glyph)	(glyph)	8
(glyph)	(glyph)	F	(glyph)	(glyph)	9

*As consonant.
†Always pronounced hard, as in "cat."
‡As vowel.
§Pronounced "zh" as in "seizure."
¶Always prounounced as a long vowel, as in "true."
\\Always pronounced as a short vowel, as in "father."

NOTES

CHAPTER 1.
OVERVIEW OF THE NINE ANGLES

1. Aquino, *The Church of Satan*, 164.
2. Aquino, *The Ceremony of the Nine Angles*, 189.
3. Aquino, *The Ceremony of the Nine Angles*, 189.
4. Aquino, *The Ceremony of the Nine Angles*, 189–90.
5. Aquino, *The Ceremony of the Nine Angles*, 190.
6. Aquino, *The Ceremony of the Nine Angles*, 190.
7. Aquino, "Charter of the Order of the Trapezoid," in *The Temple of Set*, 81.
8. Aquino, *The Ceremony of the Nine Angles*, 191.
9. Aquino, *The Ceremony of the Nine Angles*, 191.
10. Aquino, *The Ceremony of the Nine Angles*, 191.
11. Aquino, *The Ceremony of the Nine Angles*, 191.

CHAPTER 2.
HISTORICAL ANTECEDENTS

1. Boyer, *A History of Mathematics*, 7.
2. LaVey, *The Satanic Rituals*, 219.
3. Bauschatz, *The Well and the Tree*, 14.
4. Webb, "Xeper: The Eternal Word of Set."
5. List, *The Secret of the Runes*, trans. Flowers, 69.
6. Levenda, *The Dark Lord*, 250.
7. Flowers and Moynihan, *The Secret King*, 43.
8. Flowers and Moynihan, *The Secret King*, 83.
9. Flowers and Moynihan, *The Secret King*, 79. Translation slightly modified.

10. Webb, *The Harmonious Circle*, 505.
11. Webb, *The Harmonious Circle*, 512.
12. LaVey, *The Satanic Bible*, 155.
13. Aquino, *The Temple of Set*, 269.
14. LaVey, *The Satanic Bible*, 192.
15. Lovecraft, *The Doom that Came to Sarnath and Other Stories*, 37.

CHAPTER 3. ANGULAR MAGIC WITHIN THE CHURCH OF SATAN AND THE TEMPLE OF SET

1. LaVey, *The Satanic Rituals*, 219.
2. LaVey, *The Satanic Rituals*, 107.
3. Long, "The Hounds of Tindalos," 247.
4. LaVey, *The Satanic Rituals*, 110–11.
5. Doreal, *The Emerald Tablets*, 44.
6. Howard, "The God in the Bowl," in *The Coming of Conan the Cimmerian*, 66.
7. Kincaid [LaVey], "An Explanation of the Role of the Council of the Trapezoid," 4.
8. LaVey, *The Satanic Rituals*, 175.
9. LaVey, *The Satanic Rituals*, 176.
10. Lovecraft, *Selected Letters*, vol. 5, 120.
11. Webb, *Uncle Setnakt's Nightbook*, 220–1.
12. Price, *The Azathoth Cycle*, v–vi.
13. Price, *The Azathoth Cycle*, vi.
14. Lovecraft, *The Dream-Quest of Unknown Kadath*, 3.
15. Lovecraft, *Bloodcurdling Tales*, 172.
16. Lovecraft, *Bloodcurdling Tales*, 304.
17. Lovecraft, *Bloodcurdling Tales*, 220.
18. Lovecraft, *Bloodcurdling Tales*, 111.
19. Lovecraft, *The Dream-Quest of Unknown Kadath*, 182.
20. Lovecraft, *Bloodcurdling Tales*, 215.
21. Lovecraft, *Selected Letters*, vol. 1, 161.
22. Lovecraft, *The Doom that Came to Sarnath and Other Stories*, 57.
23. Lovecraft, *Bloodcurdling Tales*, 83.
24. Lovecraft, *Bloodcurdling Tales*, 84.
25. Lovecraft, *Bloodcurdling Tales*, 214.

26. Lovecraft, *Bloodcurdling Tales,* 298.

27. Aquino, *The Ceremony of the Nine Angles,* 189.

28. Lovecraft, *Bloodcurdling Tales,* 304.

29. Aquino, *The Ceremony of the Nine Angles,* 189.

30. Aquino, *The Ceremony of the Nine Angles,* 189–90.

31. Aquino, *The Ceremony of the Nine Angles,* 189.

32. Aquino, *The Ceremony of the Nine Angles,* 190.

33. Flowers, "Wisdom for the Wolf-Age."

34. Flowers, "Wisdom for the Wolf-Age."

35. Flowers, *Rúnarmál I,* 9.

36. Flowers, "The Alchemy of Yggdrasill," 20–21.

37. Flowers, "The Alchemy of Yggdrasill," 23.

38. Aquino, *The Ceremony of the Nine Angles,* 190.

CHAPTER 4. THE FOUNDATIONS OF GEOMETRY IN MAGICAL PRACTICES

1. Arthur C. Clarke, *2001,* 243–44.

2. Grant, *The Magical Revival,* 4.

3. Kincaid [LaVey], "An Explanation of the Role of the Council of the Trapezoid," 4.

4. Frater U∴D∴, *High Magic,* 69.

5. Aquino, *The Ceremony of the Nine Angles,* 189.

6. Lawlor, *Sacred Geometry,* 6.

7. Barrie, *The Sacred In-Between,* 35.

8. Lawlor, *Sacred Geometry,* 8.

9. Lovecraft and Price, "Through the Gates of the Silver Key," 197–98.

CHAPTER 5. A THEORY OF MAGIC

1. Flowers, *Runes and Magic,* 9.

2. Flowers, *Runes and Magic,* 12.

3. Baal, *Symbols for Communication,* 263.

4. Aquino, *The Church of Satan,* 164

5. Mortensen, *The Command to Look,* 44.

6. Mortensen, *The Command to Look,* 51.

7. Mortensen, *The Command to Look,* 63.

8. Mortensen, *The Command to Look,* 45.

9. Mortensen, *The Command to Look,* 47.

10. Mortensen, *The Command to Look,* 47.

11. Mortensen, *The Command to Look,* 47–49.

12. Aquino, *The Church of Satan,* 377.

CHAPTER 6. THE THREE RITES OF ANGULAR MAGIC ANALYZED

1. *Satanis: The Devil's Mass,* dir. Ray Laurent, 66:06.

2. Aquino, *The Church of Satan,* 248–49.

3. LaVey, *The Satanic Rituals,* 111.

4. LaVey, *The Satanic Bible,* 189.

5. LaVey, *The Satanic Bible,* 192.

6. Cook and Russell, *Heinrich Himmler's Camelot,* 3–4.

7. Cook and Russell, *Heinrich Himmler's Camelot,* 22.

8. LaVey, *The Satanic Rituals,* 117.

9. LaVey, *The Satanic Rituals,* 117.

10. LaVey, *The Satanic Rituals,* 118.

11. LaVey, *The Satanic Rituals,* 118.

12. LaVey, *The Satanic Rituals,* 108.

13. LaVey, *The Satanic Rituals,* 119.

14. LaVey, *The Satanic Rituals,* 119.

15. Doreal, *The Emerald Tablets,* 46.

16. LaVey, *The Satanic Rituals,* 121.

17. LaVey, *The Satanic Rituals,* 122–23.

18. Aquino, *The Church of Satan,* 164.

19. LaVey, *The Satanic Rituals,* 122.

20. LaVey, *The Satanic Rituals,* 123.

21. LaVey, *The Satanic Rituals,* 123.

22. LaVey, *The Satanic Rituals,* 123.

23. LaVey, *The Satanic Rituals,* 124.

24. LaVey, *The Satanic Rituals,* 126.

25. LaVey, *The Satanic Rituals,* 126.

26. LaVey, *The Satanic Rituals,* 127.

27. LaVey, *The Satanic Rituals,* 127–28.

28. LaVey, *The Satanic Rituals*, 129.

29. Aquino, *The Ceremony of the Nine Angles*, 182.

30. Aquino, *The Ceremony of the Nine Angles*, 183.

31. Aquino, *The Church of Satan*, 1099.

32. Fowles, *The Magus*, 540–41.

33. Aquino, *The Ceremony of the Nine Angles*, 184.

34. Aquino, *The Ceremony of the Nine Angles*, 186.

35. Aquino, *The Ceremony of the Nine Angles*, 186.

36. Aquino, *The Ceremony of the Nine Angles*, 187.

37. Aquino, *The Ceremony of the Nine Angles*, 187.

38. Aquino, *The Ceremony of the Nine Angles*, 188.

39. Aquino, *The Ceremony of the Nine Angles*, 189.

40. Aquino, *The Ceremony of the Nine Angles*, 189.

41. Aquino, *The Ceremony of the Nine Angles*, 189.

42. Aquino, *The Ceremony of the Nine Angles*, 189–90.

43. Aquino, *The Ceremony of the Nine Angles*, 190.

44. Aquino, *The Ceremony of the Nine Angles*, 190.

45. Aquino, *The Ceremony of the Nine Angles*, 191.

46. Aquino, *The Ceremony of the Nine Angles*, 191.

47. Aquino, *The Ceremony of the Nine Angles*, 191.

48. Aquino, *The Ceremony of the Nine Angles*, 191.

49. Aquino, *The Ceremony of the Nine Angles*, 191.

50. Aquino, *The Ceremony of the Nine Angles*, 191.

51. Aquino, *The Ceremony of the Nine Angles*, 193.

52. Aquino, *The Call to Cthulhu*, 198.

53. Aquino, *The Call to Cthulhu*, 199.

54. Aquino, *The Call to Cthulhu*, 199.

55. Aquino, *The Call to Cthulhu*, 200.

56. Aquino, *The Ceremony of the Nine Angles*, 184.

57. Aquino, *The Call to Cthulhu*, 200.

58. Aquino, *The Call to Cthulhu*, 200.

CHAPTER 7. THE FOUNDATIONS OF WORK WITH THE NINE ANGLES

1. Aquino, *The Ceremony of the Nine Angles*, 189–91.

CHAPTER 8. ILLUSTRATIVE AND OPERATIVE WORK WITH THE ANGLES

1. Aquino, *The Ceremony of the Nine Angles,* 191.

2. Aquino, *The Ceremony of the Nine Angles,* 191.

3. Aquino, *The Ceremony of the Nine Angles,* 190.

4. Aquino, *The Ceremony of the Nine Angles,* 184.

5. Aquino, *The Ceremony of the Nine Angles,* 189.

6. Aquino, *The Ceremony of the Nine Angles,* 191.

7. Aquino, *The Ceremony of the Nine Angles,* 191.

8. Aquino, *The Ceremony of the Nine Angles,* 189–90.

9. Kircher, as quoted in Webb, *The Harmonious Circle,* 508.

APPENDIX C. THE NINE ANGLES OF THE SEAL

1. Aquino, *The Ceremony of the Nine Angles,* 191.

2. Aquino, *The Ceremony of the Nine Angles,* 189.

3. Aquino, *The Ceremony of the Nine Angles,* 189.

4. Aquino, *The Ceremony of the Nine Angles,* 189–90.

5. Aquino, *The Ceremony of the Nine Angles,* 190.

6. Aquino, *The Ceremony of the Nine Angles,* 190.

7. Aquino, *The Ceremony of the Nine Angles,* 191.

8. Aquino, *The Ceremony of the Nine Angles,* 191.

9. Aquino, *The Ceremony of the Nine Angles,* 191.

10. Aquino, *The Ceremony of the Nine Angles,* 191.

BIBLIOGRAPHY

Alinder, Mary Street. *Seeing Straight: Group f.64*. Oakland: The Oakland Museum, 1992.

Aquino, Michael A. *The Call to Cthulhu*. In *The Satanic Rituals* by Anton LaVey, 197–201. New York: Avon, 1972.

———. *The Ceremony of the Nine Angles*. In *The Satanic Rituals* by Anton LaVey, 181–93. New York: Avon, 1972.

———. "The Metaphysics of Lovecraft." In *The Satanic Rituals* by Anton LaVey, 175–78. New York: Avon, 1972.

———. "Commentary on the Seal of the Nine Angles." *Runes* 6, no. 3 (June 1988): 1–4.

———. *The Church of Satan*. Self-published, CreateSpace, 2013.

———. *Extreme Prejudice: The Presidio "Satanic Abuse" Scam*. Self-published, CreateSpace, 2014.

———. *The Temple of Set*. Self-published, CreateSpace, 2016.

———. *FindFar*. Self-published, CreateSpace, 2017.

Asprem, Egil. *Arguing with Angels: Enochian Magic and Modern Occulture*. Albany: SUNY Press, 2013.

Austin, James L. *How to Do Things with Words*. Cambridge, Mass.: Harvard University Press, 1962.

Baal, Jan van. *Symbols for Communication: An Introduction to the Anthropological Study of Religion*. Assen: Van Gorcum, 1971.

Barrie, Thomas. *The Sacred In-Between: The Mediating Roles of Architecture*. Abingdon, UK: Routledge, 2010.

Barrow, John D. *Pi in the Sky: Counting, Thinking and Being*. Boston: Little, Brown, 1992.

Bauschatz, Paul. *The Well and the Tree: World and Time in Early Germanic Culture*. Amherst, Mass.: University of Massachusetts Press, 1982.

Boyer, Carl B. *A History of Mathematics.* New York: Wiley, 1911.

Buckingham, Will. "The I-Ching is an Uncertainty Machine." Available on the Aeon magazine website, posted October 11, 2013.

Casaubon, Meric. *A True and Faithful Relation of What Passed for Many Years between Dr. John Dee and Some Spirits.* London: T. Garthwait, 1659.

Chappell, Toby. "Angular Divination." *Runes* 32, no. 1 (March 2014): 1–3.

———. "Charter of the House of Infernal Geometry." *Runes* 32, no. 2 (June 2014): 1–3.

———. "Angular Rites of Passage." *Runes* 32, no. 4 (December 2014): 1–2.

Clarke, Arthur C. *2001: A Space Odyssey.* New York: Ace Books, 2000. Originally published in 1968.

———. *Childhood's End.* New York: Ballantine Books, 1953.

Cook, Stephen, and Stuart Russell. *Heinrich Himmler's Camelot: The Wewelsburg, Ideological Center of the SS 1934–1945.* Andrews, N.C.: Kressmann-Backmeyer, 1999.

Crowley, Aleister. *Magick (Book 4).* York Beach, Maine: Red Wheel/Weiser, 1998.

———. *The Vision and the Voice.* New York: Samuel Weiser, 1972.

De Bono, Edward. *Serious Creativity: Using the Power of Lateral Thinking to Create New Ideas.* New York: Harperbusiness, 1992.

Denny, J. Peter. "Cultural Ecology of Mathematics: Ojibway and Inuit Hunters." In *Native American Mathematics,* edited by Michael P. Closs, 129–80. Austin: University of Texas Press, 1986.

Doreal, Maurice. *The Emerald Tablets of Thoth-the-Atlantean.* Nashville: Source Books, 1996.

Dunn, Patrick. *Magic, Power, Language, Symbol: A Magician's Exploration of Linguistics.* Woodbury, Minn.: Llewelyn, 2008.

Flowers, Stephen E. "The Alchemy of Yggdrasill." In *Blue Rûna: Edred's Shorter Works Vol. III (1988–1994),* 17–24. Smithville, Tex.: Rûna-Raven, 2001.

———. "The Nine Angles of the Seal." *Runes* 6, no. 2 (March 1988): 3–7.

———. "V'Yn'Khe Rohz: The Cycle of Nine." *Runes* 10, no. 5 (September 1992): 1–10.

———. *Black Rûna: Being the Shorter Works of Stephen Edred Flowers Produced for the Order of the Trapezoid of the Temple of Set (1985-1989).* Smithville, Tex.: Rûna-Raven, 1995.

———. *Runes and Magic: Magical Formulaic Elements in the Older Runic*

Tradition. 3rd revised and expanded edition. Smithville, Tex.: Rûna-Raven, 2010.

———. *Lords of the Left-Hand Path.* Revised and expanded edition. Rochester, Vt.: Inner Traditions, 2012.

———. *Icelandic Magic: Practical Secrets of the Northern Grimoires.* Rochester, Vt.: Inner Traditions, 2016.

———. *The Fraternitas Saturni: History, Doctrine, and Rituals of the Magical Order of the Brotherhood of Saturn.* Rochester, Vt.: Inner Traditions, 2018.

———. "Wisdom for the Wolf-Age—A Conversation with Dr. Stephen Flowers." Interview by Michael Moynihan. Available on the Rune Gild website, posted June 27, 2012.

———. *Rûnarmâl I: The RÛNA-Talks, Summer 1991ev.* Smithville, Tex.: Rûna-Raven, 1996.

Flowers, Stephen E., and Michael Moynihan. *The Secret King: The Myth and Reality of Nazi Occultism.* Port Townsend, Wash.: Dominion/Feral House, 2007.

Fowles, John. *The Magus.* New York: Dell, 1985.

Frater U.'.D.'.. *High Magic: Theory and Practice.* Woodbury, Minn.: Llewellyn, 2005.

———. *Practical Sigil Magic: Creating Personal Symbols for Success.* Woodbury, Minn.: Llewellyn, 1990.

Gennep, Arnold van. *The Rites of Passage.* London: Routledge & Kegan Paul, 1960.

Girdler, William, dir. *Asylum of Satan.* 1972; Chatsworth, Calif.: Image Entertainment, 2002. DVD.

Goodrick-Clarke, Nicholas. *Black Sun: Aryan Cults, Esoteric Nazism and the Politics of Identity.* New York: New York University Press, 2002.

———. *The Occult Roots of Nazism.* Wellingborough, UK: Aquarian, 1985.

Grabinski, Stefan. *The Dark Domain.* Sawtry, Cambridgeshire, UK: Dedalus, 1993.

Grant, Kenneth. *The Magical Revival.* London: Frederick Muller Limited, 1972.

Hardy, Patty. "Charter of the Starry Wisdom Hyperlodge of the Order of the Trapezoid." *Runes* 12, no. 2 (May 1994): 11–14.

Hardy, Patty. "Keystone." *Runes* 10, no. 3 (June 1992): 3–8.

Hawkins, Gerald. *Mindsteps to the Cosmos.* New York: Harper & Row, 1983.

Hinton, Charles. "What is the Fourth Dimension?" 1880.

Hodgson, William Hope. "The Gateway of the Monster." In *Carnacki: The Ghost-Finder*, 39–64. London: Grafton Books, 1991.

Hofstadter, Douglas. *Gödel, Escher, Bach: An Eternal Golden Braid*. New York: Basic, 1979.

Howard, Robert E. *The Coming of Conan the Cimmerian*. New York: Ballantine, 2003.

———. "The Shadow Kingdom." in *Shadow Kingdom: The Weird Works of Robert E. Howard, Volume 1*, 150–81. Rockville, Md.: Wildside, 2015.

Kincaid, John M. [Anton LaVey]. "An Explanation of the Role of the Council of the Trapezoid." *The Cloven Hoof* 5, no. 12 (December 1970): 4–5.

Kingsepp, Eva. "The Power of the Black Sun." Paper presented at the First International Conference on Contemporary Esotericism, Stockholm University, August 27–29, 2012. Available on the Contemporary Esoteric Research Network website.

Kircher. *Arithmologia Sive De Abditis Numerorum Mysterijs*. Rome: Ex Typographia Varesij, 1665.

Lafforest, Roger de. *Houses that Kill*. New York: Berkley, 1974.

Lang, Fritz, dir. *Metropolis*. 1927; New York: Kino, 2010. DVD.

Laurent, Ray, dir. *Satanis: The Devil's Mass*. 1970; Seattle, Wash.: Something Weird Video, 2003. DVD.

LaVey, Anton Szandor. "The Law of the Trapezoid." In *The Devils Notebook*, 111–16. Port Townsend, Wash.: Feral House, 1992.

———. *The Satanic Bible*. New York: Avon, 1969.

———. *The Satanic Rituals*. New York: Avon, 1972.

Lawlor, Robert. *Sacred Geometry: Philosophy and Practice*. New York: Thames & Hudson, 1982.

Leman, Andrew H., dir. *The Call of Cthulhu*. 2005; Glendale, Calif.: H. P. Lovecraft Historical Society, 2007. DVD.

Levenda, Peter. *The Dark Lord: H. P. Lovecraft, Kenneth Grant, and the Typhonian Tradition in Magic*. Lake Worth, Fla.: Ibis, 2013.

List, Guido von. *The Secret of the Runes*. Translated by Stephen E. Flowers. Rochester, Vt.: Destiny, 1988.

Livio, Mario. *The Golden Ratio: The Story of PHI, the World's Most Astonishing Number*. New York: Broadway, 2002.

Long, Frank Belknap. "The Hounds of Tindalos." Sauk City, Wisc.: Arkham House, 1946.

Lovecraft, Howard Phillips. *Selected Letters, Vol. 1: 1911–1924,* (Sauk City, Wisc.: Arkham House, 1965.

———. *Selected Letters, Vol. 5: 1934–1937.* Sauk City, Wisc.: Arkham House, 1976.

———. "The Dreams in the Witch-House." In *The Best of H. P. Lovecraft: Bloodcurdling Tales of Horror and the Macabre,* 296–324. New York: Del Ray, 1982.

———. "The Haunter of the Dark" In *The Best of H. P. Lovecraft: Bloodcurdling Tales of Horror and the Macabre,* 207–24. New York: Del Ray, 1982.

———. "Polaris," in *The Doom that Came to Sarnath and Other Stories,* 34–38. New York: Del Ray, 1971.

———. "The Silver Key." In *The Dream-Quest of Unknown Kadath,* 151–67. New York: Del Ray, 1986.

Lovecraft, Howard Phillips, and E. Hoffman Price. "Through the Gates of the Silver Key." In *The Dream-Quest of Unknown Kadath,* 168–219. New York: Del Ray, 1986.

Luske, Hamilton, dir. *Donald in Mathmagic Land.* 1959; Burbank, Calif.: Disney, 2009. DVD.

Lytle, Larry, and Michael Moynihan, eds. *American Grotesque: The Life and Art of William Mortensen.* Port Townsend, Wash.: Feral House, 2014.

McCarty, Louis P. *The Great Pyramid Jeezeh.* San Francisco: McCarty, 1907.

McGranahan, Timothy. "Charter of the Y'n-Khe Rohz Lodge of the Order of the Trapezoid." *Runes* 11, no. 1 (February 1993): 5–12.

McGranahan, Timothy. "Ye Yuggothic Lexicon." *Runes* 10, no. 1 (April 1992): 2–17.

Mortensen, William. *The Command to Look: A Master Photographer's Method for Controlling the Human Gaze.* Port Townsend, Wash.: Feral House, 2014.

Orwell, George. *1984.* New York: Signet Classic, 1950.

Ostrander, Sheila, and Lynn Schroeder. *Psychic Discoveries Behind the Iron Curtain.* Englewood Cliffs, N.J.: Prentice-Hall, 1970.

Pauwels, Louis, and Jacques Bergier. *The Morning of the Magicians: Secret Societies, Conspiracies, and Vanished Civilizations.* New York: Stein and Day, 1964.

Plato. *Timaeus.* Translated by Peter Kalkavage. Indianapolis, Ind.: Hackett, 2016.

Price, Robert M. *The Azathoth Cycle.* Ann Arbor, Mich.: Chaosium, 1994.

Raaflaub, Kurt A. *The Adventure of the Human Intellect: Self, Society, and the Divine in Ancient World Cultures.* New York: Wiley & Sons, 2016.

Robson, Mark, dir. *The Seventh Victim*. 1943; Burbank, Calif.: Warner Brothers, 2005. DVD.

Rucker, Rudy. *The Fourth Dimension*. Boston: Houghton Mifflin, 1984.

Samuels, Mike and Nancy. *Seeing with the Mind's Eye: The History, Techniques and Uses of Visualization*. New York: Random House, 1975.

Schneider, Michael S. *A Beginner's Guide to Constructing the Universe: The Mathematical Archetypes of Nature, Art, and Science*. New York: Harper Perennial, 1994.

Siepe, Daniela. "Esoterische Sichtweisen auf die Wewelsburg: Rezeption in 'satanischen' Kreisen." In *Mythos Wewelsburg: Fakten und Legenden*, edited by Kirsten John-Stucke and Daniela Siepe, 207–48. Paderborn: Schöningh, 2015.

Stanley, Thomas. *Pythagoras: His Life and Teachings*. Lake Worth, Fla.: Ibis, 2010.

Tambiah, S. J. "Form and Meaning of Magical Acts: A Point of View." In *Modes of Thought: Essays on Thinking in Western and Non-Western Societies*, edited by Robin Horton and Ruth Finnegan, 199–229. London: Faber and Faber, 1973.

———. "The Magical Power of Words." *Man*. New series, vol. 3, no. 2 (June 1968): 175–208.

Taylor, Thomas. *The Theoretic Arithmetic of the Pythagoreans*. Whitefish, Mont.: Kessinger Legacy Reprints, 2010.

Thorsson, Edred [Stephen E. Flowers]. *Runelore*. York Beach, Maine: Weiser, 1987.

VandenBroeck, André. *Philosophical Geometry*. Rochester, Vt.: Inner Traditions, 1987.

Veldman, Frederick. *Theurgy and Numbers: Purification, Liberation, and Salvation of the Soul*. Cold Spring, N.Y.: Waning Moon, 2010.

Webb, Don. "From a Letter on the Seal of Rûna." *Runes* 10, no. 4 (December 1992): 4–7.

———. "Knowing the Knot." *Runes* 13, no. 1 (March 1995): 2–8.

———. *Mysteries of the Temple of Set*. Smithville, Tex.: Rûna-Raven, 2011.

———. "Why Do Magicians Write Fiction?" in *Uncle Setnakt's Nightbook*, 217–22. Smithville, Tex.: Lodestar, 2016.

———. *Uncle Setnakt's Essential Guide to the Left Hand Path*. Smithville, Tex.: Rûna-Raven, 1999.

———. "Xeper: The Eternal Word of Set." Available on the Resources page of the Temple of Set website.

Webb, James. *The Harmonious Circle: The Lives and Work of G. I. Gurdjieff, P. D. Ouspensky, and Their Followers.* Boston: Shambhala, 1980.

Weine, Robert, dir. *Das Cabinet des Dr. Caligari.* 1920; New York: Kino, 2014. DVD.

Wolfram von Eschenbach. *Parzifal.* Translated by A. T. Hatto. New York: Penguin, 1980.

INDEX

Page numbers in *italics* refer to illustrations.

315

Hounds of Tindalos, 67, 161–62, 164, 186, 266

"Hounds of Tindalos, The" (Long), 1, 25, 66–68, 71, 211

curved and angular time in, 66–68

Howard, Robert E., 69, 69n, 160

hypercube, 284

hypertetrahedron, 283

ice, fire and, 60–62

Illuminati, 286–87

illustrative rituals, 147–48

Impact, 135

indirect object, 128–29

indulgence, Satanic concept of, 261

infernal geometry, 119–20. *See also* Nine Angles, the

defined, 47, 120

inspiration, 28

Is-To-Be, 158–59

Kelley, Edward, 52–53

keywords, of the Nine Angles, 3, 21–24

Khnum, 100

Kircher, Athanasius, 48, 48n, 246

lateral thinking, 211, 226–27

LaVey, Anton. *See also* angular magic

creation of *Die Elektrischen Vorspiele,* 150–52

and Enochian Keys, 52–54

and eternal return, 57

and Law of the Trapezoid, 62–64

non-belief in Satan and magic, 150–51

reinvention of himself, 150–51

revelation of rites by, 1–2

and Thomas Carnacki, 71

law of contagion, 123

Law of Fives, 287

Law of Octaves, 50

Law of Seven, 50, 61–62

law of similarity, 123, 129, 159, 165, 168

Law of the Octave, 61–62

Law of the Trapezoid, 18, 62–64, 115, 134–37

Law of Three, 50

Left-Hand Path, 248

and angular magic, 124

defined, 4

goals of, 139

and Nine Angles, 3–5

Right-Hand Path vs., 56

and Starry Wisdom, 55–58

Lesser Law, 162–63

Lévi-Strauss, Claude, on magic, 122

Liebenfels, Jörg Lanz von, 42n

linear time, 25

List, Guido von, 34–35

litany, in *Die Elektrischen Vorspiele,* 158–67

Livio, Mario, 109–10

Llull, Ramon, 48

Loki, 167

Lovecraft, H. P.

as astronomer, 288

"conviction" in his writing, 256

ideas on magic, 72–75

individual Angles and Lovecraft connection, 83–88

influence of mythology on, 74–75

influence on Left-Hand Path, 55–58

influence on Satanic Rites, 1

Lovecraftian rites in *The Satanic Rituals,* 79–90